Learning Apache Apex

Real-time streaming applications with Apex

Thomas Weise
Munagala V. Ramanath
David Yan
Kenneth Knowles

BIRMINGHAM - MUMBAI

Learning Apache Apex

First published: November 2017

Production reference: 2061217

Published by Packt Publishing Ltd.
Livery Place
35 Livery Street
Birmingham
B3 2PB, UK.
ISBN 978-1-78829-640-3

www.packtpub.com

Credits

Authors
Thomas Weise
Munagala V. Ramanath
David Yan
Kenneth Knowles

Reviewer
Ananth Gundabattula

Acquisition Editor
Frank Pohlmann

Content Development Editor
Monika Sangwan

Technical Editor
Joel D'Souza

Copy Editors
Safis Editing
Tom Jacob

Project Coordinator
Suzanne Coutinho

Indexer
Pratik Shirodkar

Graphics
Jason Monteiro

Production Coordinator
Arvindkumar Gupta

About the Authors

Thomas Weise is the Apache Apex PMC Chair and cofounder at Atrato. Earlier, he worked at a number of other technology companies in the San Francisco Bay Area, including DataTorrent, where he was a cofounder of the Apex project. Thomas is also a committer to Apache Beam and has contributed to several more of the ecosystem projects. He has been working on distributed systems for 20 years and has been a speaker at international big data conferences. Thomas received the degree of Diplom-Informatiker (MSc in computer science) from TU Dresden, Germany. He can be reached on Twitter at: `@thweise`.

I'd like to thank the Apache Apex community and project cofounder, Chetan Narsude, for creating this advanced streaming platform. I'd also like to thank Dean Lockgaard, Ananth G., and my coauthors for their help with the book, and Packt editors for their support.

Dr. Munagala V. Ramanath got his PhD in Computer Science from the University of Wisconsin, USA and an MSc in Mathematics from Carleton University, Ottawa, Canada. After that, he taught Computer Science courses as Assistant/Associate Professor at the University of Western Ontario in Canada for a few years, before transitioning to the corporate sphere. Since then, he has worked as a senior software engineer at a number of technology companies in California including SeeBeyond, EMC, Sun Microsystems, DataTorrent, and Cloudera. He has published papers in peer reviewed journals in several areas including code optimization, graph theory, and image processing.

David Yan is based in the Silicon Valley, California. He is a senior software engineer at Google. Prior to Google, he worked at DataTorrent, Yahoo!, and the Jet Propulsion Laboratory. David holds a master of science in Computer Science from Stanford University and a bachelor of science in Electrical Engineering and Computer Science from the University of California at Berkeley.

Kenneth Knowles is a founding PMC member of Apache Beam. Kenn has been working on Google Cloud Dataflow—Google's Beam backend—since 2014. Prior to that, he built backends for startups such as Cityspan, Inkling, and Dimagi. Kenn holds a PhD in Programming Language Theory from the University of California, Santa Cruz.

About the Reviewer

Ananth Gundabattula is a senior application architect in the Decisioning and Advanced Analytics architecture team for Commonwealth Bank of Australia. Ananth holds a PhD in Computer Science Security and is interested in all things related to data, including low latency distributed processing systems, machine learning, and data engineering domains. He holds three patents granted by USPTO and has one application pending.

Prior to joining CBA, Ananth was an architect at Threatmetrix and the member of the core team that scaled the Threatmetrix architecture to 100 million transactions per day, which runs at very low latencies using Cassandra, ZooKeeper, and Kafka. He also migrated Threatmetrix data warehouse into the next generation architecture based on Hadoop and Impala. Prior to Threatmetrix, he worked for the IBM software labs and IBM CIO labs, enabling some of the first IBM CIO projects onboarding HBase, Hadoop, and Mahout stack.

Ananth is a committer for Apache Apex and is currently working for the next generation architectures for the CBA fraud platform and Advanced Analytics Omnia platform at CBA.

www.PacktPub.com

For support files and downloads related to your book, please visit `www.PacktPub.com`. Did you know that Packt offers eBook versions of every book published, with PDF and ePub files available? You can upgrade to the eBook version at `www.PacktPub.com` and as a print book customer, you are entitled to a discount on the eBook copy. Get in touch with us at `service@packtpub.com` for more details. At `www.PacktPub.com`, you can also read a collection of free technical articles, sign up for a range of free newsletters and receive exclusive discounts and offers on Packt books and eBooks.

`https://www.packtpub.com/mapt`

Get the most in-demand software skills with Mapt. Mapt gives you full access to all Packt books and video courses, as well as industry-leading tools to help you plan your personal development and advance your career.

Why subscribe?

- Fully searchable across every book published by Packt
- Copy and paste, print, and bookmark content
- On demand and accessible via a web browser

Customer Feedback

Thanks for purchasing this Packt book. At Packt, quality is at the heart of our editorial process. To help us improve, please leave us an honest review on this book's Amazon page at `https://www.amazon.com/dp/1788296400`.

If you'd like to join our team of regular reviewers, you can email us at `customerreviews@packtpub.com`. We award our regular reviewers with free eBooks and videos in exchange for their valuable feedback. Help us be relentless in improving our products!

Table of Contents

Preface

With business demand for faster insights derived from a growing number of information sources, the stream data processing technology is gaining popularity. Open-source-based products have become the prevailing implementation choice, and there has been a shift from the early MapReduce-based batch processing paradigm to newer, more expressive frameworks designed to process data as streams with minimal latency, high reliability, and accuracy guarantees.

Apache Apex is a large-scale stream-first big data processing framework that can be used to build low-latency, high-throughput complex analytics pipelines that execute on clusters. Apex was developed in 2012, and is continuously improving, and today it is being used in production by a number of companies for real time and batch processing at scale.

The big data landscape has a wide array of technology components and choices, and it remains a challenge for end users to piece everything together to be successful with their big data projects and realize value from their technology investments.

This book will focus on how to apply Apex to big data processing use cases. It is written by experts in the area, including key contributors of Apache Apex who built the platform and have extensive experience working with users in the field that use Apex in their enterprise solutions. This book is an instructional and example-driven guide on how to build Apex applications for developers and hands-on enterprise architects. It will help identify use cases, the building blocks needed to put together solutions, and the process of implementing, testing and tuning applications for production. Fully functional example projects are provided to cover key aspects of data processing pipelines such as connectors for sources and sinks and common transformations. These projects can also be used as starting points for custom development.

To connect with the Apache Apex project, please visit the website (`http://apex.apache.org/`), subscribe to the mailing lists mentioned there, or follow @ApacheApex on Twitter (`https://twitter.com/apacheapex`) or on SlideShare (`http://www.slideshare.net/ApacheApex/presentations`).

What this book covers

`Chapter 1`, *Introduction to Apex*, tells us how processing of data-in-motion is realized by Apache Apex. It also gives us a few Apex stream processing use cases and applications, and talks about their value propositions.

Chapter 2, *Getting Started with Application Development*, shows us how the Apex development process works from project creation to application deployment; the result is a simple working application.

Chapter 3, *The Apex Library*, talks about the Malhar library, which contains functional building blocks for writing real-world Apex applications.

Chapter 4, *Scalability, Low Latency, and Performance*, teaches us how Apex can scale and parallize processing, how to achieve dynamic scaling and better resource allocation in general, and why low latency and high throughput are both achievable without trading one off against the other. Operator partitioning and related techniques are central to this endeavor and are shown in practice in a sample application.

Chapter 5, *Fault Tolerance and Reliability*, explores the implementation of fault-tolerance and reliability in Apex including exactly-once semantics via distributed checkpointing and effective state management.

Chapter 6, *Example Project – Real-Time Aggregation and Visualization*, puts together all the building blocks to show a streaming analytics project and how to integrate it with a UI and existing infrastructure.

Chapter 7, *Example Project – Real-Time Ride Service Data Processing*, relies on a historical dataset to simulate a real-time ride service data stream. We are using event time and out-of-order processing, in particular, to build a simple analytics application that can serve as a template for more complicated event stream data pipelines.

Chapter 8, *Example Project – ETL Using SQL*, shows how to build a classic ETL application using Apex and Apache Calcite.

Chapter 9, *Introduction to Apache Beam*, introduces the Beam stream processing framework and an approach that allows a stream application engine such as Apex to be swapped in if needed.

Chapter 10, *The Future of Stream Processing*, looks at the road ahead for Apex and stream processing in general. We are going to examine the role of machine learning, as well as the role of SQL and why it is important for streaming.

What you need for this book

Apex applications can be built and run locally on the user's development machine via a properly written JUnit test. To do this, the user need only ensure that recent versions of the following software packages are present:

- Java JDK (please note that the JRE alone is not adequate).
- Maven build system
- Git revision control system (optional)
- A Java IDE such as Eclipse or IntelliJ (optional)

To run Apex applications on a cluster, one needs a cluster with Hadoop installed and a client to launch them. This client needs to be installed on the edge node (sometimes referred to as the gateway node or the client node); there is no need to install anything on the entire cluster.

There are several options to install the client, and some of them are listed on the Apex download page: `http://apex.apache.org/downloads.html`.

Without an existing Hadoop cluster, an easy way to get started for experimentation is a sandbox VM that already has a single node cluster configured (sandbox VMs are available from Hadoop vendors, as docker images and so on).

Who this book is for

This book is a practical and example-oriented guide on how to use Apache Apex to successfully implement solutions for real-world big data problems. The book assumes knowledge of application development with Java and familiarity with distributed systems. It does not require prior knowledge of Apex or stream processing, although knowledge of other big data processing frameworks is helpful.

Conventions

In this book, you will find a number of styles of text that distinguish between different kinds of information. Here are some examples of these styles, and an explanation of their meaning.

Code words in text (such as database table names, folder names, filenames, file extensions, pathnames, dummy URLs, user input, and Twitter handles) are shown as follows where the code word is "10011": "This result tells the driver to drive toward the zip code `10011`."

A block of code is set as follows:

```
PubSubWebSocketAppDataResult wsResult = dag.addOperator("QueryResult", new
PubSubWebSocketAppDataResult());
  wsResult.setTopic("nyctaxi.result");
  try {
    wsResult.setUri(new URI("ws://localhost:8890/pubsub"));
  } catch (URISyntaxException ex) {
    throw Throwables.propagate(ex);
  }
dag.addStream("server_to_query_output", dataServer.queryResult,
wsResult.input);
```

Any command-line input or output is written as follows:

```
bash> apex
apex> launch target/malhar-examples-nyc-taxi-3.8.0-SNAPSHOT.apa
```

New terms and important words are shown in bold.

Warnings or important notes appear like this.

Tips and tricks appear like this.

Reader feedback

Feedback from our readers is always welcome. Let us know what you think about this book—what you liked or may have disliked. Reader feedback is important for us to develop titles that you really get the most out of.

To send us general feedback, simply send an email to feedback@packtpub.com, and mention the book title in the subject of your message.

If there is a topic that you have expertise in and you are interested in either writing or contributing to a book, see our author guide on www.packtpub.com/authors.

Customer support

Now that you are the proud owner of a Packt book, we have a number of things to help you to get the most from your purchase.

Downloading the example code

You can download the example code files for this book from your account at `http://www.packtpub.com`. If you purchased this book elsewhere, you can visit `http://www.packtpub.com/support` and register to have the files emailed directly to you.

You can download the code files by following these steps:

1. Log in or register to our website using your email address and password.
2. Hover the mouse pointer on the **SUPPORT** tab at the top.
3. Click on **Code Downloads & Errata**.
4. Enter the name of the book in the Search box.
5. Select the book for which you're looking to download the code files.
6. Choose from the drop-down menu where you purchased this book from.
7. Click on **Code Download**.

Once the file is downloaded, please make sure that you unzip or extract the folder using the latest version of:

- WinRAR / 7-Zip for Windows
- Zipeg / iZip / UnRarX for Mac
- 7-Zip / PeaZip for Linux

The code bundle for the book is also hosted on GitHub at `https://github.com/PacktPublishing/Learning-Apache-Apex`. We also have other code bundles from our rich catalog of books and videos available at `https://github.com/PacktPublishing/`. Check them out!

Downloading the color images of this book

We also provide you with a PDF file that has color images of the screenshots/diagrams used in this book. The color images will help you better understand the changes in the output. You can download this file from `https://www.packtpub.com/sites/default/files/downloads/LearningApacheApex_ColorImages.pdf`.

Errata

Although we have taken every care to ensure the accuracy of our content, mistakes do happen. If you find a mistake in one of our books—maybe a mistake in the text or the code—we would be grateful if you would report this to us. By doing so, you can save other readers from frustration and help us improve subsequent versions of this book. If you find any errata, please report them by visiting http://www.packtpub.com/submit-errata, selecting your book, clicking on the errata submission form link, and entering the details of your errata. Once your errata are verified, your submission will be accepted and the errata will be uploaded on our website, or added to any list of existing errata, under the Errata section of that title. Any existing errata can be viewed by selecting your title from http://www.packtpub.com/support.

Piracy

Piracy of copyright material on the Internet is an ongoing problem across all media. At Packt, we take the protection of our copyright and licenses very seriously. If you come across any illegal copies of our works, in any form, on the Internet, please provide us with the location address or website name immediately so that we can pursue a remedy.

Please contact us at copyright@packtpub.com with a link to the suspected pirated material.

We appreciate your help in protecting our authors, and our ability to bring you valuable content.

Questions

You can contact us at questions@packtpub.com if you are having a problem with any aspect of the book, and we will do our best to address it.

1
Introduction to Apex

The world is producing data at unprecedented levels, with a rapidly growing number of mobile devices, sensors, industrial machines, financial transactions, web logs, and so on. Often, the streams of data generated by these sources can offer valuable insights if processed quickly and reliably, and companies are finding it increasingly important to take action on this **data-in-motion** in order to remain competitive. MapReduce and Apache Hadoop were among the first technologies to enable processing of very large datasets on clusters of commodity hardware. The prevailing paradigm at the time was batch processing, which evolved from MapReduce's heavy reliance on disk I/O to Apache Spark's more efficient, memory-based approach.

Still, the downside of batch processing systems is that they accumulate data into batches, sometimes over hours, and cannot address use cases that require a short time to insight for continuous data in motion. Such requirements can be handled by newer stream processing systems, which can process data in **real time**, sometimes with latency as low as a few milliseconds. Apache Storm was the first ecosystem project to offer this capability, albeit with prohibitive trade-offs such as reliability versus latency. Today, there are newer and production-ready frameworks that don't force the user to make such choices. Rather, they enable low latency, high throughput, reliability, and a unified architecture that can be applied to both streaming and batch use cases. This book will introduce **Apache Apex**, a next-generation platform for processing data in motion.

In this chapter, we will cover the following topics:

- Unbounded data and continuous processing
- Use cases and case studies
- Application Model and API
- Value proposition of Apex

Unbounded data and continuous processing

Datasets can be classified as unbounded or bounded. Bounded data is finite; it has a beginning and an end. Unbounded data is an ever-growing, essentially infinite data set. The distinction is independent of how the data is processed. Often, unbounded data is equated to stream processing and bounded data to batch processing, but this is starting to change. We will see how state-of-the-art stream processors, such as Apache Apex, can be used to (and are very capable of) processing both unbounded and bounded data, and there is no need for a batch processing system just because the data set happens to be finite.

 For more details on these data processing concepts, you can visit the following link: `https://www.oreilly.com/ideas/the-world-beyond-batch-streaming-101`.

Most **big datasets** (high volume) that are eventually processed by big data systems are unbounded. There is a rapidly increasing volume of such infinite data from sources such as IoT sensors (such as industrial gauge sensors, automobile data ports, connected home, and quantified self), stock markets and financial transactions, telecommunications towers and satellites, and so on. At the same time, the legacy processing and storage systems are either nearing performance and capacity limits, or total cost of ownership (TCO) is becoming prohibitive.

Businesses need to convert the available data into meaningful insights and make data-driven, real-time decisions to remain competitive.

Organizations are increasingly relying on very fast processing (high velocity), as the value of data diminishes as it ages:

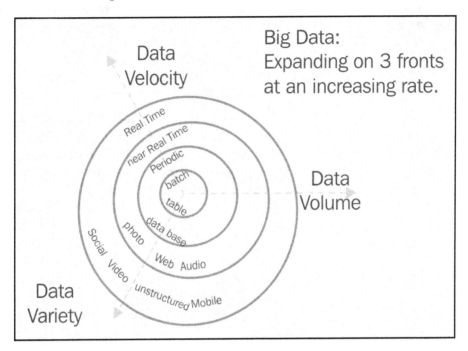

How were these unbounded datasets processed without streaming architecture?

To be consumable by a batch processor, they had to be divided into bounded data, often at intervals of hours. Before processing could begin, the earliest events would wait for a long time for their batch to be ready. At the time of processing, data would already be old and less valuable.

Stream processing

Stream processing means processing event by event, as soon as it is available. Because there is no waiting for more input after an event arrives, there is no artificially added latency (unlike with batching). This is important for real-time use cases, where information should be processed and results available with minimum latency or delay. However, stream processing is not limited to **real-time** data. We will see there are benefits to applying this continuous processing in a uniform manner to historical data as well.

Consider data that is stored in a file. By reading the file line by line and processing each line as soon as it is read, subsequent processing steps can be performed while the file is still being read, instead of waiting for the entire input to be read before initiating the next stage. Stream processing is a pipeline, and each item can be acted upon immediately. Apart from low latency, this can also lead to even resource consumption (memory, CPU, network) with steady (versus bursty) throughput, when operations performed inherently don't require any blocking:

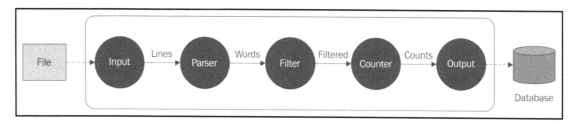

An example of a data pipeline

Data flows through the pipeline as individual events, and all processing steps are active at the same time. In a distributed system, operations are performed on different nodes and data flows through the system, allowing for parallelism and high throughput. Processing is decentralized and without inherent bottlenecks, in contrast to architectures that attempt to move processing to where the data resides.

Stream processing is a natural fit for how events occur in the real world. Sources generate data continuously (mobile devices, financial transactions, web traffic, sensors, and so on). It therefore makes sense to also process them that way instead of artificially breaking the processing into batches (or micro-batches).

The meaning of real time, or time for fast decision making, varies significantly between businesses. Some use cases, such as online fraud detection, may require processing to complete within milliseconds, but for others multiple seconds or even minutes might be sufficiently fast. In any case, the underlying platform needs to be equipped for fast and correct low-latency processing.

Streaming applications can process data fast, with low latency. Stream processing has gained popularity along with growing demand for faster processing of current data, but it is not a synonym for real-time processing. Input data does not need to be real-time. Older data can also be processed as stream (for example, reading from a file) and results are not always emitted in real-time either. Stream processing can perform operations such as *sum, average,* or *top,* that are performed over multiple events before the result becomes available.

To perform such operations, the stream needs to be sliced at temporal boundaries. This is called **windowing**. It demarcates finite datasets for computations. All data belonging to a window needs to be observed before a result can be emitted and windowing provides these boundaries. There are different strategies to define such windows over a data stream, and these will be covered in Chapter 3, *The Apex Library:*

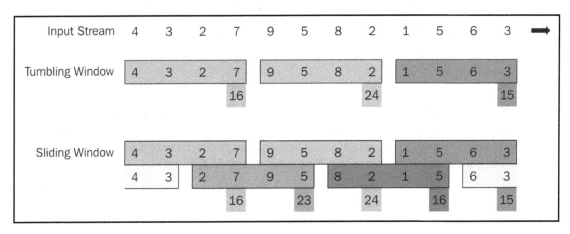

Windowing of a stream

In the preceding diagram we see the sum of incoming readings computed over tumbling (non-overlapping) and sliding (overlapping) windows. At the end of each window, the result is emitted.

With windowing, the final result of an operation for a given window is only known after all its data elements are processed. However, many windowed operations still benefit from event-by-event arrival of data and incremental computation. Windowing doesn't always mean that processing can only start once all input has arrived. In our example, the sum can be updated whenever the next event arrives vs. storing all individual events and deferring computation until the end of the window. Sometimes, even the intermediate result of a windowed computation is of interest and can be made available for downstream consumption and subsequently refined with the final result.

Stream processing systems

The first open source stream processing framework in the **big data** ecosystem was Apache Storm. Since then, several other Apache projects for stream processing have emerged. Next-generation streaming first architectures such as Apache Apex and Apache Flink come with stronger capabilities and are more broadly applicable. They are not only able to process data with low latency, but also provide for state management (for data that an operation may require across individual events), strong processing guarantees (correctness), fault tolerance, scalability, and high performance.

Users can now also expect such frameworks to come with comprehensive libraries of connectors, other building blocks and APIs that make development of non-trivial streaming applications productive and allow for predictable project implementation cycles. Equally importantly, next-generation frameworks should cater to aspects such as operability, security, and the ability to run on shared infrastructure (multi-tenancy) to satisfy DevOps requirements for successful production launch and uptime.

Streaming can do it all!

Limitations of early stream processing systems lead to the so-called **Lambda Architecture**, essentially a parallel setup of stream and batch processing path to obtain fast but potentially unreliable results through the stream processor and, in parallel, correct but slow results through a batch processing system like **Apache Hadoop MapReduce**:

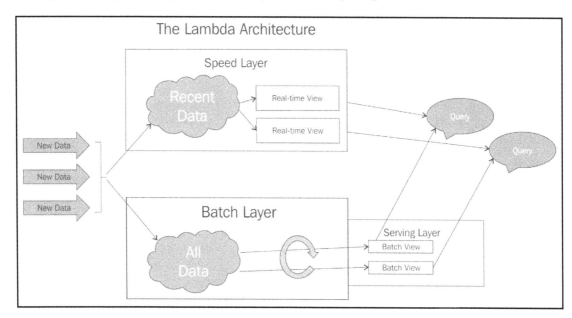

The fast processing path in the preceding diagram can potentially produce incorrect results, hence the need to re-compute the same results in an alternate batch processing path. Correctness issues are caused by previous technical limitations of stream processing, not by the paradigm itself. For example, if events are processed multiple times or lost, it leads to double or under counting, which would be a problem for an application that relies on accurate results, for example, in the financial sector.

This setup requires the same functionality to be implemented with two different frameworks, as well as extra infrastructure and operational skills, and therefore, results in longer time to production and higher **Total Cost of Ownership (TOC)**. With recent advances in stream processing, Lambda Architecture is no longer necessary. Instead, a unified streaming architecture can be used for reliable processing in a much more TOC effective solution.

This approach based on a single system was outlined in 2014 as **Kappa Architecture**, and today there are several stream processing technology options, including Apache Apex, that support batch as a special case of streaming.

 To know more about the Kappa Architecture, please refer to following link: https://www.oreilly.com/ideas/questioning-the-lambda-architecture.

These newer systems are fault-tolerant, produce correct results, can achieve low latency as well as high throughput, and provide options for enterprise-grade operability and support. Potential users are no longer confronted with the shortcomings that previously justified a parallel batch processing system. We will later see how Apache Apex ensures correct processing, including its support for exactly-once processing.

What is Apex and why is it important?

Apache Apex (http://apex.apache.org/) is a stream processing platform and framework that can process data in-motion with low latency in a way that is highly scalable, highly performant, fault-tolerant, stateful, secure, distributed, and easily operable. Apex is written in Java, and Java is the primary application development environment.

In a typical streaming data pipeline, events from sources are stored and transported through a system such as **Apache Kafka**. The events are then processed by a stream processor and the results delivered to sinks, which are frequently databases, distributed file systems or message buses that link to downstream pipelines or services.

The following figure illustrates this:

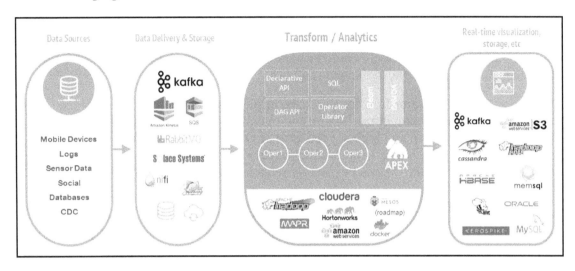

In the end-to-end scenario depicted in this illustration, we see Apex as the processing component. The processing can be complex logic, with operations performed in sequence or in parallel in a distributed environment.

Apex runs on cluster infrastructure and currently supports and depends on Apache Hadoop, for which it was originally written. Support for Apache Mesos and other Docker-based infrastructure is on the roadmap.

Apex supports integration with many external systems out of the box, with connectors that are maintained and released by the project, including but not limited to the systems shown in the preceding diagram. The most frequently used connectors include Kafka and file readers. Frequently used sinks for the computed results are files and databases, though results can also be delivered directly to frontend systems for purposes such as real-time reporting directly from the Apex application, a use case that we will look at later.

Origin of Apex

The development of the Apex project started in 2012, with the original vision of enabling fast, performant, and scalable real-time processing on Hadoop. At that time, batch processing and MapReduce-based frameworks such as Apache Pig, Hive, or Cascading were still the standard options for processing data. Hadoop 2.x with YARN (Yet Another Resource Negotiator) was about to be released to pave the way for a number of new processing frameworks and paradigms to become available as alternatives to MapReduce. Due to its roots in the Hadoop ecosystem, Apex is very well integrated with YARN, and since its earliest days has offered features such as dynamic resource allocation for scaling and efficient recovery. It is also leading in high performance (with low latency), scalability and operability, which were focus areas from the very beginning.

The technology was donated to the Apache Software Foundation (ASF) in 2015, at which time it entered the Apache incubation program and graduated after only eight months to achieve Top Level Project status in April 2016.

Apex had its first production deployments in 2014 and today is used in mission-critical deployments in various industries for processing at scale. **Use cases** range from very low-latency processing in the real-time category to large-scale batch processing; a few examples will be discussed in the next section. Some of the organizations that use Apex can be found on the **Powered by Apache Apex** page on the Apex project web site at
`https://apex.apache.org/powered-by-apex.html`.

Use cases and case studies

Apex is a platform and framework on top of which specific applications (or solutions) are built.

As such, Apex is applicable to to a wide range of use cases, including real-time machine learning model scoring, real-time ETL (**Extract, Transform, and Load**), predictive analytics, anomaly detection, real-time recommendations, and systems monitoring:

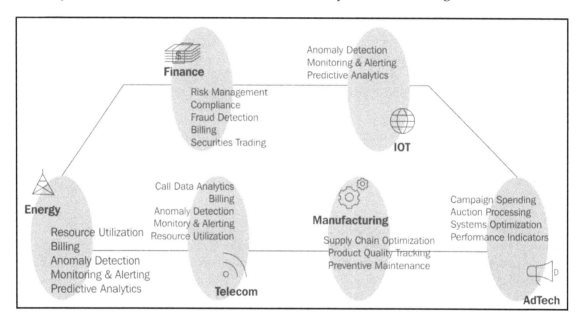

As organizations realize the financial and competitive importance of making data-driven decisions in real time, the number of industries and use cases will grow.

In the remainder of this section, we will discuss how companies in various industries are using Apex to solve important problems. These companies have presented their particular use cases, implementations and findings at conferences and meetups, and references to this source material are provided with each case study when available.

Real-time insights for Advertising Tech (PubMatic)

Companies in the advertising technology (AdTech) industry need to address data increasing at breakneck speed, along with customers demanding faster insights and analytical reporting.

PubMatic is a leading AdTech company providing marketing automation for publishers and is driven by data at a massive scale. On a *daily* basis, the company processes over 350 billion bids, serves over 40 billion ad impressions, and processes over 50 terabytes of data. Through real-time analytics, yield management, and workflow automation, PubMatic enables publishers to make smarter inventory decisions and improve revenue performance. Apex is used for real-time reporting and for the allocation engine.

In PubMatic's legacy batch processing system, there could be a delay of five hours to obtain updated data for their key metrics (revenues, impressions and clicks) and a delay of nine hours to obtain data for auction logs.

PubMatic decided to pursue a real-time streaming solution so that it could provide publishers, demand side platforms (DSPs), and agencies with actionable insights as close to the time of event generation as possible. PubMatic's streaming implementation had to achieve the following:

- Ingest and analyze a high volume of clicks and views (200,000 events/sec) to help their advertising customers improve revenues
- Utilize auction and client log data (22 TB/day) to report critical metrics for campaign monetization
- Handle rapidly increasing network traffic with efficient utilization of resources
- Provide a feedback loop to the ad server for making efficient ad serving decisions.

This high volume data would need to be processed in real-time to derive actionable insights, such as campaign decisions and audience targeting.

PubMatic decided to implement its real-time streaming solution with Apex based on the following factors:

- Time to value - the solution was able to be implemented within a short time frame
- The Apex applications could run on PubMatic's existing Hadoop infrastructure
- Apex had important connectors (files, Apache Kafka, and so on) available out of the box
- Apex supported event time dimensional aggregations with real-time query capability

With the Apex-based solution, deployed to production in 2014, PubMatic's end-to-end latency to obtain updated data and metrics for their two use cases fell from hours to seconds. This enabled real-time visibility into successes and shortcomings of its campaigns and timely tuning of models to maximize successful auctions.

Additional Resources

- Video: PubMatic presents High Performance AdTech Use Cases with Apache Apex at `https://www.youtube.com/watch?v=JSXpgfQFcU8`
- Slides: `https://www.slideshare.net/ashishtadose1/realtime-adtech-reporting-targeting-with-apache-apex`

Industrial IoT applications (GE)

General Electric (GE) is a large, diversified company with business units in energy, power, aviation, transportation, healthcare, finance, and other industries. Many of these business units deal in industrial machinery and devices such as wind turbines, aviation components, locomotive components, healthcare imaging machines, and so on. Such industrial devices continually generate high volumes of real-time data, and GE decided to provide advanced IoT analytics solutions to the thousands of customers using these devices and sensors across its various business units and industries.

The GE Predix platform enables users to develop and execute Industrial IoT applications to gain real-time insights about their devices and their usage, as well as take actions based on these insights. Certain services offered by Predix are powered by Apache Apex. GE selected Apex for these services based on the following features (feature details will be covered later in this book):

- High performance and distributed computing
- Dynamic partitioning
- Rich library of existing operators
- Support for at-least-once, at-most-once, and exactly-once processing
- Hadoop/YARN compatibility
- Fault tolerance and platform stability
- Ease of deployment and operability
- Enterprise grade security

One Predix service that runs on Apex is the Time Series service, which leverages Apex due to its speed, scalability, high performance, and fault tolerance capabilities.

The service provides:

- Efficient storage of time series data
- Data indexing for quick retrieval
- Industrial focused query modes
- High availability and horizontal scalability
- Millisecond data point precision

By running Apex, users of the Time Series service are able to:

- Ingest and analyze high-volume, high speed data from thousands of devices, sensors per customer in real-time without data loss
- Run predictive analytics to reduce costly maintenance and improve customer service
- Conduct unified monitoring of all connected sensors and devices to minimize disruptions
- Have fast application development cycles
- Meet changing business and application workloads due to Apex's high scalability

Another Predix service leveraging Apex is the Stream Processing service, which provides predefined flows to support data conversion, manipulation, or processing of large volumes of real-time data before delivering it to the event hub or storage layer. This service provides the following capabilities to users:

- Raw data ingestion
- Fault tolerance, allowing data to be processed despite machine or node failures
- Apex as the runtime engine (Spark and other engines will be supported in future releases)
- Multi-tenancy support
- Security (UAA integrated)

Apex's integration into the GE Predix platform and ability to be used across a broad spectrum of industrial devices and Industrial IOT use cases speaks volumes about Apex and its capabilities.

Additional Resources

- Video: GE presents Industrial IOT with Apache Apex - `https://www.youtube.com/watch?v=hmaSkXhHNu0`
- Slides: GE presents Industrial IOT Time Series and Ingestion with Apache Apex - `https://www.slideshare.net/secret/kqgcUZoDY5WNxj`
- Video: An Overview of Predix, GE's Platform for the Industrial Internet - `https://www.youtube.com/watch?v=cTKDDy8cHfg`
- Website: GE Predix Developer Network - Stream Processing - `https://www.predix.io/services/service.html?id=2229`

Real-time threat detection (Capital One)

Capital One is currently the eighth largest bank in the U.S. One of its core areas of business was facing vast and increasing costs for an existing solution to guard against digital threats. The bank set out to find a new solution that would deliver better performance while also being more cost effective.

At the time, Capital One was processing several thousand transactions every second. The bank's innovation team established that the solution must be able to process data within low double-digit milliseconds latency, scale easily, ensure that it runs internal algorithms with zero data loss, and also be highly available. Additionally, the team realized that tackling this challenge would require dynamic and flexible machine learning algorithms in a real-time distributed environment.

The team launched a rigorous process of evaluating numerous streaming technologies including Apache Apex, Apache Flink, Apache Storm, Apache Spark Streaming, IBM Infosphere Streams, Apache Samza, Apache Ignite, and others. The evaluation process involved developing parallel solutions using each of the technologies, and comparing the quantitative results generated by each technology as well as its qualitative characteristics.

At the conclusion of the evaluation, only one technology emerged as being able to meet all of Capital One's requirements. In the team's own words:

> *"Of all evaluated technologies, Apache Apex is the only technology that is ready to bring the decision making solution to production based on: Maturity, Fault Tolerance, Enterprise-Readiness, and Performance."*

With Apache Apex, Capital One was able to:

- Achieve latency in single-digit milliseconds, which is significantly lower than the double digit millisecond latency that the bank set out to achieve and which is a hard requirement for use cases such as online transactions
- Meet the SLA requirements of continuously running the data pipeline applications with
  99.999% uptime on 24x7 basis, with automatic failover
- Reduce the total cost of ownership, based on Apex's ability to run on Hadoop and scale out with commodity grade hardware
- Easily add newer applications and features to accurately detect suspicious events without being tied to the vendor roadmap and timeline
- Focus on core business algorithms and innovation, while the platform took care of fault tolerance, operability, scalability, and performance

Furthermore, Capital One's implementation of Apex enabled the following:

- Parallel Model Scoring
- Dynamic Scalability based on Throughput or Latency
- Live Model Refresh, parallelized model scoring

Parameter	Capital One's Goal	Result With Apex
Latency	< 40 milliseconds	0.25 milliseconds
Throughput	2,000 events/sec	70,000 events/sec
Durability	No loss, every message gets exactly one response	Yes
Availability	99.5% uptime, ideally 99.999% uptime	99.99925% uptime
Scalability	Can add resources and still meet latency requirements	Yes
Integration	Transparently connected to existing systems: Hardware, Messaging, HDFS	Yes
Open Source	All components licensed as open source	Yes
Extensibility	Rules can be updated, Model is regularly refreshed	Yes

A complete set of Capital One's goals, and the results it achieved with Apex

Additional Resources

- Video: Capital One presents Toppling the Mainframe with Apache Apex - https://www.youtube.com/watch?v=98EW5NGM3u0
- Slides: Capital One presents Next Gen Decisions in Less Than 2ms with Apache Apex - http://www.slideshare.net/ApacheApex/capital-ones-next-generation-decision-in-less-than-2-ms

Silver Spring Networks (SSN)

Silver Spring Networks (SSN) helps global utilities and cities connect, optimize, and manage smart energy and smart city infrastructure. It provides smart grid products and also develops software for utilities and customers to improve their energy efficiency. SSN is one of the world's largest IOT companies, receiving data from over 22 million smart meters and connected devices, reading over 200 billion records per year, and conducting over two million remote operations per year.

As SSN's network and volume, variety, and velocity of data began to grow, it started to ponder:

- How to obtain more value out of its network of connected devices
- How to manage the growing number of devices, access their data, and ensure the safety of their data
- How to integrate with third party data applications quickly

SSN's answer to these questions would be informed by its needs, which included:

- A broad variety of incoming data, including sensor data, meter data, interval data, device metadata, threshold events, and traps
- Multi-tenancy and shared resources to save costs, with centralized management of software and applications
- Security, including encryption of both data-at-rest and data-in-motion, auditing of data, and no loss of data across tenants
- Ability to scale, based on the millions of connected devices in its network, as well as over eight billion events per day and volume of over 500 GB each day
- High availability and disaster recoverability of its cluster, with automated failovers as well as rolling upgrades

SSN chose Apex as its solution due to the following factors:

- The availability of pre-existing and prebuilt operators as part of the Apex Malhar library
- The ability to develop applications quickly
- Apex's operability and auto-scaling capabilities
- Apex's partitioning capabilities, leading to scalability
- Java programmers are able to learn Apex application development quickly
- Operations are handled by Apex and don't require hands on management

In addition to meeting SSN's requirements, Apex was able to make SSN data accessible to applications without delay to improve customer service and was able to capture and analyze historical data to understand and improve grid operations.

Additional Resources

- **Video**: Silver Spring Networks presents Utilities & Smart Meter IOT with Apex - `https://www.youtube.com/watch?v=98EW5NGM3u0`
- **Slides**: Silver Spring Networks presents IOT Big Data Ingestion and Processing with Apex - `http://www.slideshare.net/ApacheApex/iot-big-data-ingestion-and-processing-in-hadoop-by-silver-spring-networks`

Application Model and API

In this section, we will look at how Apex applications are specified by the user. Apex applications can be written in a number of ways, using different APIs. We will introduce the Java-based lower-level compositional API, the more recently added high-level stream API, and the ability to define pipelines with SQL.

Later in this book, we will also look at how applications developed with **Apache Beam** can be executed with the Apex engine. Each of these varied source specifications are ultimately translated into a logical Apex **Directed Acyclic Graph** (**DAG**), which is then provided to the Apex engine for execution.

Directed Acyclic Graph (DAG)

An Apex application is represented by a DAG, which expresses processing logic as **operators** (vertices) and **streams** (edges). Streams are unbounded sequences of pieces of data, also called events or **tuples**. The logic that can be executed is arranged in the DAG in sequence or in parallel.

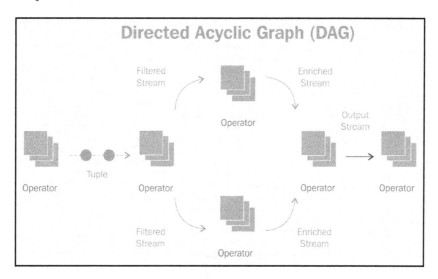

The resulting graph must be acyclic, meaning that any given tuple is processed only once by an operator. An exception to this is iterative processing, also supported by Apex, whereby the output of an operator becomes the input of a predecessor (or upstream operator), introducing a loop in the graph as far as the streams are concerned. This construct is frequently required for machine learning algorithms.

The concept of a DAG is not unique to Apex. It is widely used, for example to represent the history in revision control systems such as Git. Several projects in the Hadoop ecosystem use a DAG to model the processing logic, including Apache Storm, Apache Spark, and Apache Tez. Apache Beam pipelines are represented as a DAG of transformations and each of the streaming engines that currently offer Beam runners also have a DAG as their internal representation.

Operators are the functional building blocks that can contain custom code specific to a single use case or generic functionality that can be applied broadly. The Apex Malhar library (to be introduced later) contains reusable operators, including connectors that can read from various sources, provide filtering or transformation functionality, or output to various destinations:

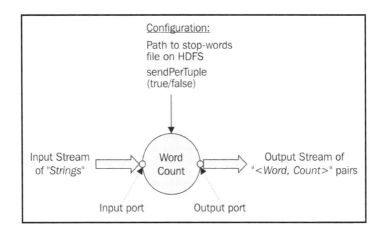

The flow of data is defined through streams, which are connections between ports. Ports are the endpoints of operators to receive data (input ports) or emit data (output ports). Each operator can have multiple ports and each port is connected to at most one stream (ports can also be optional, in which case they don't have to be connected in the DAG). We will look at ports in more detail when discussing operator development. For now, it is sufficient to know that ports provide the type-safe endpoints through which the application developer specifies the data flow by connecting streams. The advantage of using ports versus just a single process and emit method on the operator is that the type of tuple or record is explicit and, when working with a Java IDE, the compiler will show type mismatches as compile errors.

In the following subsections, we will introduce the different APIs that Apex offers to develop applications. Each of these representations is eventually translated into the native DAG, which is the input required by the Apex engine to launch an application.

Apex DAG Java API

The low-level DAG API is defined by the Apex engine. Any application that runs on Apex, irrespective of the original specification format, will be translated into this API. It is sometimes also referred to as **compositional**, as it represents the logical DAG, which will be translated into a physical plan and mapped to the execution layer by the Apex runtime.

The following is the *Word Count* example application, briefly introduced in the *Stream Processing* section earlier written with the DAG API:

```
LineReader lineReader = dag.addOperator("input", new LineReader());
Parser parser = dag.addOperator("parser", new Parser());
UniqueCounter counter = dag.addOperator("counter", new UniqueCounter());
ConsoleOutputOperator cons = dag.addOperator("console", new
  ConsoleOutputOperator());
dag.addStream("lines", lineReader.output, parser.input);
dag.addStream("words", parser.output, counter.data);
dag.addStream("counts", counter.count, cons.input);
```

The developer implements a method that is provided with a DAG handle by the engine (in this case, dag) through which operators are added and then connected with streams.

As mentioned, the Apex library provides many prebuilt operators. Operators can also be custom and encapsulate use case specific logic, or they can come from a library of an organization to share reusable logic across applications.

The DAG API is referred to as **low level** because many aspects are explicit. The developer identifies the operators and is aware of the ports for stream connections. In the case of larger applications, the wiring code can become more challenging to navigate. At the same time, the DAG API offers the most flexibility to the developer and is often used in larger projects that typically involve significant operator development and customization and where the complexity of wiring the DAG is normally not a concern.

High-level Stream Java API

The high-level Apex Stream Java API provides an abstraction from the lower level DAG API. It is a declarative, fluent style API that is easier to learn for someone new to Apex. Instead of identifying individual operators, the developer works with methods on the stream interface to specify the transformations.

The API will internally keep track of the operator(s) needed for each of the transformations and eventually translate it into the lower level DAG. The high-level API is part of the Apex library and outside of the Apex engine.

Here is the *Word Count* example application written with the high-level API (using Java 8 syntax):

```
StreamFactory.fromFolder("/tmp")
    .flatMap(input -> Arrays.asList(input.split(" ")), name("Words"))
    .window(new WindowOption.GlobalWindow(),
            new
```

```
TriggerOption().accumulatingFiredPanes().withEarlyFiringsAtEvery(1))
    .countByKey(input -> new Tuple.PlainTuple<>(new KeyValPair<>(input,
1L)),
        name("countByKey"))
    .map(input -> input.getValue(), name("Counts"))
    .print(name("Console"))
    .populateDag(dag);
```

Windowing is supported and stateful transformations can be applied to a windowed stream, as shown with countByKey in the preceding code listing. The individual windowing options will be explained later in the *Windowing and time* section, as they are applicable in a broader context.

In addition to the transformations that are directly available through the Stream API, the developer can also use other (possibly custom) operators through the addOperator(..) and endsWith(..) methods. For example, if output should be written to JDBC, the connector from the library can be integrated using these generic methods instead of requiring the stream API to have a method like toJDBC.

The ability to add additional operators is important, because not all possible functionality can be baked into the API and larger projects typically require customizations to operators or additional operators that are not part of the Apex library. Additionally, there are many connectors available as part of the library, each with its own set of dependencies and, sometimes, these dependencies and connectors may conflict. In this situation it isn't practical or possible to add a method for each connector to the API. Instead, the developer needs to be able to plug-in the required connector and use it along with the generally applicable transformations that are part of the Stream API.

It is also possible to extend the Stream API with custom methods to provide new transformations without exposing the details of the underlying operator. An example for this extension mechanism can be found in the API unit tests.

 For readers interested to explore the API further, there is a set of example applications in the apex-malhar repository at https://github.com/apache/apex-malhar/tree/master/examples/highlevelapi.

The Stream API is relatively new and there are several enhancements planned, including expansion of the set of windowed transforms, watermark handling, and custom trigger support. The community is also discussing expanding the language support to include a native API for Scala and Python.

SQL

SQL is widely used for data transformation and access, not only with traditional relational databases but also in the Apache big data space with projects like Hive, Drill, Impala, and several others. They all let the user process bounded data at rest using familiar SQL syntax without requiring other programming skills. SQL can be used for ETL purposes but the most common use is for querying data, either directly or through the wide range of SQL compatible BI tools.

Though it has been in use in the Hadoop space for years, SQL is relatively new in the stream processing area as a declarative approach to specify a streaming application. Apex is using **Apache Calcite** for its SQL support, which has already been adopted by many other big data processing frameworks. Instead of every project coming up with its own declarative API, Calcite aims to make SQL the common language. Calcite accepts standard SQL, translates it into relational algebra, facilitates query planning and optimization to physical plan and allows for integration of any data source that can provide collections of records with columns (files, queues, and so on).

There are different use cases for Calcite, including ETL, lookups, search, and so on. With unbounded data sources, the processing of SQL becomes continuous and it is necessary to express windows on the stream that define boundaries at which results can be computed and emitted. Calcite provides streaming SQL extensions to support unbounded data (`https://calcite.apache.org/docs/stream.html`).

The initial SQL support in Apex covers `select`, `insert`, `inner join`, `where` clause and `scalar` functions. Endpoints (sources and sinks) can be files, Kafka or streams that are defined with the DAG API (fusion style) and CSV is supported as a data format.

Here is a simple example to illustrate the translation of SQL into an Apex DAG:

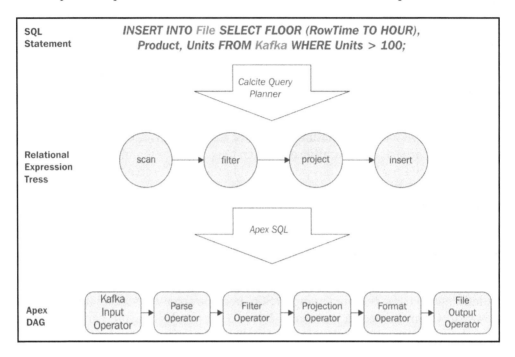

Translation of SQL into Apex DAG

 For more information, you can visit `http://apex.apache.org/docs/ malhar/apis/calcite/`.

The community is working on the support for windowed transformations (required for aggregations), which will be based on the scalable window and accumulation state management of the Apex library (refer to `Chapter 3`, *The Apex Library*).

JSON

Another way of assembling applications without writing Java code is through JSON.

This format can be created manually, but it could also be used to generate the DAG from a different frontend, like a visual tool. Here is the word count written in JSON:

```
{
    "displayName": "WordCountJSON",
    "operators": [
    { "name": "input", ... }, { "name": "parse", ... },
    {
        "name": "count",
        "class": "com.datatorrent.lib.algo.UniqueCounter",
         "properties": { "com.datatorrent.lib.algo.UniqueCounter": {
"cumulative":
            false } }
    },
    { "name": "console", ... } ],
    "streams": [
    { "name": "lines",
      "sinks": [ { "operatorName": "parse", "portName": "input" } ],
      "source": { "operatorName": "input", "portName": "output" }
    },
    { "name": "words", ... },
    { "name": "counts", ... }
    ]
}
```

Just like applications that are written in Java, the JSON files will be included in the application package, along with the operator dependencies. Upon launch of the application, the Apex client will parse these files and translate them into a native DAG representation.

Windowing and time

Streams of unbounded data require windowing to establish boundaries to process data and emit results. Processing always occurs in a window and there are different types of windows and strategies to assign individual data records to windows.

Often, the relationship of data processed and time is explicit, with the data containing a timestamp identifying the **event time** or when an event occurred. This is usually the case with streaming sources that emit individual events. However, there are also cases where time can be derived from a container. For example, when data arrives batched in hourly files, time may be derived from the file name instead of individual records. Sometimes, data may arrive without any timestamp, and the processor at the source needs to assign a timestamp based on **arrival time** or **processing time** in order to perform stateful windowed operations.

The windowing support provided by the Apex library largely follows the Apache Beam model. It is flexible and broadly applicable to different use cases. It is also completely different from and not to be confused with the Apex engine's native arrival time based **streaming window** mechanism.

The streaming window is a processing interval that can be applied to use cases that don't require handling of out-of-order inputs based on event time. It assumes that the stream can be sliced into fixed time intervals (default 500 ms), at which the engine performs callbacks that the operator can use to (globally) perform aggregate operations over multiple records that arrived in that interval.

The intervals are aligned with the internal **checkpointing** mechanism and suitable for processing optimizations such as flushing files or batching writes to a database. It cannot support transformation and other processing based on event time, because events in the real world don't necessarily arrive in order and perfectly aligned with these internal intervals. The windowing support provided by the Apex library is more flexible and broadly applicable, including for processing based on event time with out-of-order arrival of events.

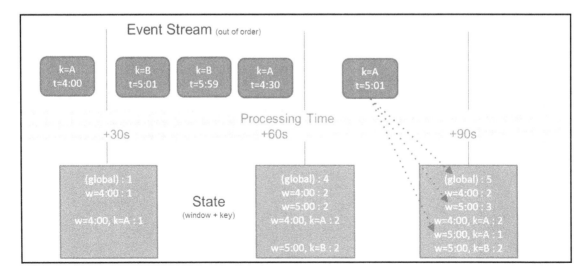

The preceding example shows a sequence of events, each with a timestamp (**t**) and key (**k**) and their processing order. Note the difference between processing and event time. It should be possible to process the same sequence at different times with the same result. That's only possible when the transformations understand event time and are capable maintaining the computational state (potentially multiple open windows at the same time with high key cardinality). The example shows how the state tracks multiple windows (**w**). Each window has an associated timestamp (4:00 and 5:00 and global for a practically infinite window) and accumulates its own counts regardless of processing time based on the timestamps of the events (and optionally by key).

Value proposition of Apex

The cases studies presented earlier showcase how Apex is used in critical production deployments that solves important business problems. This section will highlight key capabilities of Apex and how they relate to the value proposition. To understand the challenges in finding the right technology and building successful solutions, it is helpful to look at the evolution of the big data technology space over the last few years, which essentially started with Apache Hadoop.

Hadoop was originally built as a Java-based platform for search indexing in Yahoo, inspired by Google's MapReduce paper. Its promise was to perform processing of big data on commodity hardware, reducing the infrastructure cost of such systems significantly. Hadoop became an Apache Software Foundation (ASF) top-level project in 2008, consisting of HDFS for storage and MapReduce for processing. This marked the beginning of an entire ecosystem of other Apache projects beyond MapReduce, including HBase, Hive, Oozie, and so on. Recently, we have started to see the shift away from MapReduce towards projects such as Apache Spark and Apache Kafka, leading to a transformation within the ecosystem that reflects the need for a different architecture and processing paradigm.

A further indication is that even leading Hadoop vendors have started to rebrand products and conferences to expand beyond the original Hadoop roots. Over the last 10 years, there has been a lot of hype around Hadoop, but the success rate of projects has not kept up. Challenges include:

- A very large number of tools and vendors with often confusing positioning, making it difficult to evaluate and identify the right options
- Complexity in development and integration, a steep learning curve, and long time to production

- Scarcity of skill set: experts in the technology are difficult to hire
- Production-readiness: often the primary focus is on features and functionality while operational aspects are sidelined, which is a problem for business critical systems.

Matt Turck of FirstMark Capital summed it up with the following declaration:

> *Big Data success is not about implementing one piece of technology (like Hadoop or anything else), but instead requires putting together an assembly line of technologies, people and processes.*

So, how does Apex help to succeed with stream data processing use cases?

High Performant	Developer Friendly
In-Memory Distributed True Stream Processing High Throughput *and* Low Latency (sub-second)	Library of Operators Easy to use API Custom Logic/Operators Unified Architecture for Streaming & Batch
Stateful Architecture	**Resiliency & Operability**
End-to-end Exactly-once Automatic Checkpointing Event Time Windowing Scalable State Management Resume from Checkpoint	Fault Tolerant / High Availability Horizontal Scalability Dynamic Scaling Dynamic Updates Multi-tenancy

Since its inception, the Apex project was focused on enterprise-readiness as a key architectural requirement, including aspects such as:

- The fault tolerance and high availability of all components, automatic recovery from failures, and the ability to resume applications from previous state.
- Stateful processing architecture with strong processing guarantees (end-to-end exactly-once) to enable mission critical use cases that depend on correctness.
- Scalability and superior performance with high throughput and low latency and the ability to process millions of events per second without compromising fault tolerance, correctness and latency.

- Security, multi-tenancy and operability, including a REST API with metrics for monitoring, and so on
- A comprehensive library of connectors for integration with the external systems typically found in enterprise architecture. The library is an integral part of the project, maintained by the community and guaranteed to be compatible with the engine.
- Ability for code reuse in the JVM environment, and Java as the primary development language, which has a very rich ecosystem and large developer base that is accessible to the kinds of customers who require big data solutions

With several large-scale, mission-critical deployments in *production*, some of which we discussed earlier, Apex has proven that it can deliver.

Apex requires a cluster to run on and, as of now, this means a Hadoop cluster with YARN and HDFS. Apex will likely support other cluster managers such as Mesos, Kubernetes, or Docker Enterprise in the future, as they gain adoption in the target enterprise space. Running on top of a cluster allows Apex to provide features such as dynamic scaling and resource allocation, automatic recovery and support for multi-tenancy.

For users who already have Hadoop clusters as well as the operational skills and processes to run the infrastructure, it is easy to deploy an Apex application, as it does not require installation of any additional components on cluster nodes. If no existing Hadoop cluster is available, there are several options to get started with varying degrees of upfront investment, including cloud deployment such as Amazon EMR, installation of any of the Hadoop distributions (Cloudera, Hortonworks, MapR) or just a Docker image on a local laptop for experimentation.

Big data applications in general are not trivial, especially not the pipelines that solve complex use cases and have to run in production 24/7 without downtime. When working with Apex, the development process, APIs, library, and examples are tailored to enable a Java developer to become productive and obtain results quickly. By using readily available connectors for sources and sinks, it is possible to quickly build an initial **proof of concept** (**PoC**) application that consumes real data, does some of the required processing, and stores results. The more involved custom development for using case-specific business logic can then occur in iterations. The process of building an Apex application will be covered in detail in the next chapter.

Apex separates the application functionality (or business logic) and the behavior of the engine. Aspects such as parallelism, operator chaining/locality, checkpointing and resource allocations for individual operators can all be controlled through configuration and modified without affecting the application code or triggering a full build/test cycle. This allows benchmarking and tuning to take place independently. For example, it is possible to run the same packaged application with different configurations to test trade-offs such as lower parallelism/longer time to completion (batch use case), and so on.

Low latency and stateful processing

Apex is a native streaming architecture. As previously discussed, this allows processing of events as soon as they arrive without artificial delay, which enables real-time use cases with very low latency. Another important capability is stateful processing. Windowing may require a potentially very large amount of computational state. However, state also needs to be tracked in connectors for correct interaction with external systems. For example, the Apex Kafka connector will keep track of partition offsets as part of its checkpointed state so that it can correctly resume consumption after recovery from failure. Similarly, state is required for reading from files and other sources. For sources that don't allow for replay, it is even necessary to retain all consumed data in the connector until it has been fully processed in the DAG.

Stateful stream processors have what is also referred to as continuous operator model. Operators are initialized once, at launch time. Subsequently, as events are processed one by one, state can be accumulated and held in-memory as long as it is needed for the computation. Access to the memory is fast, which allows for very low latency.

So, what about fault tolerance? The platform is responsible for checkpointing the state. It can do so efficiently and provides everything needed to guarantee that state can be restored and is consistent in the event of failure. Unlike the early days of Apache Storm with per tuple acknowledgement overhead and user responsibility for state handling, the next generation streaming architectures provide fault tolerance mechanisms that do not compromise performance and latency. How Apex solves this, will be covered in detail in Chapter 5, *Fault Tolerance and Reliability*.

Native streaming versus micro-batch

Let's examine how the stateful stream processing (as found in Apex and Flink) compares to the micro-batch based approach in Apache Spark Streaming.

Let's look at the following diagram:

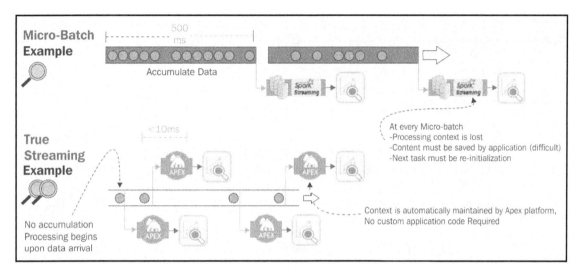

On top, we see an example of processing in Spark Streaming and below we see an example in Apex in the preceding diagram. Based on its underlying "stateless" batch architecture, Spark Streaming processes a stream by dividing it into small batches (**micro-batches**) that typically last from 500 ms to a few seconds. A new task is scheduled for every micro-batch. Once scheduled, the new task needs to be initialized. Such initialization could include opening connections to external resources, loading data that is needed for processing and so on. Overall this implies a per task overhead that limits the micro-batch frequency and leads to a latency trade-off.

In classical batch processing, tasks may last for the entire bounded input data set. Any computational state remains internal to the task and there is typically no special consideration for fault tolerance required, since whenever there is a failure, the task can restart from the beginning.

However, with unbounded data and streaming, a stateful operation like counting would need to maintain the current count and it would need to be transferred across task boundaries. As long as the state is small, this may be manageable. However, when transformations are applied to large key cardinality, the state can easily grow to a size that makes it impractical to swap in and out (cost of serialization, I/O, and so on). The correct state management is not easy to solve without underlying platform support, especially not when accuracy, consistency and fault tolerance are important.

Performance

Even with big data scale out architectures on commodity hardware, efficiency matters. Better efficiency of the platform lowers cost. If the architecture can handle a given workload with a fraction of the hardware, it will result in reduced Total Cost of Ownership (TCO). Apex provides several advanced mechanisms to optimize efficiency, such as stream locality and parallel partitioning, which will be covered in `Chapter 4`, *Scalability, Low Latency, and Performance*.

Apex is capable of very low latency processing (< 10 ms), and is well suited for use cases such as the real-time threat detection as discussed earlier. Apex can be used to deliver latency processing Service Level Agreement (SLA) in conjunction with speculative execution (processing the same event multiple times in parallel to prevent delay) due to a unique feature: the ability to recover a path or subset of operators without resetting the entire DAG.

Only a fraction of real-time use cases may have such low latency and SLA requirements. However, it is generally desirable to avoid unnecessary trade-offs. If a platform can deliver high throughput (millions of events per second) with low latency and everything else is equal, why not choose such a platform over one that forces a throughput/latency trade-off? Various benchmarking studies have shown Apex to be highly performant in providing high throughput while maintaining very low latency.

Where Apex excels

Overall, Apex has characteristics that positively impact time to production, quality, and cost. It is a particularly good fit for use cases that require:

- High performance and low latency, possibly with SLA
- Large scale, fault tolerant state management and end-to-end exactly-once processing guarantees
- Computationally complex production pipelines where accuracy, functional stability, security and certification are critical and ad hoc changes not desirable

The following figure provides a high-level overview of the business value Apex is capable of delivering:

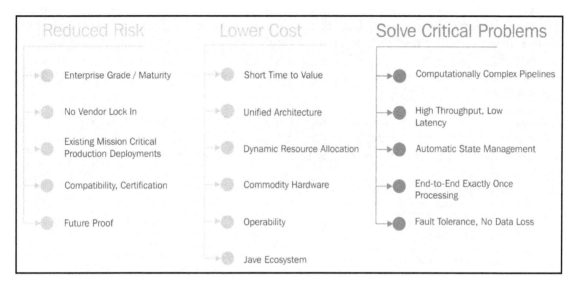

Where Apex is not suitable

On the other hand, there are a few related areas of interest that Apex does not target or is less suited for (as of this writing):

- Data exploration in ad hoc, experimental environments such as Spark's interactive shell.
- Machine learning. Apex currently does not have its own library of machine learning algorithms, although it does have the capability for iterative processing and can be used as execution engine as seen in Apache SAMOA.
- Interactive SQL. Apex has basic support for streaming SQL transformations, but is not comparable to Hive or similar tools.
- At the time of writing, Apex does not have support for Python, although it is being discussed within the community and likely to happen in the future. (The Apex library has a Jython operator, but users typically want to run native Python code and also specify the pipeline in Python.)

Summary

This chapter introduced stream processing and Apache Apex as a next-generation, data-in-motion processing platform. The case studies that were presented illustrate how Apex can be used to solve important business problems and implement solutions that deliver value and succeed in production. We looked at the application development model and various APIs that are available to develop Apex applications. Finally, the value proposition of Apex was covered.

The next chapter will cover the development process in detail. Supporting technical capabilities and architectural characteristics such as fault tolerance, performance, integration with other systems, and scalability will be covered in detail in subsequent chapters.

2

Getting Started with Application Development

The previous chapter introduced concepts, use cases, and application model. This chapter will be about application development and guide the reader through the process of building and running their first application. The examples will be simple; more comprehensive applications will be covered in subsequent chapters.

In this chapter we will cover the following topics:

- Development process and methodology
- Setting up the development environment
- Creating a new Maven project
- Custom operator development
- Testing within the IDE
- Running application on the cluster

Development process and methodology

Development of an Apex application starts with mapping the functional specification to operators (smaller functional building blocks), which can then be composed into a DAG to collectively provide the functionality required for the use case.

This involves identifying the data sources, formats, transformations and sinks for the application, and finding matching operators from the Apex library (which will be covered in the next chapter). In most cases, the required connectors will be available from the library that support frequent sources, such as files and Kafka, along with many other external systems that are part of the Apache Big Data ecosystem.

With the comprehensive operator library and set of examples to cover frequently used I/O cases and transformations, it is often possible to assemble a preliminary end-to-end flow that covers a subset of the functionality quickly, before building out the complete business logic in detail.

 Examples that show how to work with frequently used library operators and accelerate the path to an initial running application can be found at `https://github.com/apache/apex-malhar/tree/master/examples`.

Having a basic pipeline working early on in the target environment (or at least close to it) allows for various important integration and operational requirements to be evaluated in parallel, such as security and access control. It also establishes a baseline for iterative and parallel development, and for testing the full-featured operators. Experience from working on complex pipelines shows how having an early basic pipeline can reduce risk and provides better visibility into the progress of a bigger project, especially when it has many integration points and a larger development team. Essentially, development dependencies can follow the modular structure of the DAG, allowing the full pipeline to be gradually built up and functions further downstream to be developed in parallel with mocked input, when needed.

A large project broken down into a series of smaller and more manageable milestones would roughly involve the following sequence of steps:

1. Writing the Java code for new or customized operator.
2. Unit testing (in IDE, no cluster environment needed).
3. Integrating the operator into DAG.
4. Integration testing (testing the DAG with potentially mocked data, in IDE).
5. Configuring operator properties for the target environment (connector setting, and so on).
6. End-to-end testing with realistic data set in the target environment.
7. Tuning (optimizing resource utilization, configuring appropriate platform attributes such as processing locality, memory and CPU allocation, scaling and so on).

Following a similar sequence will ensure that basic functional issues are discovered early on (ideally within the IDE environment where it is far more efficient to debug and fix) before fully packaging and deploying the pipeline to a cluster.

In subsequent sections, we will look at each of these phases in more detail.

Setting up the development environment

Development of Apex applications requires a Java development environment with the following:

- **Java Development Kit (JDK)**: Apex applications are mostly written in Java, and Apex itself is implemented in Java. Other Java Virtual Machine (JVM) languages such as Scala can also be used, but this is outside the scope of this book.
- **Maven**: Apex comes with a Maven Archetype to bootstrap new projects and the Apex project itself also uses Maven as build tool.

In addition to the above, it is recommended to have an IDE with Maven support such as IntelliJ or Eclipse. Apex provides code style settings for these IDEs that can optionally be used.

It is further recommended to have Git installed. Git is not required to build an application, but it is a convenient way to fetch the Apex source code and is especially useful for easily navigating the full operator library (*apex-malhar*) project within the IDE when working on operator customizations.

 For the latest details on setting up a development environment, please refer to http://apex.apache.org/docs/apex/apex_development_setup/.

Application development can be done on any host operating system that can provide the above, including macOS, Windows, and Linux. Much of the development and functional testing can be done on the local machine within the IDE. Apex applications can run in embedded mode for this purpose, which eliminates the need to have a Hadoop cluster, which typically runs on Linux. Options for running Hadoop will be covered later as well.

Creating a new Maven project

Apex applications are packaged in a special ZIP file format that contains everything needed for an application to be launched on a cluster (dependency jars, configuration files, and so on). It is roughly comparable to the uber jar approach that some other frameworks employ, with the difference that dependencies in the Apex package remain as individual JAR files, rather than being flattened into a standard JAR.

 More information about Apex application packages can be found at
`http://apex.apache.org/docs/apex/application_packages/#apache-apex-packages`.

It would be a rather involved task to set up a new Maven project from scratch. The Apex application archetype simplifies the process of creating an application skeleton for the expected artifact structure. Here is an example of the Maven command to create an Apex application archetype:

```
mvn archetype:generate \
  -DarchetypeGroupId=org.apache.apex \
  -DarchetypeArtifactId=apex-app-archetype -DarchetypeVersion=RELEASE \
  -DgroupId=com.example -Dpackage=com.example.myapexapp -
DartifactId=myapexapp \
  -Dversion=1.0-SNAPSHOT
```

In this case, we are using `RELEASE` as the archetype version to refer to the latest available Apex release (`http://apex.apache.org/downloads.html`). You can replace it with a specific version you want to use instead, which will then also become the Apex engine dependency version in the generated `pom.xml`.

The newly generated project does not depend on or inherit anything from a parent POM. So, if your organization requires a common parent POM, then you will be able to use that without extensive changes to this project.

If, instead of creating a brand new project, you would like to start from a similar existing project and modify it to cater to your use case, have a look at the examples that come with the Apex library at `https://github.com/apache/apex-malhar/tree/master/examples` that also cover many operators that are frequently needed in projects.

The generated project has the following typical Maven project structure:

```
$ tree myapexapp/
myapexapp/
├── pom.xml
├── src
```

```
|     ├──── assemble
|     |     └──── appPackage.xml
|     ├──── main
|     |     ├──── java
|     |     |     └──── com
|     |     |           └──── example
|     |     |                 └──── myapexapp
|     |     |                       ├──── Application.java
|     |     |                       └──── RandomNumberGenerator.java
|     |     └──── resources
|     |           └──── META-INF
|     |                 └──── properties.xml
|     ├──── site
|     |     └──── conf
|     |           └──── my-app-conf1.xml
|     └──── test
|           ├──── java
|           |     └──── com
|           |           └──── example
|           |                 └──── myapexapp
|           |                       └──── ApplicationTest.java
|           └──── resources
|                 └──── log4j.properties
└──── XmlJavadocCommentsExtractor.xsl
```

In addition to the usual Java main and test directories, the project contains an assembly specification that defines the structure of the resulting application package. There is also an optional site/conf directory that can be used for additional configuration files that the user can select when launching the application. To try out the project, run the simple placeholder application with the JUnit test:

```
cd myapexapp
mvn test
...
hello world: 0.25805982800750105
hello world: 0.8945864455634059
...
Tests run: 1, Failures: 0, Errors: 0, Skipped: 0, Time elapsed: 11.78 sec
```

The test runs for about 10 seconds and prints generated numbers. Successful execution validates the project and environment setup.

The test is actually an integration test for the entire placeholder application, not just a unit test for a single class or a method within a class. It uses the embedded execution mode that will run the application DAG within the unit test JVM. This is the preferred way for functional testing your application and does not require a cluster.

We will now examine various aspects of the application and the process of making changes to its logic and configuration.

Application specifications

Let's start by transforming this placeholder application into an application that counts words – the Hello World equivalent for big data processing frameworks. The functionality is easy to understand and not very important, as our focus here is on the development process.

The full source code of the modified application is available at `https://github.com/tweise/apex-samples/tree/master/wordcount`. Here is the modified application assembly in `Application.java`:

```
@Override
  public void populateDAG(DAG dag, Configuration conf)
  {
   LineByLineFileInputOperator lineReader = dag.addOperator("input",
       new LineByLineFileInputOperator());
    LineSplitter parser = dag.addOperator("parser", new LineSplitter());
    UniqueCounter counter = dag.addOperator("counter", new
UniqueCounter());
    GenericFileOutputOperator<Object> output = dag.addOperator("output",
       new GenericFileOutputOperator<>());
    output.setConverter(new ToStringConverter());
    dag.addStream("lines", lineReader.output, parser.input);
    dag.addStream("words", parser.output, counter.data);
    dag.addStream("counts", counter.count, output.input);
  }
```

The pipeline reads from a file (`LineByLineFileInputOperator`), then each line is split into words (`LineSplitter`), then occurrences of each word are counted (`UniqueCounter`), and finally the result is written to the file (`GenericFileOutputOperator`). Apart from the `LineSplitter` operator, all other operators are part of the Apex library. After all the operators are added to the DAG, the pipeline is completed connecting the operator (through their ports) using `addStream`. This is the explicit style of composing the logical DAG (rather than using the high level API), hence the name compositional API. Note that ports must always be defined in their respective operators, and may not always be named input and output.

Custom operator development

As our example application has the `LineSplitter` operator, which is not part of the Apex library, we will use it as an example to illustrate the process of developing a custom operator.

Splitting a line into words is, of course, a simple stateless operation. Connectors and stateful transformations will be more involved, and there are many examples in the Apex library to look at for this.

Here is the line splitter:

```
public class LineSplitter extends BaseOperator
{
  // default pattern for word-separators
  private static final Pattern nonWordDefault =     Pattern.compile
    ("[\\p{Punct}\\s]+");

  private String nonWordStr;              // configurable regex
  private transient Pattern nonWord;      // compiled regex

  /**
    * Output port on which words from the current file are emitted
    */
  public final transient DefaultOutputPort<String> output = new
    DefaultOutputPort<>();

  /**
    * Input port on which lines from the current file are received
    */
  public final transient DefaultInputPort<String> input = new
    DefaultInputPort<String>()
  {

    @Override
    public void process(String line)
    {
      // line; split it into words and emit them
      final String[] words = nonWord.split(line);
      for (String word : words) {
        if (word.isEmpty()) {
          continue;
        }
        output.emit(word);
      }
    }
  };
```

```
/**
 * Returns the regular expression that matches strings between words
 * @return Regular expression for strings that separate words
 */
public String getNonWordStr()
{
  return nonWordStr;
}

/**
 * Sets the regular expression that matches strings between words
 * @param regex New regular expression for strings that separate words
 */
public void setNonWordStr(String regex)
{
  nonWordStr = regex;
}

/**
 * {@inheritDoc}
 * Set nonWord to the default pattern if necessary
 */
@Override
public void setup(OperatorContext context)
{
  if (null == nonWordStr) {
    nonWord = nonWordDefault;
  } else {
    nonWord = Pattern.compile(nonWordStr);
  }
}
}
```

The operator has two ports: one input port to receive the lines and one output port to emit the words that result from splitting the lines. The processing logic (line splitting) is in the process method of the input port and that is really the logic of the operator. The rest of the code is not related to splitting lines, but more to the usability and efficient working of the operator.

We see a property `nonWordStr` (with getter and setter), which allows the user to configure the regular expression used to split the lines. We will later in this chapter see how operators can be configured without changing the Java code of the pipeline. The existence of respective operator properties is a prerequisite for this.

There is also a setup method, which is used to perform one-time initialization. This is an opportunity to perform operations that we don't want repeated on every event, for example, because they take time or would waste resources. In this case, the regular expression needs to be compiled only once, as there is no need to do it for every event. The compiled regex is assigned to a transient field, indicating that it isn't part of the operator state and should not be checkpointed. If the operator fails, it will be re-deployed and the setup will be executed again. This operator is stateless- it does not have any fields that the engine needs to manage as part of checkpointing for fault tolerance. If the operator were a counter, for example, then it would have state that needs to be recovered on a failure and we would want the fields that represent the counter's state to be checkpointed. Hence, they would not be transient.

The Apex operator model

Now that we have seen an example of a custom operator implementation, let's have a closer look at the Apex operator life cycle interfaces. The operators that are specified in the logical DAG will be deployed into the execution layer container (worker process) before they can do actual work. The Apex engine defines an execution life cycle for operators with corresponding interfaces and callback methods—the operator API. Operators that can be used in Apex applications have to be implemented in a way that conforms to the operator API. There are many prebuilt and ready to use operators in the Apex library, but the user isn't limited to those, as we have just seen (in the previous example) with the custom operator example.

The following diagram illustrates the operator life cycle after deployment in a container:

In the case of an input operator (which has no port to receive incoming events), the engine will call `emitTuples()` instead of the `process()` method on the port. Let's have look at the individual callbacks in more detail:

- `setup`: This is a one-time call when the operator gets deployed. This is the opportunity to perform initialization work such as creation of caches, connections to external systems, and so on. This method should not perform actual data processing work. It is for preparation only.
- `beginWindow`: This marks the start of a streaming window (the Apex engine's processing time slice of a stream that was discussed in `Chapter 1`, *Introduction to Apex* and not to be confused with event time windowing). This is a repeating callback, as the operator is now in processing mode and can therefore also emit results on output ports or write data to external systems. The most typical work done in `beginWindow` is the resetting of transient state that lasts for the duration of the interval. It is also possible to emit tuples during this callback, such as for recovery logic that requires replay of previously emitted tuples from a log.

- `emitTuples` (`input operator`): This is periodically called by the engine, it provides an opportunity for the operator to emit data tuples to an output stream (which transports them for further processing to downstream operators). As an example, the Kafka connector emits tuples received from the consumer API to the output port. The engine will call `emitTuples` as many times as possible within the streaming window interval. Therefore, it is recommended that the operator code return control to the engine as fast as possible and does not block. In fact, most of the connectors that read from external systems do that in a separate IO thread (managed in setup/teardown) that will place available data into a holding buffer from which `emitTuples` will only transfer whatever is available up to a limit before returning control.

- `InputPort.process`: For operators other than the input operators we just discussed, this is the entry point to the processing logic when new data is available on the stream. The engine will pass individual tuples to process (one at a time) and that can repeat many times within a streaming window. The type of tuples is that of the stream and the user's schema, it can be any Java object (POJO, Map, and so on). Examples of processing logic are simple stateless operation such as filtering that immediately emits a result as seen in the earlier example or stateful transformation, such as counting where accumulation occurs within the operator and aggregate results emitted later. Just like for `emitTuples`, the operator logic should not block and return control as fast as possible to not interfere with the overall processing in the DAG.

- `endWindow`: When a streaming window interval has lapsed, the engine will call this method. This is an opportunity to perform operations on data that would be too expensive to do individually such as database commit, flushing files. It can also be used to emit an aggregate result, such as a count per interval or update metric fields in an operator.

 As a side note, there is an attribute, `APPLICATION_WINDOW_COUNT`, for the application developer to control the frequency of `beginWindow` and `endWindow` callbacks in the form of multiples of streaming window intervals. It won't be further discussed here, as the recommended way to optimize resources consistent with fault tolerant state management is the `CheckpointNotificationListener`.

- `teardown`: This should perform the opposite of setup. Like setup, `teardown` isn't part of the data processing flow and should not be used to affect any related state. For example, it would be invalid to commit to the database in `teardown`. There is also no guarantee that this method will be called. When the process terminates unexpectedly the engine may not be able to perform the callback and logic in the operator should be written with that expectation. For example, it is ideal and best effort to close files or connections, but it may not be possible and the operator needs to be prepared for it. An example would be a file lease in HDFS that will prevent from a replacement operator to write to the same file, making it necessary to use intermediate file name until they are final.

CheckpointListener/CheckpointNotificationListener

This interface provides hooks for the operator developer to align behavior with the engine's checkpointing mechanism (which will be covered in detail in the `Chapter 5`, *Fault Tolerance and Reliability*). For now, it will be sufficient to understand that during checkpointing the state of the operator is externalized and saved to durable storage. In order to optimize this and align any additional fault tolerance support that the operator requires, the interfaces provide:

- `beforeCheckpoint`: This is called before the engine extracts the state from the operator. This is an opportunity to update the state. For example, suppose the operator implementation needs to write state to a write ahead log and needs to remember the file name(s) and offset range(s) so that when there is a need to recover, it knows what to read. In this example, the operator would flush pending data to the file and the update it's state containing the offset information, so that the meta information is checkpointed and available during recovery.
- `checkpointed`: This is called immediately after a checkpoint is completed. This could be used to optimize resources or record information about a completed checkpoint. In most cases, the operator or developer would implement `beforeCheckpoint`, however.
- `committed`: This is called with the latest known streaming window interval identifier that was fully processed in the entire DAG and therefore will never need to be replayed during recovery. This is an opportunity for operator implementations to finalize state and make it available to external consumers. For example, a file writer could close intermediate files and move/rename them to the final location. Alternatively, incremental state saving mechanisms can materialize that state and drop recovery logs.

ActivationListener

This optional interface enables callbacks that are somewhat similar to setup and teardown but they occur at a different point during deployment and there are a few cases where using this interface may be necessary.

- `activate`: This is called after the operator along with its ports was initialized (set up) and immediately before processing of tuples starts. As an example, this is a place for initialization logic that depends on the initialization of the operator ports, such as obtaining the tuple schema or other port attributes.
- `deactivate`: This should perform the opposite of activate.

IdleTimeHandler

Sometimes, an operator is *idle*, which means there is no work to do because no tuples are available on the input stream for processing (or in the case of an input operator, no data is produced on the output port(s)). Some operators could make use of the idle time to do bookkeeping work, such as maintaining caches or other other background processing. Apex provides the **IdleTimeHandler** interface that operators may implement to use the extra CPU time in the engine managed operator thread.

- `handleIdleTime`: This is called whenever the engine detects that the operator isn't doing any processing. If the implementation also doesn't have any work to do, it should block the call for a short duration to prevent a busy loop, as the method is called again and again until the operator is no longer idle.

This section was an introduction to developing custom operators. Note that, in many cases, it isn't necessary to develop a complete custom operator from scratch. Often it is sufficient to extend an existing operator with a few overrides or configure a generic operator with the desired behavior. An example would be the `FunctionOperator` that accepts a user defined function (equivalent of Java 8 Lambda Expression) as property. It eliminates the needs to write boilerplate code that deals with operator ports and life cycle methods, which are in many cases not required to express the business logic. The high-level Java API, which was introduced in the first chapter, provides the same benefit of concise specification of custom logic for those cases where the predefined primitive functions are sufficient.

 For more information about custom operator development, please refer to http://apex.apache.org/docs/apex/operator_development/ #developing-custom-operators.

Application configuration

In the previous sections, we have seen how applications can be specified and how custom operators can be developed (with an example for configurable property). Most operators have properties that need to be configured, for example, a file reader will need to be supplied with the directory path or a Kafka consumer the broker address and topic. Whoever deploys the application needs to know and be able to supply values for these properties.

In addition to properties that are directly related to the functionality of an operator, there is another category of settings called **attributes** that control behavior of the platform (as opposed to the functionality of operators).

Attributes are defined for three different scopes:

- **Application**: Platform behavior for the application as a whole, such as streaming window interval, container JVM options, container heartbeat interval and timeout, and so on. See the complete list of attributes here `https://ci.apache.org/projects/apex-core/apex-core-javadoc-release-3.6/com/datatorrent/api/Context.DAGContext.html`.

- **Operator**: Platform behavior for individual operators like resource requirements (memory, CPU), partitioner, checkpoint interval. See the complete list of attributes here `https://ci.apache.org/projects/apex-core/apex-core-javadoc-release-3.6/com/datatorrent/api/Context.OperatorContext.html`.

- **Port**: Settings related to ports of an operator that, for example, affect how data is moved between operators. Examples include buffer memory, queue capacity, stream codec. See complete list of attributes here `https://ci.apache.org/projects/apex-core/apex-core-javadoc-release-3.6/com/datatorrent/api/Context.PortContext.html`.

Since settings can vary between environments or refer to security sensitive information like credentials, they should not be embedded into the application code, but defined externally and provided when the application is launched. Source and format of the configuration depends on the tool that is used the launch the application and the following example will apply to the Apex command line interface (CLI), that expects files in Hadoop configuration file format:

```
<property>
<name>apex.application.MyFirstApplication.operator.input.prop.directory</name>
  <value>./src/test/resources</value>
</property>
```

```
<property>
<name>apex.application.MyFirstApplication.operator.output.prop.filePath</na
me>
   <value>./target</value>
</property>
<property>
   <name>apex.application.MyFirstApplication.operator.output.prop
     .outputFileName</name>
   <value>wordcountresult</value>
</property>
<property>
<name>apex.application.MyFirstApplication.operator.output.prop.maxLength</n
ame>
   <value>500</value>
</property>
<property>
   <name>apex.application.MyFirstApplication.operator.output.prop
     .alwaysWriteToTmp</name>
   <value>false</value>
</property>
```

The configuration block shows how the operator properties of input file reader and output file writer of our word count application are configured for execution inside the project directory on the local machine.

Individual properties match the operator's getters and setters per Java bean convention. The extra application prefix allows multiple DAGs to be configured with a single file, separated by application name (`MyFirstApplication` was the name annotated to the application class). Operator names like `output` match the names that were used in the `addOperator()` calls.

 Examples for attributes, streams, and other details on the available settings and ways to specify them can be found at `http://apex.apache.org/docs/ apex/application_packages/#application-configuration`.

Testing in the IDE

This section will show how the previously created example application can be configured and run as a JUnit test within the IDE. Setting up an integration test that can be executed after every change will avoid a full package/deploy cycle to run on a cluster just to find basic issues. It allows for efficient debugging and will also come in handy when setting up continuous integration for a project.

Writing the integration test

The test covers the entire DAG and will run the application in embedded mode. In embedded mode, all operators and containers share the JUnit JVM. Containers are threads (instead of separate processes) but the data flow still behaves as if operators lived in separate processes. This means operators execute asynchronously as they would in a distributed cluster and data is transferred over the loopback interface (if that's how the streams are configured).

```
@Test
public void testApplication() throws Exception {
  EmbeddedAppLauncher<?> launcher =
Launcher.getLauncher(LaunchMode.EMBEDDED);
  Attribute.AttributeMap launchAttributes = new
    Attribute.AttributeMap.DefaultAttributeMap();
  launchAttributes.put(EmbeddedAppLauncher.RUN_ASYNC, true);
  Configuration conf = new Configuration(false);
  conf.addResource(this.getClass().getResourceAsStream("/META-
    INF/properties.xml"));
  conf.addResource(this.getClass().getResourceAsStream("/wordcounttest-
    properties.xml"));

  File resultFile = new File("./target/wordcountresult_4.0");
  if (resultFile.exists() && !resultFile.delete()) {
    throw new AssertionError("Failed to delete " + resultFile);
  }
  AppHandle appHandle = launcher.launchApp(new Application(), conf,
    launchAttributes);
  long timeoutMillis = System.currentTimeMillis() + 10000;
  while (!appHandle.isFinished() && System.currentTimeMillis() <
timeoutMillis) {
    Thread.sleep(500);
    if (resultFile.exists() && resultFile.length() > 0) {
      break;
    }
  }
  appHandle.shutdown(ShutdownMode.KILL);
  Assert.assertTrue(resultFile.exists() && resultFile.length() > 0);
  String result = FileUtils.readFileToString(resultFile);
  Assert.assertTrue(result, result.contains("MyFirstApplication=5"));
}
```

The flow of the test is as follows:

1. The test driver creates a launcher for embedded mode.
2. Load the configuration (from the standard location as well as overrides that are needed for the test.
3. Make sure that the result area is clean, which means any residual from previous runs should be removed as part of the test initialization.
4. Instantiate the application and launch it with the embedded cluster, keep the returned handle to check and control the asynchronous execution.
5. In a loop, check if the application has terminated or cancel it after the expected results are in. In case the logic checks for the expected result files and with the timeout also makes sure that the test does not turn into a runaway process if the application fails to produce the expected results.
6. After the results are available, check the details with assertions.

The test completes within a few seconds and can easily be run within the IDE whenever a change is made. At this stage, there is no need to package the application, launch it on a Hadoop cluster, and diagnose issues by collecting logs and other information from distributed workers. Instead, when a test fails it is most of the time straightforward to identify the cause and where appropriate step through the code with a debugger.

Running the application on YARN

Once the application is functionally complete and passes the tests in embedded mode, it is time to take it for a test drive on the cluster. Compared to working within the IDE, execution in distributed mode requires a different approach and tools for deployment, testing and troubleshooting of the application. In this section, we will introduce YARN as the execution layer and how to setup and navigate the cluster for various tasks. Note that, as of release 3.6, Apex supports YARN as cluster manager, support for other infrastructure is likely to follow in one of the next releases.

Execution layer components

YARN (Yet Another Resource Negotiator) originates from an effort to separate processing resource management from the application framework MapReduce, which was tightly coupled in the first version of Hadoop. Today, many of the big data processing frameworks, including Apache Spark, support YARN.

 The following blog is one of many resources that provide a good overview of the history of YARN, why it is important and how it works: `https://blog.acolyer.org/2017/01/09/apache-hadoop-yarn-yet-another-resource-negotiator/`.

Let's first have a look at how an Apex application would execute on YARN:

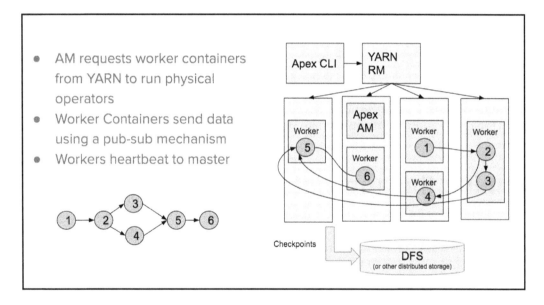

To launch a YARN application, a client executable is needed. That client is normally provided by the framework (in this case Apex) and understands how to interpret the user's application specification and submit it as YARN application (for historic reasons also often still referred to as job) to the YARN resource manager (RM), which will launch it on the cluster. In a typical cluster, the client runs on what is called a *gateway* or *edge node*, a machine that has access to all other nodes in the cluster but is not a worker node (that does not have a YARN nodemanager running on it).

Apex comes with the `apex` CLI (command line interface). Beyond the client, there is nothing that needs to be installed on the node managers to run Apex applications. All dependencies will be deployed with the application through YARN. The `CLI launch` command will take the application package, process it to derive the YARN application specification and submit it to the RM. The RM provides a unique application ID (such as `application_1489955964301_0001`) for subsequent interaction. The CLI client at this point is no longer involved in the application execution or needed to keep it running, it can be terminated or used to monitor and manage the application.

When the resource manager receives the launch request, it will, among other things, look for a suitable node to host the application master (AM). The AM is responsible to control the application and is framework specific. The AM is the first YARN container (a process) to be launched it will be responsible to orchestrate the application, including requesting additional resources and launching further containers as needed.

Once the Apex AM is running, it will determine how many worker containers are needed. It does that by translating the logical DAG into a physical plan by applying the attributes that were specified in the configuration. The physical plan is the blueprint for the execution layer; it arranges the operators into containers, taking into consideration required parallelism, locality constraints, and other attributes. After the physical plan is created, the AM will request the required resources for the execution layer from the YARN RM. One key feature of Apex is the ability to augment the physical plan at runtime and thereby change the resource allocation dynamically. That's possible because it can request and release containers from the YARN RM as needed, with Apex there is no need to statically fix it at launch time.

After the AM has acquired all required containers, it will launch the processes. Each worker process will communicate with the AM periodically through a heartbeat protocol, which allows the master to keep track of the progress of the workers and monitor their health.

The master is not involved in the actual stream processing. Processing is decentralized, asynchronous and distributed over the containers and the workers communicate through a publish subscribe (often abbreviated as **pub-sub**) mechanism to transfer the data. These aspects will be examined in more detail in subsequent chapters, at this point it is sufficient to understand the different components and their interaction at a higher level to be able to run and troubleshoot our own application.

Next, we explain how to setup a single node Hadoop cluster on the local machine. From the download options listed on `http://apex.apache.org/downloads.html`, we will use the Apex Docker Sandbox.

If you already have an existing YARN cluster (for Apex 3.6.0, it should be YARN version 2.6 or higher) that you would like to use instead, you can install the Apex CLI from `https://github.com/atrato/apex-cli-package/releases/tag/v3.6.0` and skip the next subsection that will explain setup of the Apex Docker sandbox.

Installing Apex Docker sandbox

The Apex Docker sandbox is built based on Apache Bigtop (`http://bigtop.apache.org/`), which brings together many of the Hadoop ecosystem components from an infrastructure perspective by providing support for packaging, testing, and deployment. Apex is part of Bigtop and there is a Docker image available with a single node Hadoop cluster and Apex pre-installed at `https://hub.docker.com/r/apacheapex/sandbox/`.

If Docker isn't already installed, visit `https://docs.docker.com/engine/installation/`.

The Apex Docker sandbox is a lightweight and friction-free solution to get a working single node Hadoop cluster and a suitable option for a typical local Apex development environment. The laptop should ideally have 16 GB (or more) RAM with 8 GB allocated to Docker so that the development environment on the host OS and the single node Hadoop cluster in the Docker container have sufficient resources.

The following steps are for macOS. The `install` command will assume a `workspace` directory that is under your home directory that will be shared with the sandbox. That `workspace` directory should contain the Git repositories and the example project, so that the application package can be accessed directly from the build directory.

We will also expose some of the Hadoop service ports so that we can access them later directly. The SSH port will be useful to add ssh tunneling later as the need for additional ports arises, without taking down the docker container. Install and start the sandbox:

```
docker run -v ~/workspace:/workspace --expose=22 -p 8022:22 -p 8088:8088 -p
50070:50070 -it -h apex-sandbox --name=apex-sandbox
apacheapex/sandbox:3.6.0
```

The port mappings in the `run` command will make the Hadoop services that run in the container appear as they would run on the host machine, and we will use that later when accessing the web UI with the browser.

The directory mapping makes the `workspace` folder (with the example project) in your host's home directory available inside the sandbox. We will later access files (including the previously built application package) from there.

Depending on your internet connection it may take a bit to download the images and finally start the cluster running inside the Docker container. The command prompt will now be inside the container. Should the container process ever stop and you get kicked out to the host terminal (for example, because the MacBook goes to sleep!), you can re-attach using the following:

```
docker start -ai apex-sandbox
```

If, after the unexpected termination and restart of the sandbox, you see an error about not being able to write to HDFS due to `safemode` of the `namenode`, run the following:

```
hdfs dfsadmin -safemode leave
```

When working with the sandbox, some links in the Hadoop web UI may not work because they refer to Docker container internal addresses (for example, `http://apex-sandbox:8042/` for the node manager). A way to overcome this without having to recreate the sandbox with additional port mappings is to use SSH port forwarding (tunneling). It allows us to expose further ports as needed while the sandbox keeps running.

We define the extra ports in the SSH configuration. Use your favorite editor (vi, nano and so on) and edit `~/.ssh/config` to add the following:

```
Host apex-sandbox
     HostName localhost
     User apex
     Port 8022     DynamicForward 8157
     LocalForward 8042 127.0.0.1:8042
```

With this change in place, open a new terminal window/tab and establish the `ssh` session that will make port 8042 available to the outside:

```
ssh apex-sandbox
(password: apex)
```

Now the port can be accessed as `localhost:8042` but the resource manager will generate the links with `apex-sandbox:8042`, and hence we still need to find a solution for the host name. Since the port forwarding (for both, SSH, and original Docker `run` command) use the same port number on host and container, we can define `apex-sandbox` as localhost. Next, we will edit the hosts file to accomplish this, which will work not only for the browser but also for other tools or protocols. An alternative that does not require changes to the hosts file would be installation of a browser proxy such as the freely available FoxyProxy (`https://getfoxyproxy.org/`). It should be configured to forward all traffic that matches **apex-sandbox** to `localhost:8157` (as defined earlier in `~/.ssh/config`).

If you go with the hosts file option, edit the `/etc/hosts` file to define `apex-sandbox` as alias for `localhost` as shown in the following code snippet. Editing the file requires root access and a password:

```
sudo vi /etc/hosts

##
# Host Database
#
# localhost is used to configure the loopback interface
# when the system is booting.  Do not change this entry.
##
127.0.0.1       localhost apex-sandbox
255.255.255.255 broadcasthost
::1             localhost
```

In conjunction with the port forwarding that we set up earlier, this will make sure the node manager links generated by the RM web UI will now work in the browser. Our single node cluster with the Apex CLI is now ready to run and monitor applications.

Running the application

Package the example application by running `mvn package -DskipTests` in the `wordcount` subdirectory of the `apex-samples` directory. This will create the `.apa` application package in the target directory:

```
/workspace/apex-samples/wordcount/target/wordcount-1.0-SNAPSHOT.apa
```

Prepare some input data:

```
apex@7bd66492cedc:~$ wget
https://raw.githubusercontent.com/apache/apex-core/master/LICENSE
apex@7bd66492cedc:~$ hdfs dfs -mkdir /tmp/wordcount
apex@7bd66492cedc:~$ hdfs dfs -put LICENSE /tmp/wordcount/LICENCE
```

Set up configuration for input and output (`src/test/resources/properties-sandbox.xml`):

```xml
<?xml version="1.0"?>
 <configuration>
  <property>
    <name>apex.application.*.operator.*.attr.MEMORY_MB</name>
    <value>256</value>
  </property>
  <property>
    <name>apex.operator.input.prop.directory</name>
    <value>/tmp/wordcount</value>
  </property>
  <property>
    <name>apex.operator.output.prop.filePath</name>
    <value>/tmp/wordcount-result</value>
  </property>
  <property>
    <name>apex.operator.output.prop.outputFileName</name>
    <value>wordcountresult</value>
  </property>
  <property>
    <name>apex.operator.output.prop.maxLength</name>
    <value>500</value>
  </property>
  <property>
    <name>apex.operator.output.prop.alwaysWriteToTmp</name>
    <value>false</value>
  </property>
</configuration&gt;
```

Compared to the unit test, the file locations now refer to the default file system. In the sandbox, that's HDFS. The input directory property needs to match the location where the file was previously placed (`/tmp/wordcount`). Now we are ready to start the CLI:

```
apex@7bd66492cedc:~$ apex
Apex CLI 3.6.0 12.06.2017 @ 12:28:11 UTC rev: 7cc3470 branch:
7cc3470d99488d985aa7c50c62ecf994121fdb05
apex>
```

Launch the application, using the application package from the `workspace` build directory and the configuration file with settings that are specific to this environment:

```
apex> launch /workspace/apex-samples/wordcount/target/wordcount-1.0-
SNAPSHOT.apa -conf /workspace/apex-
samples/wordcount/src/test/resources/properties-sandbox.xml
```

Now, the application should be launched and the id of the application should be displayed:

```
{"appId": "application_1490404466322_0001"}
apex (application_1490404466322_0001) >
```

Note that the CLI also permits you to directly specify properties through the launch command. There are also several commands to obtain information about the running application, such as listing the operators and containers along with system metrics. Enter `help` for available commands and options. Enter `exit` to leave the Apex CLI and return back to the shell prompt. After a few seconds, the results will be available in the HDFS output directory:

```
apex@7bd66492cedc:~$ hdfs dfs -ls /tmp/wordcount-result/
Found 4 items
-rwxrwxrwx   1 apex supergroup       5425 2017-03-20 04:24 /tmp/wordcount-
result/wordcountresult_4.0
-rwxrwxrwx   1 apex supergroup        501 2017-03-20 04:25 /tmp/wordcount-
result/wordcountresult_4.1
-rwxrwxrwx   1 apex supergroup        501 2017-03-20 04:27 /tmp/wordcount-
result/wordcountresult_4.2
-rwxrwxrwx   1 apex supergroup          0 2017-03-20 04:27 /tmp/wordcount-
result/wordcountresult_4.3
```

Cat the first file to see the output (the remaining files contain empty lines, because the unique counter happens to emit empty maps even when no input was received):

```
apex@7bd66492cedc:~$ hdfs dfs -cat /tmp/wordcount-
result/wordcountresult_4.0
{using=1, 2004=1, incurred=1, party=2, free=2, event=1, solely=1,
interfaces=1, sublicense=1, Legal=4, meet=1, fee=1, conditions=9, 3=1, 2=4,
1=2, 0=3, 7=1, 6=1, 5=1, 4=1, retain=1, 9=2,
...
```

All output was produced in a single streaming interval, so that the first part file contains a long line with all word counts. This is the consequence of reading from a small file. With a streaming source and continuous data, we would see multiple part files with counts continuously written.

Congratulations, we have built and run our first Apex application on a Hadoop cluster. Even though the functionality is simple, it covered a lot of ground in terms of environment setup and getting an overview of the development process.

Working on the cluster

This section will cover some of the tools and techniques to monitor and debug the application in the distributed environment. We will also look at some of the options to apply changes to the application without rebuilding or packaging it. The tools we use in this section are standard components of Apex, Hadoop, and the operating system (nothing distribution or vendor specific).

Let's begin with some of the basic tools and commands that will allow us to gather information. YARN provides a basic web interface to look at information about running applications and container processes. Examples are based on the local Docker environment which was discussed earlier. The tools are all standard and available when working with a different cluster setup as well, although machine addresses and access may differ.

YARN web UI

Following is the RM web UI. It provides information about the cluster and running and terminated applications. Here, there are two applications of type **ApacheApex** shown that were run since the sandbox was started (when exactly following the sequence of instructions in this chapter the reader would at this point see only one entry). In a multi-tenant cluster there could be many applications belonging to multiple users and different types (frameworks).

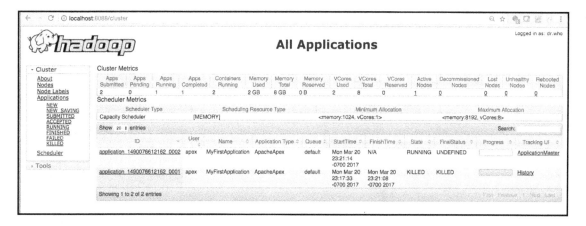

When navigating to the application details (click on **running application**), we see the following:

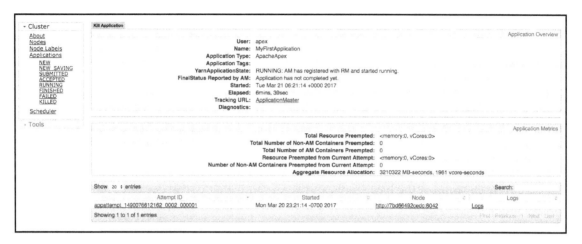

When debugging an application we often need to find the container processes and log files. Click on the **application** attempt for the list of all containers with link to their logs will appear:

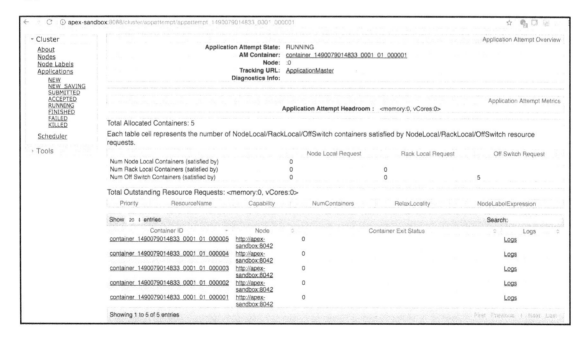

Use the links to see additional details about the containers, specifically to view the logs. The application details that we have accessed so far were generic at the YARN level. In order to see framework-specific details and understand the execution at the DAG level, we need to obtain information from the Apex application master. The Apex AM does not have a web UI, but exposes a REST API that makes detailed information about the application available.

Apex CLI

The REST API can be used by automation tools and is also used by the Apex CLI, for which we will now provide a few examples.

 More information about available commands can be found at `http://apex.apache.org/docs/apex/apex_cli/`.

Assuming the example application is still running, let's attach with the CLI and collect some details from it:

```
apex@apex-sandbox:~$ apex
Apex CLI 3.5.0 14.03.2017 @ 08:14:36 UTC rev: d86f0da branch:
d86f0da78b7be9bffb30b73c5fa762711dbce379
apex> list-apps
{"apps": [{
  "startTime": "2017-03-22 04:42:04 +0000",
  "id": 2,
  "name": "MyFirstApplication",
  "state": "RUNNING",
  "trackingUrl": "http:\/\/apex-
    sandbox:8088\/proxy\/application_1490156780107_0001\/",
  "finalStatus": "UNDEFINED",
  "tags": []
}]}
1 active, total 1 applications.
```

This is summary information, similar to that we had seen earlier in the RM web UI. Now, we connect to the only running application (the number specified with the command is the last part if the ID of the running application) and list the containers:

```
apex> connect 1
Connected to application application_1490156780107_0001
apex (application_1490156780107_0001) > list-containers
{"containers": [
  ...
  {
```

```
      "id": "container_1490156780107_0001_01_000002",
      "host": "apex-sandbox:34449",
      "state": "ACTIVE",
      "jvmName": "2510@apex-sandbox",
      "lastHeartbeat": "1490158053699",
      "numOperators": "1",
      "operators": {"4": "output"},
      "memoryMBAllocated": "1024",
      "memoryMBFree": "118",
      "gcCollectionTime": "228",
      "gcCollectionCount": "4",
      "containerLogsUrl": "http:\/\/apex-sandbox:8042\/node\/containerlogs\/
        container_1490156780107_0001_01_000002\/apex",
      "startedTime": "1490157739962",
      "finishedTime": "-1",
      "rawContainerLogsUrl": "http:\/\/apex-sandbox:8042\/logs\/containers\/
  application_1490156780107_0001\/container_1490156780107_0001_01_000002"
    },
    {
      "id": "container_1490156780107_0001_01_000004",
      "host": "apex-sandbox:34449",
  ...
    }
  ]}
  apex (application_1490156780107_0001) >
```

For brevity, only one complete container entry is shown. Along with details that would also be available from YARN, there are now Apex specific metrics that are useful to examine the application, including resource allocation and utilization, the operators that are deployed in the container and other process level system metrics.

Another command is list-operators; it will provide us insights about the execution of operators, and we can identify and filter them based on the logical plan:

```
  apex (application_1490156780107_0001) > list-operators
  LineByLineFileInputOperator
   {"operators": [{
     "id": "1",
     "name": "input",
     "className":
  "org.apache.apex.malhar.lib.fs.LineByLineFileInputOperator",
     "container": "container_1490156780107_0001_01_000004",
     "host": "apex-sandbox:45479",
     "totalTuplesProcessed": "0",
     "totalTuplesEmitted": "404",
     "tuplesProcessedPSMA": "0",
     "tuplesEmittedPSMA": "0",
     "cpuPercentageMA": "0.5161704845014089",
```

```
      "latencyMA": "0",
      "status": "ACTIVE",
      "lastHeartbeat": "1490252509420",
      "failureCount": "0",
      "recoveryWindowId": "6400552219472575747",
      "currentWindowId": "6400552219472575761",
      "ports": [{
        "name": "output",
        "type": "output",
        "totalTuples": "404",
        "tuplesPSMA": "0",
        "bufferServerBytesPSMA": "16",
        "queueSizeMA": "0",
        "recordingId": null
      }],
      "unifierClass": null,
      "logicalName": "input",
      "recordingId": null,
      "counters": {
        "LOCAL_NUMBER_OF_RETRIES": "0",
        "PENDING_FILES": "0",
        "GLOBAL_NUMBER_OF_FAILURES": "0",
        "LOCAL_NUMBER_OF_FAILURES": "0",
        "GLOBAL_NUMBER_OF_RETRIES": "0",
        "GLOBAL_PROCESSED_FILES": "0",
        "LOCAL_PROCESSED_FILES": "2"
      },
      "metrics": {},
      "checkpointStartTime": "1490252502359",
      "checkpointTime": "44",
      "checkpointTimeMA": "48"
    }]}
```

This is quite a bit of data, and normally, there isn't a need to get into the details until the application does not behave as expected and the metrics can be used in various ways to gain insight or diagnose issues. Here are a few examples:

- `tuplesProcessed/Emitted`: These measure throughput. The moving averages measure current activity, the totals can be used to measure how balanced a partitioning scheme is or whether there is significant skew (partitions are multiple instances that process portions of a stream for scalability).

- `currentWindowId/recoveryWindowId`: These are indicators of progress of the operator. If the current window does not progress steadily, an operator may fall behind with its processing.

- `Status, heartbeat`: Operator deployment state and periodic reporting of metrics from the worker container to the AM.
- `Checkpointing`: Excessive checkpoint times may indicate that the operator cannot transfer its state fast enough (possible reasons include size of the state, efficiency of serialization or performance of the checkpoint backend).
- `Counters/metrics`: operators can expose metrics such as the file I/O specific counters in the `LineByLineFileInputOperator`.

It is not necessary to understand all metrics and possible causes for non-optimal execution at this point. The examples are mentioned to give a glimpse of how is involved in diagnosing issues that may come up as part of testing and tuning. Subsequent chapters will cover important Apex concepts and provide more context.

Let's wrap up this section about the CLI by demonstrating how changes can be made to a running application. Apex supports that in several ways and, here, we will use the example of adding an additional operator to the application while it is running. We will execute the logical plan change, then check that the operator was successfully added and deployed into a new worker container, and finally verify its functional by adding some more input to the file scanner.

The new operator will be a console operator, which will be attached to the lines stream, essentially copying the input file content into the console. The console is redirected to the `stdout` container log and we will locate and look at the log file for verification. This scenario not only illustrates the CLI but also some of the operability features for Apex!

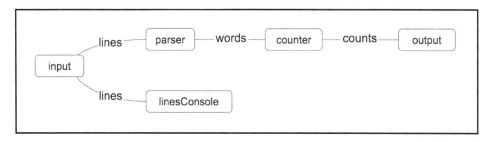

Execute the logical plan change (for this, we need to know the operator class name and the names of ports and streams (either by using other CLI commands or utilizing our knowledge from building the application):

```
apex (application_1490156780107_0001) > begin-logical-plan-change
  logical-plan-change (application_1490156780107_0001) > create-operator
linesConsole com.datatorrent.lib.io.ConsoleOutputOperator
  logical-plan-change (application_1490156780107_0001) > add-stream-sink
lines linesConsole input
```

```
logical-plan-change (application_1490156780107_0001) > submit
{}
```

Confirm operator was added and successfully deployed:

```
apex (application_1490156780107_0006) > list-operators Console
{"operators": [{
  "id": "5",
  "name": "linesConsole",
  "className": "com.datatorrent.lib.io.ConsoleOutputOperator",
  "container": "container_1490156780107_0006_01_000006",
  "host": "apex-sandbox:34449",
```

Add some more input data:

apex@apex-sandbox:~$ hdfs dfs -put LICENSE /tmp/wordcount/LICENCE2

Check the log file of the container into which the console operator was deployed for the expected lines output (using the container ID obtained above):

```
apex (application_1490156780107_0006) > list-containers
  {
    "id": "container_1490156780107_0006_01_000006",
    "host": "apex-sandbox:34449",
    "state": "ACTIVE",
    "jvmName": "12313@apex-sandbox",
    "lastHeartbeat": "1490164067991",
    "numOperators": "1",
    "operators": {"5": "linesConsole"},
    "memoryMBAllocated": "1024",
    "memoryMBFree": "177",
    "gcCollectionTime": "37",
    "gcCollectionCount": "4",
    "containerLogsUrl": "http:\/\/apex-sandbox:8042\/
      node\/containerlogs\/container_1490156780107_0006_01_000006\/apex",
    "startedTime": "1490163666306",
    "finishedTime": "-1",
    "rawContainerLogsUrl": "http:\/\/apex-sandbox:8042\/logs\/containers\/
application_1490156780107_0006\/container_1490156780107_0006_01_000006"
  }
]}
```

We can take the log files link for the container and enter it into the browser, then navigate to the `stdout` file:

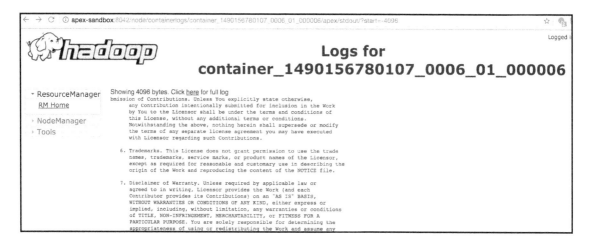

It shows the last portion of the license file that we used as input, which concludes our fun experiment of dynamic application change as part of the CLI overview.

We can also pull the log file from the node manager and compare it with the source:

```
curl
http://apex-sandbox:8042/logs/containers/application_1490156780107_0006/con
tainer_1490156780107_0006_01_000006/stdout > stdout

apex@apex-sandbox:~$ diff -s stdout LICENSE
Files stdout and LICENSE are identical
```

Logging

Applications, by default, use the **log4j** configuration that is part of the Hadoop configuration. That way, centrally configured defaults for file rotation and so on will be picked up. Often, it is necessary to fine-tune the logging for an application and we will show how logging levels can be changed for individual classes as part of the Apex application configuration or even on the running application!

Note that it is possible to use a custom log4j configuration file, more info can be found at `https://apex.apache.org/docs/apex/application_packages/#logging-configuration`.

Logging levels for specific classes (or packages) can be adjusted through configuration or dynamically through the AM web service. Explicit class paths or patterns such as `org.apache.apex.*` can be used to adjust logging to valid log4j levels such as DEBUG or INFO. For permanent changes to logging levels, use the application configuration file. For example:

```
<property>
  <name>dt.loggers.level</name>
  <value>org.apache.apex.*:DEBUG,org.apache.*:INFO</value>
</property>
```

Dynamically adjusting logging levels

Apex provides the ability to query and change log levels at runtime. The commands aren't part of the CLI yet, so we can use this opportunity to show how the AM web service can be accessed via curl:

```
apex@apex-sandbox:~$ curl
http://apex-sandbox:8088/proxy/application_1490233572332_0003/ws/v2/stram/l
oggers/
{"loggers":[]}
```

The preceding request reaches the AM web service through the RM proxy. The corresponding direct AM URL can be derived by obtaining the AM web service port via the CLI `get-app-info` response (for example, `"appMasterTrackingUrl":"apex-sandbox:39809"`):

```
apex@apex-sandbox:~$ curl http://apex-sandbox:39809/ws/v2/stram/loggers/
{"loggers":[]}
```

Sometimes, it is very useful to be able to change the log level of specific classes when debugging a problem and the system is in a state that would be lost on restart and hard to reproduce. The following is an example of increasing the verbosity of logging for the file output operator:

```
curl -H "Content-Type: application/json" -X POST \
  -d '{"loggers":
    [{"target":"com.datatorrent.lib.io.fs.AbstractFileOutputOperator",
    "logLevel":"DEBUG"}]}' \
      http://apex-sandbox:39809/ws/v2/stram/loggers/

apex@apex-sandbox:~$ curl http://apex-sandbox:39809/ws/v2/stram/loggers/
{"loggers":
  [{"target":"com.datatorrent.lib.io.fs.AbstractFileOutputOperator",
  "logLevel":"DEBUG"}]}
```

The resulting changes can be observed in the container log (the container that hosts the file output operator can be found with the `list-containers CLI` command):

It shows more verbose output for the file writer, providing details about the handling of the output files. This would be helpful in a situation where the expected output is missing and there are no exceptions of other information available.

Summary

In this chapter, we introduced the end-to-end process of developing applications with Apex, including how to create a new project, write a custom operator, assemble the DAG, integration test within the IDE, deploy the application package to the cluster, and how to navigate the distributed environment. The functionality was intentionally basic to keep the focus on the process.

Subsequent chapters will expand from here; we will cover the operators that are available in the Apex library, how to scale and tune applications, and how they are fault tolerant with exactly-once processing guarantee, as well as providing comprehensive examples that put it all together.

3
The Apex Library

The previous chapter introduced the application development process resulting in a simple *Hello World* application. Now, we will introduce the Apex library and look at more meaningful functional building blocks that are used to assemble real applications.

This chapter will cover:

- An overview of the library
- Integration with existing infrastructure
- Messaging systems, files, and databases as frequently used sources and sinks
- Transformations to build the pipeline functionality

An overview of the library

The Apex Malhar library (referenced as **Apex library** throughout this book) contains operators as well as APIs and other components that are useful to assemble applications and build customized operators (for example, stream codecs, partitioners, state management, and windowing support). The aim of the Apex library is to provide many common building blocks as readily usable (configurable, as opposed to having to write code).

 The Apex library is maintained as part of the Apache Apex project in its own repository: `https://github.com/apache/apex-malhar` (whereas the Apex core engine is under `https://github.com/apache/apex-core`). Releases of the Apex library and Apex core engine are made at different frequencies, mostly because operators, which are the functional building blocks for applications, receive more contributions and evolve at a faster pace than the core engine.

The API of the engine is designed so that development can be separated and new functionality added without requiring changes to the core. This is important, as it typically enables users to upgrade their applications (the Apex library is part of the Apex application packages discussed in the previous chapter) without having to upgrade their Apex engine/CLI installation on the edge node (or Hadoop client). In larger organizations, the two components would typically be maintained by separate groups and the barrier for upgrades on the cluster would be much higher than an application dependency that is controlled by the development team.

The Apex library provides out-of-the-box functionality that can be used to develop applications. Because the Apex library is maintained by the Apex community, compatibility with the engine is better than it would be the case with third party components.

The following is an overview of various categories of operators available in the Apex library with examples for each category:

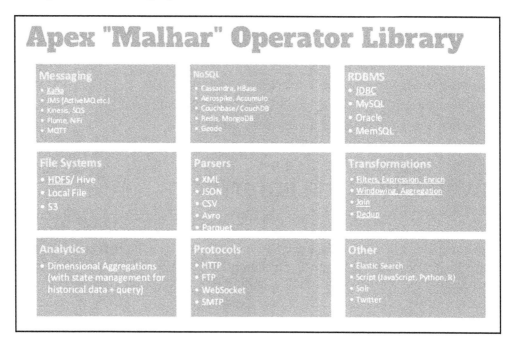

Since its inception, Apex has covered a wide range of integrations with other systems and ecosystem projects.

- The first category of integrations is messaging systems, with connectors that continuously consume or produce streams of real-time (or historical) data. Apache Kafka is most prevalent, based on current usage of Apex. The Kafka connector was also (along with the (H)DFS file reader) one of first operators developed in the early days of the Apex project.

- Apex can read from and write to Kafka and works well with streaming sources on Amazon AWS (Kinesis, SQS), various systems under the JMS (Java Message Service) umbrella, and more.

- The next categories shown are **NoSQL and RDBMS**. Apex currently has connectors to integrate most of the important Apache projects. For RDBMS, Apex has generic JDBC operators, which function as a catch-all (read and write). Note that several of the NoSQL systems have, since their origin, also added support for SQL or similar query language.

- Aside from Kafka, file systems are the most frequently used source for Apex applications, and are also the most commonly used sink (data processed in Apex applications often lands in files). The generic file operators are written against the Hadoop DFS interface, which has various implementations (HDFS, MapR FS, S3, and so on). Apex has operators to poll directories for continuously arriving files, for reading files fast and in parallel (**FileSplitter** and **BlockReader**) and a few other variations such as for optimized to write to S3 and so on. That there are several options that target different use case patterns stems from the fact that file I/O is used extensively, not just to write results or for batch applications, but (perhaps surprisingly) also as a **streaming** source.

- As a matter of fact, the first production deployment of Apex in 2014 was a streaming use case, but, initially, the data could only be brought in through continuously arriving files (this is when the directory scanner was developed). When, a few months later, the source was switched to Kafka, it led to the first production-ready version of the Kafka input operator. Overall, Kafka and files are the top two data sources (and stores) whose corresponding Apex operators have seen most mileage (data flowing through). This is likely reflected in number of bugs fixed, features added, and changes committed against them.

- The next category is parsers, which, like sources, are needed in every data processing pipeline. The most common cases such as CSV, JSON, and XML parsers are covered at the following link, along with examples: `https://github.com/apache/apex-malhar/tree/master/examples/parser`.

- Following the typical pipeline sequence, next come filters and transformations. Examples for enrichment, join, de-duplication (dedup), and others can all be found here: `https://github.com/apache/apex-malhar/tree/master/examples/`.
- Join and dedup are stateful transformations, as are various windowed accumulations that are available through the window operator (we introduced windowing in the first chapter, and in this chapter, we will see how it can be applied using the **WindowedOperator**).

The Apex library has many more operators than those mentioned here, with varying degrees of maturity. As a rule of thumb, if an operator has good test coverage, user documentation, and examples, then it would generally be more reliable and dependable than other operators that are lacking in these areas. As an additional check for maturity, it may be prudent to confirm the operator's support for partitioning and fault tolerance (which all of the frequently-used operators have).

You can find the links here:

- User documentation: `http://apex.apache.org/docs/malhar/`
- Javadoc: `https://ci.apache.org/projects/apex-malhar/apex-malhar-javadoc-release-3.8/index.html`
- Examples: `https://github.com/apache/apex-malhar/tree/master/examples`
- Latest documentation links for released Apex library versions can be found at: `http://apex.apache.org/downloads.html`

Yet another guiding factor about an operator's maturity is the location where the operator is placed within the source code hierarchy. Operators under `/lib` are generally more mature, covered with decent tests and battle tested compared with those under `/contrib`. The latter is informally a staging area for development initiatives that aren't entirely mature yet, though there are exceptions. The intention is to break out those operators that deserve a seat in the first row into separate dedicated modules that cleanly indicate dependencies (such as Kafka and Hive).

Integrations

The following subsections we will cover important external system integrations for Apex applications and the corresponding connectors provided by the Apex library. The section will start with the streaming data connectors, used for continuous processing and low latency use cases. Next, we will look at the file connectors, which are frequently used, especially for batch use cases, where massive amounts of data need to be processed and the ability to read or write with high throughput in a scalable manner is important. Finally, we will look at a few database connectors.

Apache Kafka

In its own words, **Apache Kafka** (`http://kafka.apache.org/`) "is used for building real-time data pipelines and streaming apps. It is horizontally scalable, fault-tolerant, wicked fast, and runs in production in thousands of companies".

Apache Kafka is a distributed, horizontally scalable, fault tolerant and high-throughput pub-sub messaging system. In contrast to similar messaging systems, Kafka was not only designed as a transport mechanism, but also functions as a durable data store that can hold huge amounts of data stored in logs on disk on commodity hardware. It provides access to consumers of the data that is quite similar to a file API. We may even think of Kafka as providing remote access to potentially very large log files. In fact, MapR Streams, a proprietary implementation of the Kafka API, is built on top of the MapR file system.

The following diagram provides a visualization of the main concepts of Kafka:

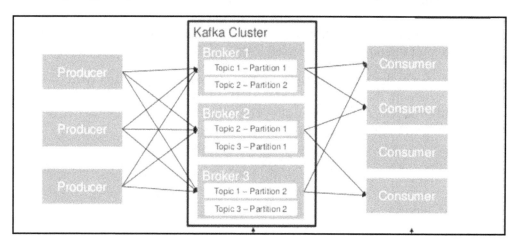

Kafka clusters consist of a set of brokers (processes that typically run on dedicated nodes). Data in Kafka is logically organized by **topic** (the reference for a particular set of unbounded data). To provide scalability, topics in the physical layout have many partitions, which may live on different machines. Data is published by **producers** and retrieved (for processing) by **consumers**.

Kafka provides high availability by replicating partitions. When there are multiple replicas of a partition, only one of them will be active and the broker that is hosting the active partition is designated the **lead broker** to which producers and consumers connect. When a broker fails, new leaders for respective partitions will be elected.

To retrieve messages, the consumer specifies an offset (number) from which to sequentially read messages. Multiple consumers (of different consumer groups) are allowed to read the same messages, and there is logically no difference whether the data is current or historical. This makes writing robust consumers much simpler than some other messaging systems, such as JMS. The client has control over the offset and does not need to be concerned about the durability of the messages, as it can always replay from the source if required.

Kafka is both a streaming source and sink for Apex applications. The Apex library has operators for the Kafka 0.8.x, 0.9.x, and 0.10.x client API. These connectors will also work with later broker versions. We will now provide an overview of the respective Kafka input and output operators in the Apex library.

Kafka input

The Kafka input operator consumes messages from the partitions of a Kafka topic and emits the message bytes to downstream operators for further processing (parsing, filtering, and so on). While this is simple functionality, let's see how aspects like scalability, efficient resource utilization, and fault tolerance are addressed.

As explained, Kafka scales with partitions; so, the operator needs the ability to automatically scale with the partitioning of the Kafka topic and the resources required for the scaling need to be allocated dynamically. The following diagram shows two different partition mapping strategies that are supported out of the box:

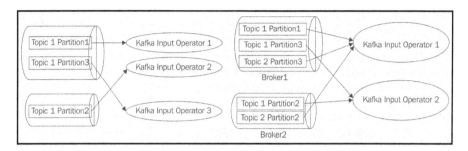

On the left-hand side, we see each Kafka partition being consumed by one partition of the Apex operator. On the right-hand side, we see multiple Kafka partitions being consumed by one Apex operator partition. The many-to-many mapping shown on the right is, in most cases, more resource efficient due to the I/O bounded nature of the operator compared to the downstream processing capacity (downstream operators can achieve higher throughput than a single Kafka consumer). Typically, multiple Kafka partitions can be consumed by a single instance, leading to a reduction of required resources on the Apex side.

The operator can, optionally, also consume from multiple Kafka clusters and topics. This support was added to better support applications that receive data from (geographically) different regions and other cases where clusters have significant throughput variation throughout the day. Having a receiver that can consume partitions from different regions allows for more optimal resource utilization.

For fault tolerance, when an error occurs and the operator needs to be recovered, it needs to resume from a saved, consistent offset for each partition and replay the messages that weren't fully processed in the DAG. Thus, the operator needs to remember the offsets relative to original Apex retrieval time. Checkpointing these offsets is required for recovery or stateful restart of an application.

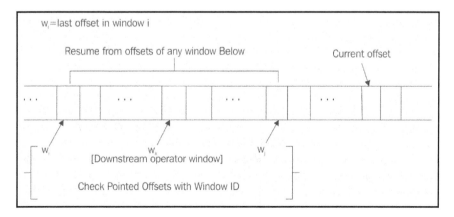

Offset checkpointing works based on the Apex streaming window. As shown in the preceding diagram, the operator will capture the streaming windows along with the offsets, and replay from the checkpointed base accordingly. Therefore, the operator guarantees no loss of data as well as idempotency (messages are emitted in the same streaming windows on replay).

Often users also need the ability to record the start offsets (for example because a stateful restart isn't possible due to the nature of upgrades made to the application or because they want external visibility into the consumer progress). For this, the operator can store the committed offset (offset that will never be used for replay on recovery) on the broker side. That offset can then be used as the (cold) start offset for the application (earliest and latest are the other options).

 More details about the input operator can be found at `http://apex.apache.org/docs/malhar-3.8/operators/kafkaInputOpera tor/`. Example code can be found at `https://github.com/apache/apex- malhar/tree/master/examples/kafka`.

Kafka output

Compared to the Kafka input operator, the Kafka output operator implementation is rather simple. The output operator takes the tuple from the input port and hands it to the Kafka producer (part of the operator configuration is to specify the appropriate message serializer). However, things get more complicated when taking fault tolerance into account. In versions prior to 0.11, Kafka did not support transactions, and therefore, the onus was on the client to make sure messages are not lost or duplicated in the event of a failure and when exactly-once output is required.

For this purpose, the library has a specialized `KafkaExactlyOnceOutputOperator`. This operator is actually both a producer and consumer, because it needs to remember what has already been written to Kafka partitions to not write any duplicates. The operator does the following for recovery:

- Uses the Kafka message key to record the source of message (application and Apex operator partition) so that multiple producers can write to the same Kafka partition, but each can identify its message in the recovery scenario.
- Fetches the offsets of the Kafka partitions at the end of the streaming interval and records them in the log for recovery.

- During recovery, reads the offset information from the log and skips the intervals that were already output to Kafka.
- Reads back the data from Kafka partitions from last recorded offset. This is data that was potentially emitted by the operator in the non-completed interval when the failure occurred.
- On replay of the partial window from upstream, checks if the message was already written or not, and skip any messages already written—a producer side dedup.

The operator makes use of the message key to uniquely identify the message written by the partition of the operator, hence the key cannot be used by the application. The operator also requires the message deserializer for the type of tuple used (unless it's a String, which is the default).

Until the 0.11 version is supported, Apex applications that require an exactly-once guarantee can benefit from this operator (at the cost of some additional processing to maintain the state needed for recovery).

Other streaming integrations

The Apex library has integrations for a number of other messaging systems besides Kafka. These are typically used as sources in real-time streaming use cases.

JMS (ActiveMQ, SQS, and so on)

Java Message Service (JMS) is an API defined as part of Java EE that provides a common interface to messaging protocols and messaging systems. The interface abstracts away from the underlying communication protocol and needs an implementation in the form of a JMS client library to actually talk to a messaging broker or system. Apex provides operators to read from and write to JMS. The input operator has been tested with Amazon SQS and Apache ActiveMQ, but should also work with other systems such as Tibco EMS or IBM MQSeries. Due to the design of the JMS protocol, and specifically, how acknowledgments work, the Apex JMS operator has to do more work for fault tolerance compared to the Kafka operator. The JMS input operator needs to write received messages to a durable log so they can be replayed in the event of a failure (functionality that Kafka provides inherently).

More details about the JMS operator can be found at: `http://apex.apache.org/docs/malhar/operators/jmsInputOperator/`. Examples are available at `https://github.com/tweise/examples/tree/master/tutorials/jmsActiveMQ` and `https://github.com/tweise/examples/tree/master/tutorials/jmsSqs`.

Kinesis streams

Kinesis is one of the Amazon AWS services for continuous delivery and storage of streaming data. It somewhat overlaps with SQS (JMS interface) in the sense that it transports messages from source to destination, but there are differences between the two with regard to message ordering, dynamic scaling and retention. Kinesis is more targeted at big data processing and analytics use cases and in that regard comparable to Kafka, although benchmarks have shown that Kafka, at similar cost, can achieve higher throughput and, unlike Kinesis with its default 24 hours retention period, does not place any such limitation and is designed to keep large volumes of logs for a long time.

Kinesis has also similar concepts to Kafka: shards divide the logical stream and allow for scale out, messages can be addressed by offset, and replay is possible within the retention period. Kinesis as a managed service is a good option to ingest streaming data for applications hosted on the AWS platform.

Apex has operators for input from and output to Kinesis. The input operator with its features follows what the Kafka equivalent provides: One or multiple shards can be consumed by an operator partition, the partitioning is automatic based on discovery of the shard metadata, and the operator is fault tolerant because it tracks the consumer offsets per streaming window, so that replay is possible in the event of failure.

The Kinesis operators can be found in the malhar-contrib module, documentation, and example are available at `https://github.com/deepak-narkhede/apex-malhar/blob/APEXMALHAR -2427/docs/operators/kinesisInputOperator.md` and `https://github.com/DataTorrent/examples/tree/master/tutorial s/kinesisInput`.

The contrib library has some more streaming connectors, such as for RabbitMQ, Apache NiFi, Splunk, ZeroMQ, and also a Tweet sampler. A connector for the Solace Message Router is about to be added.

Apache NiFi is commonly found in IoT (Internet of Things) use cases.

 For readers interested in the NiFi integration and how it can be used together with Apex, there is a presentation here: `https://www.slideshare.net/ApacheApex/integrating-ni-fiandapex-b y-bryan-bende`.

Files

Now we are going to look at the support Apex offers for file I/O, another important category of sources and destinations for processing. Streaming sources are on the rise, which is evident by the growing popularity of Kafka. At the same time, many integrations still have to rely on files and a batch oriented ingestion, even when the processing framework is stream based like Apex. That kind of integration puts the brakes on the stream processor, but in large organizations pieces of end-to-end solutions are often owned by different groups and involve legacy systems that take time to change.

Then, there is still the segment of batch-based analytics that typically consume very large amounts of data from files. Processing results are also often stored in files and we will also cover the support Apex provides for writing to files.

File input

The first operator (or group of operators) rely on scanning a directory for available files and then read the file incrementally while emitting records. The operator works based on the Hadoop filesystem abstraction and can therefore be used with HDFS, S3, MaprFS, FTP, local/mounted filesystems like NFS, and other supported systems. How the file content is split and what types of records are produced is defined by specializations of a common base class to support various file formats.

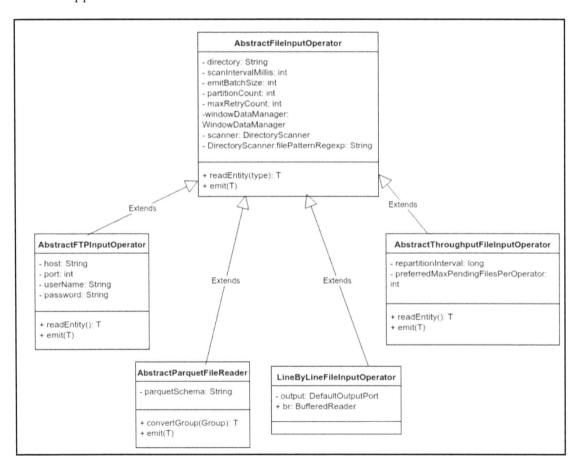

The preceding diagram shows some of the specialization available and the properties that the user can configure. It is impossible to support all file formats that can possibly be used and so the abstract base class is designed to make it easy to incorporate the required splitting and parsing logic by overriding a few hooks that provide access to the input stream and allow handling opening and closing of the files. Everything else, which is a surprising amount of detail, is taken care of, for example:

- Discovery of the files in the source with pluggable directory scanner
- Tracking of which files have already been consumed
- Tracking the file offsets for each streaming window (similar to what is needed for Kafka)
- Recovery of the state after a failure and replay of the data from checkpoint in idempotent manner
- Partitioning of the input file set through scanners

For more information about the operator, see the following links: http://apex.apache.org/docs/malhar/operators/fsInputOperator/
and https://www.slideshare.net/ApacheApex/faulttolerant-file-input-output-61713267.

File splitter and block reader

The input operator, although it is quite flexible for customization and simple to use, has one disadvantage that is important for use cases where input files can get very large and the size of files fluctuates. Since the smallest unit of input is an entire file, reading of a very large file cannot be parallelized.

The combination of file splitter and block reader can solve this. The splitter creates metadata of blocks of a file and those become the work items for downstream block readers, which can read/parse the (non-overlapping) blocks without dependency on other partitions. Essentially, the previous input operator is divided into two steps.

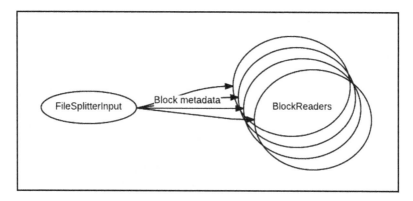

The first operator discovers the files and emits the block instructions, which are shuffled to the block readers. Now, the level of parallelism can be controlled independent of the source file size. Of course, this pattern only works with splittable file formats and sources that allow sufficiently parallel reads. That is particularly the case for frequently used CSV and other line oriented file formats.

An example for this composite pattern is the `FSRecordReaderModule`, which encapsulates splitter and block reader into a single building block that can be used when assembling the application and internally expands the atomic operators.

For more information, you can visit following links: `http://apex.apache.org/docs/malhar/operators/file_splitter/` and `https://github.com/apache/apex-malhar/tree/master/library/src/main/java/org/apache/apex/malhar/lib/fs`.

File writer

The job of the file output operators (subclasses of `AbstractFileOutputOperator`) is to write results of the processing pipelines to files, based on the Hadoop filesystem abstraction. The operator is feature rich and battle hardened, one of the most used operators in the library. It supports:

- Output of tuples to one or multiple files (output file can be selected on a per record basis for logical output partitioning).

- Exactly-once results.
- Partitioning of the writer is supported, each partition writes to separate part files with unique names.
- File rotation based on file size or time or customizable criteria. This provides sufficient flexibility to the application to balance latency and number of files (also, HDFS is not suited for managing a huge amount of small files).
- Efficient handling of open files and flushing to allow for pipelined writes. The operator holds a cache of file output streams (repeated close/open would be inefficient). The writes to the files are non-blocking in the case of HDFS, flush only occurs at the checkpoint boundary when the offsets need to be tracked in the operator state. Between those flush events, the work is left to the HDFS write pipeline for optimal throughput.
- Support for compression and encryption of data (`FilterStreamProvider`).

The file output operator is fault tolerant and can guarantee exactly-once results, given idempotent input. Let's have a look at what is involved to provide this guarantee:

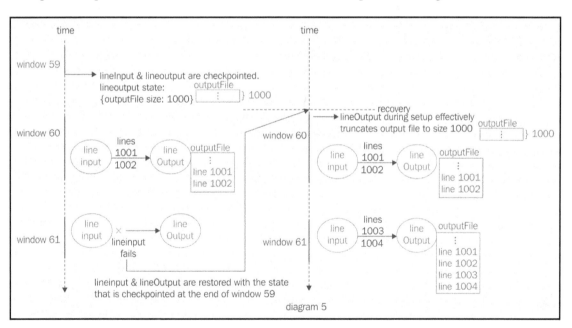

diagram 5

The preceding diagram shows the recovery sequence for a file writer. After the operator is restored to the checkpointed state at streaming window 60, it needs to rewind by logically truncating the non-finalized files that were in-progress at the time of failure to reach consistent state. It does that by using the file names and offsets that are tracked in the operator's checkpointed state, similar to how the input operators would adjust the consumer offset. The difference is that, here, the state in the file system needs to be modified to allow for replay of the stream while ensuring exactly-once output.

When working with HDFS this becomes much more complicated due to immutable state (a truncate operation is not available in Hadoop versions prior to 2.7 and the HDFS lease model makes working with partially written files quite complex in general). In short, under the covers the operator has to write to unique temporary files that can only be renamed into final files (and made visible) when the state in the DAG is committed and no replay is possible.

Typically, files produced by the writer will be consumed by other systems, but that is not always the case. An example where the file writer is used in conjunction with a consumer in the same DAG is when writing data to Hive. Finalized files are propagated to a downstream operator, which will add them to Hive partitions. The code for this composite operator can be found at the following
link: `https://github.com/apache/apex-malhar/blob/master/hive/src/main/java/org/a pache/apex/malhar/hive/HiveOutputModule.java`.

More information and examples and can be found at the following links:

- `http://apex.apache.org/docs/malhar/operators/file_ output/`
- `https://github.com/tweise/examples/tree/master/ tutorials/fileOutput`
- `https://github.com/apache/apex-malhar/tree/master/ examples/exactly-once`

Finally, there is an optimized operator for parallelized write of large files to S3. This operator used the native S3
API: `http://apex.apache.org/docs/malhar/operators/s3outputmodule/`.

Databases

Databases are often used in frontend systems to capture the results of transactions (OLTP) and in the backend for data warehousing. In the past, relational databases have been used to broadly cover many different storage needs and every other system was built to depend on them. With today's data processing demands, those architectures have reached capacity limits, especially for high throughput and high volume use cases that we discuss in this book.

Traditional OLTP and OLAP systems are increasingly complemented with newer data management infrastructure, not just to enable previously unreachable use cases but also for TCO reason. NoSQL columnar databases, such as HBase and Cassandra, became popular as they promised to overcome the scalability and performance limitations of incumbent relational database systems at a lower cost. Batch analytics based on MapReduce-based frameworks and SQL interfaces like Hive were early approaches in a continuing larger trend to offload use cases from bottlenecked central database systems.

Nevertheless, most enterprise architectures today remain database-centric, with different serving and backend processing systems depending on and tightly coupled through a shared database. The underlying assumption that data first needs to land in a central database before anything useful can be done with it is, increasingly, challenged by practical needs and push changes. New systems likely still need to be able to integrate with existing infrastructure. At the same time, they don't need to follow the same old ways.

Martin Kleppmann outlined in his excellent post *Turning the Database Inside Out* (`https://www.confluent.io/blog/turning-the-database-inside-out-with-apache-samza/`) how the concepts of change logs, streams, caches, and materialized views can be rearranged to arrive at a radically different and better architecture. This idea has gained traction with several other stream processors like Apex, that offer (or develop) the ability to use locally materialized state for processing of incoming events. Those events can mutate the state (like change capture events or transactions), but they can also be queries. An example how an Apex application can answer queries for current and historical data without external database will be presented in `Chapter 6`, *Example Project – Real-Time Aggregation and Visualization*.

For this section, it is sufficient to know that Apex needs to be able to consume data from existing databases and be able to write to those databases. That's not because Apex needs those systems to function, but because users are constrained by existing infrastructure, budgets, and timelines. Therefore, at some point need to integrate their end-to-end stream processing solution. We will now look at some of the operators that are available in the library to accomplish that task.

JDBC input

The *JDBC Poll Input Operator* reads records from a table in the source database and emits them as tuples into the Apex processing pipeline.

The operator can function as bounded or unbounded source (it can continuously discover new rows as they are inserted into the table). The operator is idempotent for exactly-once processing and is designed to handle very large tables with parallel reads of non-overlapping key ranges through multiple partitions (the user specifies the partition count as operator property).

The operator requires an ordered column, based on which range queries can be formed. This is a given for those relational databases that use sequences for primary keys or the table should have an alternate (composite) unique index that is ordered, so that newly inserted rows represent higher values than existing ones.

The operator can be used to mirror a table into the stream processing pipeline. An example for copying the data to files can be found at the following link: `https://github.com/apache/apex-malhar/tree/master/examples/jdbc`.

There are readily usable and configurable operator classes that produce POJO and CSV streams and the abstract base class can be configured for alternative output schema. More information about the operator can be found at the following link: `http://apex.apache.org/docs/malhar-3.8/operators/jdbcPollInputOperator/`.

JDBC output

The output operator can write the data produced by the processing pipeline to a table in the JDBC database. A concrete implementation is provided that maps fields of a POJO to columns in the target table and performs an insert operation. The operator is partitionable, although with most JDBC sinks the throughput will typically be limited by the external system and not by the operator writing to a single table.

Details about the operator and example can be found at the following links: `http://apex.apache.org/docs/malhar-3.8/operators/AbstractJd bcTransactionableOutputOperator/`
and `https://github.com/tweise/examples/tree/master/tutorials/fil eToJdbc`.
An example for the use of the operator to achieve exactly-once results (using MERGE) can be found at the following link: `https://github.com/ apache/apex-malhar/blob/master/examples/exactly-once/src/main/ java/org/apache/apex/examples/exactlyonce/ ExactlyOnceJdbcOutputApp.java`.

Other databases

The Apex library has support for many other data stores besides those with JDBC interface. These corresponding operators can all be found in the contrib package: `https://github.com/apache/apex-malhar/tree/master/contrib`.

Here are some of them:

- **Apache Cassandra**: Cassandra is a highly scalable, high-performance distributed database designed to handle large amounts of data across many commodity servers, providing high availability with no single point of failure. It is a NoSQL database. Apex supports read from and write to Cassandra. Examples are available at `https://github.com/tweise/examples/tree/master/tutorials`.
- **Apache HBase**: HBase is a column-oriented key/value data store built to run on top of the Hadoop Distributed File System (HDFS), based on the Google Bigtable model. Apex library has support to read from and write to HBase.
- **Apache Geode**: Geode is an in-memory, distributed database with strong consistency, reliable transaction processing, and a shared-nothing architecture to maintain very low-latency performance with high concurrency processing. Apex has input and output operators and also an implementation of the storage agent, which enables Geode as a backend for operator checkpointing.
- **Other supported systems**: Accumulo, Aerospike, Couchbase, CouchDB, Elasticsearch, Kudu, Memcache, Memsql, Mongodb, Redis, and Solr.

This section introduced the most commonly used integrations. For more connectors in the Apex library, please see the following links:

- http://apex.apache.org/docs/malhar/
- https://ci.apache.org/projects/apex-malhar/apex-malhar-javadoc-release-3.8/index.html
- https://github.com/tweise/examples/tree/master/tutorials
- https://github.com/apache/apex-malhar/tree/master/contrib/src/main/java/com/datatorrent/contrib

Transformations

So far, we have looked at the operators that connect Apex pipelines to the outside world, to read data from messaging systems, files, and other sources and to write results to various destinations. We have seen that the Apex library has comprehensive support to integrate various external systems with feature rich connectors.

Now it is time to look at the support available for the actual functionality of the pipeline. These building blocks are transformations: their purpose is to modify or accumulate the tuples that flow through the processing pipeline. Examples of typical transformations are parsing, filtering, aggregation by key, and join:

Stateless Transformations	Stateful Transformations
• Parsers: XML, JSON, CSV, Avro	• Windowing: sliding, tumbling, session
• Filter	• Accumulations: sum, merge, join, sort, top n, …
• Enrich	• Triggering, Watermarks
• Configurable POJO schema	• Dimensional Aggregations (with state management for historical data + query)
• Map, FlatMap (custom Java function)	• Deduplication
• Script (JavaScript, Jython)	

The preceding diagram categorizes transformations into those that are applied to individual tuples and those that aggregate tuples based on keys and windows. Often, per tuple transforms are stateless and windowed transforms require state for the accumulation. Most pipelines are composed of several of these transforms. It is common to see sources (Apex input operators) followed by operations such as decrypt, decompress, parsing, and filtering, and then keyed and windowed transforms that compute aggregates before results are written to sinks (Apex output operators):

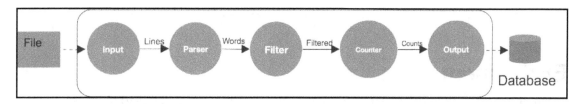

The basic word count example that accompanied the previous chapters contains some of the transforms from the library. The parsing (tokenization of lines) and filtering are per tuple operations. Counting is an aggregation performed by key and window.

Parser

Some input operators, like the Kafka input operator, will emit the message they receive as generic byte array or string and the next operator needs to turn it into a tuple according to the schema of the stream. The library contains a few parsers for common formats that can be used to turn incoming messages into POJO objects based on the configured schema.

- http://apex.apache.org/docs/malhar/operators/csvParserOperator/
- http://apex.apache.org/docs/malhar/operators/jsonParser/

Examples for CSV, JSON, fixed width, and XML parsers can be found at the following links:

- https://github.com/apache/apex-malhar/tree/master/examples/parser
- https://github.com/tweise/examples/tree/master/tutorials/parser/src/main/java/com/datatorrent/tutorial

Filter

The filter operator can be used to decide if an incoming record should be accepted or not and optionally route rejected records to an error port. The condition for the filter can be configured as Java expression. Here are some useful links to know more about the filter operator:

- http://apex.apache.org/docs/malhar/operators/filter/
- https://github.com/apache/apex-malhar/tree/master/examples/filter

Enrichment

Often, it is necessary to transform incoming tuples by adding new fields to them. As an example, an incoming transaction may contain a customer ID and the corresponding customer name or address should be added from a lookup source. The enricher operator essentially joins a stream with a lookup source and supports lookup from files or JDBC source (**Loader**) as well as from custom sources.

Lookups are cached. Input and output stream schema are configured with the POJO class and the operator will transform the incoming objects by adding fields from the lookup source. Here are some useful links:

- http://apex.apache.org/docs/malhar/operators/enricher/
- https://github.com/apache/apex-malhar/tree/master/examples/enricher

Map transform

The **transform** operator corresponds to **map** in the declarative API; it is a way to configure a mapping instead of writing the mapping function in Java. This can be useful in situations where the mapping isn't known at application assembly time and needs to be configured or modified during deployment. Refer to the following links for more information:

- http://apex.apache.org/docs/malhar/operators/transform/
- https://github.com/apache/apex-malhar/tree/master/examples/transform

Custom functions

Previous operators are focused on providing the functionality through configuration, without writing additional code. In some situations, the prebuilt logic may not be sufficient and for those cases the user would have to write a custom operator (or extend an existing one). We covered the Apex operator model in the previous chapter. It is very flexible but, on the flipside (when writing operators from scratch), the user has to deal with ports and other code that often isn't necessary, unless the requirements are very advanced.

The high-level API has removed that complexity and one of the operators that internally powers the high-level API is the function operator, which allows the user to implement a map, flat map, or filter function by specifying just the Java lambda expression without having to build a whole new operator. The function operator can be used directly when writing the pipeline with the low level DAG API.

The operator can be found at the following link: `https://github.com/apache/apex-malhar/blob/master/library/src/main/java/org/apache/apex/malhar/lib/function/FunctionOperator.java`.

Windowed transformations

As discussed in `Chapter 1`, *Introduction to Apex*, the streaming window in Apex more or less represents the ingression time of the data tuples within it. The accumulation of state based on the `beginWindow()` and the `endWindow()` callbacks is sufficient if the application intends to process the data based on ingression time or processing time. This is usually not the case. Applications often need to process the incoming tuples based on the timestamps of the individual events, not when the tuples enter the system.

If the incoming data tuples arrive in order, processing the data based on event time would be straightforward. In such cases, since we know the next incoming event always has the newest timestamp, we would not have to worry about changing the data in previous time buckets. For unbounded streaming data, this is often not true. Data often arrives out of order and we need a way to handle that.

The **WindowedOperator** provides the framework to handle unbounded, unordered, event-time based data. It borrows the windowing semantics from Apache Beam (`https://beam.apache.org/`). We will discuss the concepts that are required to use the WindowedOperator effectively.

The high-level Java stream API (introduced in the `Chapter 1`, *Introduction to Apex*) relies on the same window operator for windowed transformations.

Windowing

When a tuple arrives, it is assigned to one or more windows, so that aggregation and processing can be done per window. Unlike **streaming windows**, which are based on ingression time, windows in the WindowedOperator are based on event time, with the exception of Global Window.

Global Window

A **Global Window** is a window that spans the entire duration of the application. This is useful for some batch applications and situations where the application does not care about the event time and the state is ever accumulating. A simple example would be the running total count of tuples.

Time Windows

Time Windows are windows that have a fixed time duration and one window is followed immediately by another window. A tuple is assigned to exactly one window based on event time.

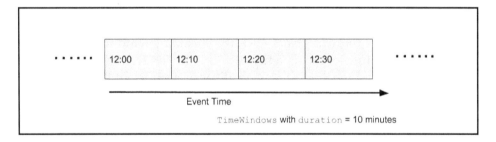

In this case, one tuple can only belong to one window.

Sliding Time Windows

Similar to Time Windows, **Sliding Time Windows** have a fixed duration. However, the configuration for SlidingTimeWindows requires an additional time duration parameter `slideBy`:

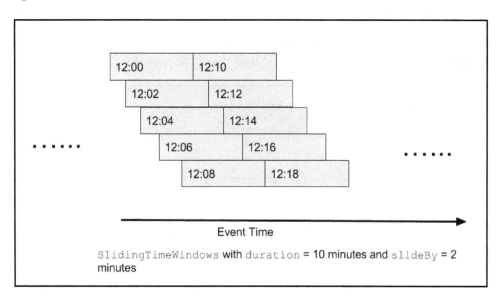

SlidingTimeWindows with duration = 10 minutes and slideBy = 2 minutes

The `slideBy` duration must be smaller than the window duration, and the window duration must be divisible by the `slideBy` duration. Each window overlaps with multiple other windows. Any timestamp would belong to the number of windows n defined by the following equation:

$$n = \text{the window duration / the slideBy duration}$$

Hence, a tuple would be assigned to n windows. As a result, Sliding Time Windows would take n times the resources compared to Time Windows.

Session Windows

Session Windows are windows that model after sessions. For example, one session could represent each time a user visits a website. Unlike Time Windows and Sliding Time Windows, Session Windows have variable durations and are based on the key of the tuple. If we want to process the activity data based on each time a user visits a website, the key of the tuple could be the user ID. Each tuple is assigned to exactly one window. It takes a duration parameter **minGap**, which specifies the minimum time gap between any two tuples that belong to two different Session Windows of the same key:

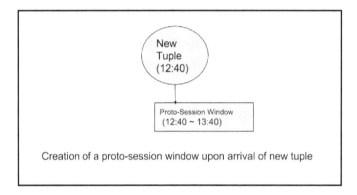

Creation of a proto-session window upon arrival of new tuple

When a tuple arrives, the **WindowedOperator** creates a temporary session window that has a time duration of **minGap**. We call this a proto-session window. In order to satisfy the minGap rule of Session Windows, the WindowedOperator does the following on the proto-session window:

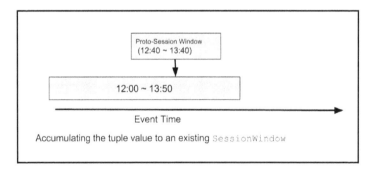

Accumulating the tuple value to an existing SessionWindow

1. **WindowedOperator** finds an existing Session Window of the same key as the tuple that can fit the entire proto-session window. In this case, the new tuple can simply be assigned to that existing Session Window:

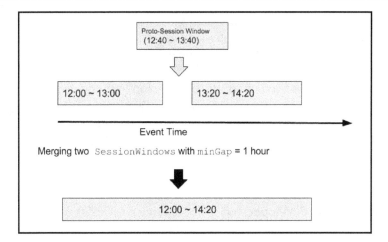

2. WindowedOperator finds two existing Session Windows of the same key as the tuple that overlap with the proto-session window. In this case, the two existing Session Windows will merge to form one new Session Window. The tuple will be assigned to the newly merged Session Window. A retraction trigger is fired, since the two old Session Windows are no longer valid. Triggers will be discussed later in this section:

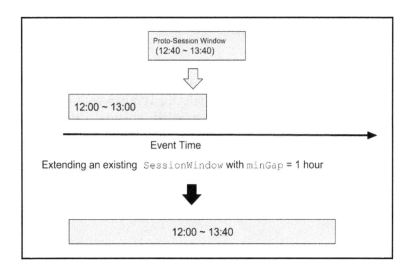

3. WindowedOperator finds one existing Session Windows of the same key as the tuple that overlap with the proto-session window. In this case, the existing Session Windows will extend to fit the proto-session window to form one Session Window. The tuple will be assigned to the newly created Session Window. A retraction trigger is fired, since the old Session Window is no longer valid.

4. WindowedOperator finds no existing Session Windows that overlap with the proto-session window. In this case, the proto-session window will be promoted to a Session Window and the tuple is assigned to that window.

Window propagation

Sometimes, an application developer may want to have a series of windowed transformations that use the same windowing scheme. WindowedOperator allows chaining of multiple instances of the operator and has only the most upstream instance assign the windows that all downstream instances inherit. This is called **Window Propagation**.

State

Each window has its own state in the WindowedOperator. If the incoming events are key-based, each key has its own state within a window. This section discusses how state is accumulated and stored.

Accumulation

When an event arrives, after it is assigned to a window, it is accumulated to the existing state of the window. The Accumulation object tells the WindowedOperator how the state for each window (and for each key if the tuple is keyed) is accumulated upon an incoming event. The Accumulation object is where the application developer can insert their own business logic, by implementing the Accumulation interface.

Accumulation Mode

Accumulation Mode tells the operator what to do with the state of the window when a trigger is fired. We will discuss triggers later in the section. There are three supported accumulation modes: **ACCUMULATING**, **DISCARDING**, and **ACCUMULATING_AND_DISCARDING**.

- **ACCUMULATING**: The state of the window is preserved until purged (usually as a result of window lying beyond the lateness horizon).
- **DISCARDING**: The state of the window is discarded immediately after firing of a trigger.
- **ACCUMULATING_AND_RETRACTING**: The state of the window is preserved until purged, but if the state has changed upon a trigger compared to the previous trigger, an additional retraction trigger is fired. This is to tell downstream operators to discard the previous state of the window and is especially useful for Session Windows, since old windows can be invalidated to form new windows.

State storage

As discussed earlier in this section, each window (or each window/key pair when keyed) has its own state. There could be millions of windows or window/key pairs at a time (see the following section for watermark and allowed lateness to limit the number of windows in the state of the operator). How the state is stored and checkpointed is likely to be the most important factor for performance. Apex provides two types of state storage. These are In-Memory Windowed Storage and Spillable Windowed Storage:

- **In-Memory Windowed Storage** stores the operator state only in memory and the entire state is copied to DFS at checkpoint. This storage is useful only if the state is expected to be small and the cardinality of valid windows and keys is small. This storage mechanism is useful for early functional testing.
- **Spillable Windowed Storage** stores the operator state in DFS with a write-ahead log and a cache in memory. This storage mechanism handles large states and incremental checkpointing. Spillable storage relies on a component called **Managed State** to interact with DFS (covered in the last subsection).

Both storage mechanisms provided by Apex require no additional external systems. However, as discussed, the state storage mechanism is likely the most important factor for performance; developers can implement the Windowed Storage interface to provide their own custom storage mechanism to optimize for performance.

Watermarks

A Watermark is a tuple that contains a timestamp that indicates all events before the watermark timestamp are expected to have arrived and influences how results are emitted from windows.

After the arrival of a watermark, if there are events with timestamps before the watermark timestamp, those events are considered late. Applications can have their Windowed Operator configured to fire *late triggers* for arrival of such events. We will discuss triggers later in this section.

Likewise, windows with a time period that lie before the watermark timestamp are considered *late*. Otherwise, they are considered *early*.

Watermarks can be generated by the input operator that generates the events, or it can be heuristically generated by the WindowedOperator.

Note that watermarks do not apply to Global Window.

Allowed lateness

When processing an unbounded streaming source, the number of possible windows is also unbounded (with the exception of Global Window). Theoretically, there is no limit on how late an incoming event can be. In practice, there is often a limit on how late an event can be for any meaningful processing to be done and there is always a limit on how much resource the system has for storing the state of the windows.

The WindowedOperator has a property called *Allowed Lateness*, which the user can specify to indicate the lateness horizon from the watermark. Events with timestamps that lie beyond the lateness horizon are dropped, and any windows that lie completely beyond the horizon are purged from the state of the operator. Thus, together with the watermarks, allowed lateness imposes a limit on the number of windows the WindowedOperator can have in its state and prevents its state storage from blowing up.

Triggering

Triggering is a way for the WindowedOperator to emit its accumulated state to downstream. A trigger is fired at the watermark for a window by default, that is, when a window is flipped from being early to being late as a result of the arrival of a watermark.

The application developer can configure the WindowedOperator to fire timed-based triggers (triggers that get fired at time intervals) or count-based triggers (triggers that get fired at tuple count intervals) when the window is early or when the window is late. A typical setup is time-based early triggers and count-based late triggers; in such a case, the WindowedOperator would periodically update the downstream the state of windows that are still expecting events and would immediately update the downstream upon arrival of events that are late.

Merging of streams

The WindowedOperator provides a way to merge two data streams for state accumulation by way of a **WindowedMergeOperator**. This operator has two incoming data streams and takes a **MergeAccumulation** instead of a regular Accumulation. The user of this operator can implement the MergeAccumulation interface to provide their custom merge or join accumulation based on their business logic. InnerJoin and Cogroup are examples of such accumulation in the Apex Library.

The WindowedMergeOperator generates its own watermarks based on the watermarks of the two input streams. The generated watermark timestamp is the earlier watermark timestamp between the two input streams. When that value changes upon the arrival of incoming watermarks, a watermark control tuple with that timestamp value will be generated and fired to downstream.

The windowing example

Examples for an augmented word count that show the use of windowing for both, the low-level DAG API and the high-level stream API, can be found at
`https://github.com/tweise/apex-samples/tree/master/windowing`.

The following code block shows the DAG construction for a keyed sum aggregation over a fixed time window of one minute that emits the intermediate sum every second and the final result at the watermark:

```
public void populateDAG(DAG dag, Configuration configuration)
  {
    WordGenerator inputOperator = new WordGenerator();
```

```
        KeyedWindowedOperatorImpl<String, Long, MutableLong,
          Long> windowedOperator =        new KeyedWindowedOperatorImpl<>();
        Accumulation<Long, MutableLong, Long> sum = new SumAccumulation();

        windowedOperator.setAccumulation(sum);
        windowedOperator.setDataStorage(new
   InMemoryWindowedKeyedStorage<String,
        MutableLong>());
          windowedOperator.setRetractionStorage(new
          InMemoryWindowedKeyedStorage<String, Long>());
          windowedOperator.setWindowStateStorage(new
          InMemoryWindowedStorage<WindowState>());
          windowedOperator.setWindowOption(new
          WindowOption.TimeWindows(Duration.standardMinutes(1)));
   windowedOperator.setTriggerOption(TriggerOption.AtWatermark()
     .withEarlyFiringsAtEvery(
        Duration.millis(1000)).accumulatingAndRetractingFiredPanes());
     ConsoleOutputOperator outputOperator = new ConsoleOutputOperator();
     dag.addOperator("inputOperator", inputOperator);
     dag.addOperator("windowedOperator", windowedOperator);
     dag.addOperator("outputOperator", outputOperator);
     dag.addStream("input_windowed", inputOperator.output,
   windowedOperator.input);
     dag.addStream("windowed_output", windowedOperator.output,
        outputOperator.input);
   }
```

The WindowOperator is set up with the windowing features. The accumulation conveys how the operator will aggregate (or combine) the incoming events that belong to a window. Prebuilt accumulations for common transformations are available here: `https://github.com/apache/apex-malhar/tree/master/library/src/main/java/org/apache/apex/malhar/lib/window/accumulation`.

This example uses the in-memory checkpointed state store. The remaining properties shown control the windowing itself (window type, duration, triggering, and so on).

More information can be found at the following link: `http://apex.apache.org/docs/malhar/operators/windowedOperator/`. Examples for use with the high-level API can be found at the following link: `https://github.com/apache/apex-malhar/tree/master/examples/highlevelapi`. Examples for use with the DAG API can be found at the following link: `https://github.com/apache/apex-malhar/tree/master/library/src/test/java/org/apache/apex/malhar/lib/window/sample`.

Dedup

Dedup (**de-duplication**) is used to remove duplicated from input datasets. Occurrence of duplicates is very common and processing pipelines often need to remove them before transformations, such as aggregation, can be applied as, otherwise, results would be inaccurate. As an example, consider calculating aggregate cost and the possibility of duplicates of the same transaction emitted from the source, which can happen due to various reasons including a message transport with non-transactional producer.

Duplicates are a fact for processing pipelines to deal with and most of the times it is necessary to discard them. The purpose of the **Dedup** operator is to identify and remove or redirect duplicate data:

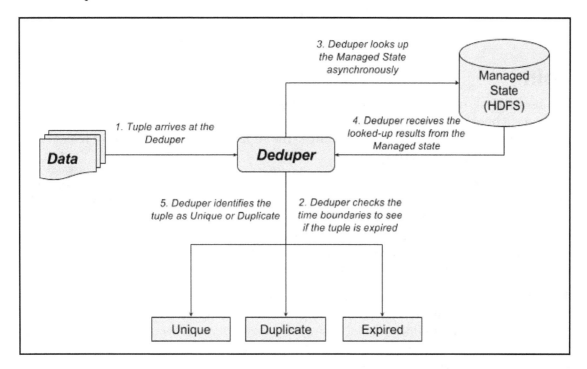

The preceding diagram shows how **Deduper** categorizes the input into a stream that contains the unique occurrences (which is what downstream processing typically needs), duplicated, and expired inputs (when working with unbounded data).

To perform its function, the operator requires state; it needs to remember which keys it has already observed. This state typically needs to be bounded by a window, as, otherwise, it could never be discarded and grow endlessly. Like other stateful transformations, dedup uses managed state to store the keys in-memory and on disk. The state management is critical for the performance, scalability, and fault tolerance of this operator despite of the seemingly simple operation it performs.

The documentation has use cases and details about the inner workings of the operator and there is also an example project at:

- http://apex.apache.org/docs/malhar/operators/deduper/
- https://github.com/apache/apex-malhar/tree/master/examples/dedup

Join

Join here refers to a transformation of multiple unbounded datasets as input. The enrichment operator covered earlier also performs a type of join, between a stream and a static bounded data set from a lookup source. The support for stream joins as of release 3.8 of the Apex library is still evolving.

Join of streams can be accomplished using the previously introduced WindowedOperator with the merge accumulation. Such accumulation can accept two incoming streams and is most efficient when it also performs incremental aggregation (because it reduces the state that the operator needs to hold until the window is complete). For a join without simultaneous aggregation, individual input records have to be maintained in the state, making this approach more suitable for keyed data with small number of records per key.

The same problem will apply to a windowed sort operation, which would require each input record to be retained. The issue could potentially be addressed with a specialized state store that allows for incremental saving of values that are collections (finer granularity than the key level), but that support isn't currently available. The operator that performs this accumulation from multiple inputs is **WindowedMergeOperatorImpl** (a subclass of WindowOperator).

State Management

Transformations such as dedup, join and windowed accumulation require state. In a pipeline that processes massive amounts of data, the state required for these transformations can grow very large. It may not fit into the operator's JVM heap memory and, even if it does, the operator wouldn't be fault tolerant, unless the state can be restored from durable storage. In addition, in a streaming use case the latency is important, which imposes additional requirements on the state management component. We need a solution that is fast, scalable, and fault tolerant.

For this purpose, the Apex library provides a utility called **Managed State**. It can persist large amounts of data on the distributed file system while allowing for asynchronous and cached I/O with fast in-memory access of frequently used data. This makes it a good fit for the streaming use cases, which has been demonstrated by the window and de-duplication operators. State management will be covered in detail in `Chapter 5`, *Fault Tolerance and Reliability*.

Summary

In previous chapters, we explored what Apex is and how applications are built using it. The examples were simple, **Hello World** style. In this chapter, we introduced the Apex library, which is of central importance to developing real-world applications. The library contains the functional building blocks that are required to integrate with existing data infrastructure and operators that implement the transformations that are frequently needed for the stream processing.

The chapter also provided links to documentation and example applications for the operators that were covered, which will be helpful as the starting point when building your own application (after all, it is much easier to start from something that works and build on top of it, as opposed to starting from scratch). Beyond functionality, we also saw how various operators support aspects such as low latency, performance, scalability, fault-tolerance, and processing guarantees that are required for production-quality applications. The next chapters will cover these topics and how they are enabled by the underlying engine in detail.

4
Scalability, Low Latency, and Performance

In traditional (non-distributed) applications, performance optimization is a substantial and ongoing effort—there are often individuals or even small teams dedicated to this effort and a vast array of techniques are employed to achieve the desired effect. These techniques include use of better algorithms, data structures with better performance characteristics, threads to parallelize computation, implementing caches, hoisting loop-invariant computations out of loops, and use of appropriate compiler options.

For distributed applications in general and Apex applications in particular, in addition to all of these techniques, a whole slew of new methods are applicable and will be covered in this chapter. Specifically, we'll cover the following topics:

- Partitioning and how it works
- Elasticity, operator state, dynamic scaling, and resource allocation
- Partitioning toolkit
- Performance optimizations (chaining of operators, stream locality, operator affinity)
- Low-latency versus throughput
- Sample application for dynamic partitioning

Partitioning and how it works

As the volume of incoming data increases, it can overwhelm the processing capabilities of the application resulting in increasing latencies and reduced throughput. It is rarely the case that the resources of the entire application are inadequate; instead, a careful analysis often reveals one or more bottlenecks. Addressing these bottlenecks will often resolve the problem. If the input data rate continues to increase, it may again cross the processability threshold, at which point the analysis must be repeated to find and resolve the new bottlenecks.

The **modus operandi** for addressing a bottleneck can take several forms, depending on the nature of the application, its configuration, the cluster environment, and other factors, for example:

- Use a faster algorithm if available and compute resources are the constraint
- Use more space-efficient algorithms and increase the memory allocation if excessive garbage collection (GC) calls are observed
- Use additional cluster nodes if a single node is resource constrained (CPU or memory).

Once optimal or near-optimal algorithms are deployed, use of additional cluster resources is often the only option for bottleneck resolution and, indeed, is the main reason why the application runs on a cluster in the first place. In the world of streaming applications, resolving the bottleneck by partitioning the input load across multiple replicated containers (each running the identical computation that was previously bottlenecking) though on different cluster nodes is formally called **partitioning**. A similar method used with web servers supporting a high-traffic website is called **load balancing**.

In Apex terminology, these replicated operators are called **partitions**. Other systems use terms such as **parallel instances** or **replicas**. Consider, for example, an input stream consisting of serialized JSON objects received from an external source, such as a TCP socket or a Kafka topic. An input operator may simply deal with the mechanics of reading from the source to maximize the input data rate and pass each record to a downstream parser.

The parser, however, has, potentially, a lot of work to do, since it has to deal with locating the delimiters for keys, values, and arrays that may be deeply nested; it also has to convert strings representing numerical values into actual numbers. All this makes the parser a likely bottleneck. If the parser is benchmarked to determine that it is rate-limited at **N** records per second, creating **P** partitions will result in a corresponding linear increase of the processing rate to $N * P$ records per second, assuming each partition has its own CPU and memory resources and can operate independent of its siblings. This is illustrated by the following diagrams which show the DAG as originally designed by the application developer (logical):

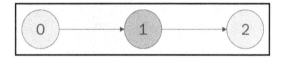

The following figure shows the DAG as embodied by the running application when partitioning is in effect (physical):

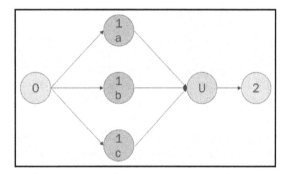

The operator labeled **U** downstream of the partitioned operator is called a **unifier**; it is used to merge the output streams of the upstream partitions and is discussed later in the *unifier* section of this chapter, entitled *Partitioning toolkit*.

Consider a second scenario where the input records are matrices and the downstream operator needs to compute some characteristics of each matrix, such as an **LU** decomposition or the eigenvalues and corresponding eigenvectors; such computations can be expensive and be severely rate limiting. Here again, partitioning such an operator is an excellent strategy to resolve the bottleneck, since each partition can perform its computations independent of all the others. The resulting effective throughput is then limited only by the available cluster resources and network bandwidth.

Partitioning can be of two types: static and dynamic. The former is applicable when the complexity of the incoming JSON and the expected maximum input rate is known in advance. The latter, when such information is not available to begin with and requires partitioning to occur at runtime based on suitable metrics computed on-the-fly. Both types are trivially easy to do with Apex. The `definePartitions()` method of `AbstractKafkaPartitioner` illustrates how the number of partitions are adjusted at runtime, based on changing external circumstances.

Sometimes, when an operator is partitioned, some of the downstream operators may become bottlenecks and may need to be partitioned as well; if they are able to operate on the partitioned streams independently, it may make sense to replicate an entire strand (or path) of the DAG, as illustrated by the following diagram:

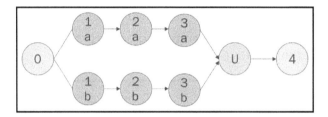

This is called parallel partitioning and is also easy to do with Apex, by setting an attribute (`PARTITION_PARALLEL`) on the input port of each operator in the replicated path. One potential issue with this scheme is that processing in the multiple paths may be heavily skewed leaving one or more paths underutilized while others are saturated. If we'd like to evenly redistribute the load, or if the number of partitions of the downstream operator does not equal the number of upstream partitions, we can simply avoid setting this attribute. Apex will then create one unifier per downstream partition and co-locate it with the corresponding partition. This is illustrated by the following diagram:

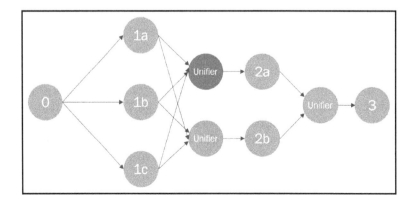

In this case, tuples from partitions **1a**, **1b**, and **1c** will get shuffled as they reach **2a** and **2b**. Parallel partitioning makes sense when we need to keep the streams segregated—for example, if each partition is processing a separate input file and the processed contents are then written to an output file. Shuffled partitioning, as noted above, may be better for CPU utilization and throughput when the input is not balanced; the particular stream locality chosen is also part of the equation and must be carefully considered when selecting the partitioning scheme.

How are tuples distributed to the partitions from an upstream operator? The platform uses a three-step process:

1. Compute an integral discriminant from the tuple data.
2. Use a partition-specific bit-mask, called the **partition mask**, to mask off appropriate bits of the discriminant.
3. Check if the resulting value is present in the partition-specific selector set called the set of **partition keys**.

By default, the object **hashCode** is used for (1)—customizable via a `StreamCodec` as discussed later—and the mask and keys are set suitably for a partition count that is a power of 2. If the actual number of partitions is not an exact power of 2, the residual tuples are distributed among the existing partitions; so, some partitions will receive a larger share of the input stream than others. Here is an illustration:

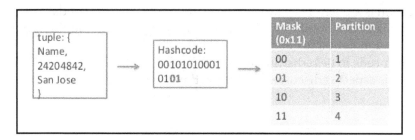

Of course, all three steps mentioned here are customizable to achieve a uniform distribution or any particular skewed distribution that the application writer desires. The details are discussed in the *StreamCodec* section later in this chapter.

Elasticity

As described in the preceding section, the number of desired partitions of each operator that is likely to be a bottleneck can be specified as part of the application configuration and the platform will ensure that the desired partitions are created at application start time. However, this is not possible when the volume of data flows can fluctuate unpredictably since we cannot forecast the number of required partitions.

The platform has the required elasticity to support such scenarios via dynamic scaling: the application writer can implement the `Partitioner` interface along with the related `StatsListener` interface, either directly in the operator or in a separate object that is set on the operator as an attribute. These interfaces allow the operator to periodically examine current metrics such as throughput, latency, or even custom metrics, and, based on those values, create new partitions or remove existing partitions, or both. All the resource allocation and deallocation is handled dynamically behind the scenes by Apex and is a significant feature that is currently absent in other platforms.

When dynamic partitioning is involved, **operator state** becomes important. Recall that an operator is simply a Java class that implements the `Operator` interface. A collection of all the fields of an operator that are *not* qualified by the `transient` Java keyword constitutes the operator state. Such fields are serialized and persisted in each checkpoint, so that it can be restored when the operator restarts after a failure.

Since serialization is a potentially expensive operation, the amount of data stored in such fields should be kept to a minimum. Operators that have no state should be annotated with the `@Stateless` annotation to ensure optimal behavior. When dynamic partitioning occurs, the state, if any, needs to be redistributed to the new set of partitions in some application-specific way. This aspect is discussed further in the next section.

Partitioning toolkit

Partitioning is appropriate, as described in the previous section, when an operator is likely to become a bottleneck. An operator is a bottleneck if it is unable to process the input stream at the required speed, causing tuples to back up in upstream buffers. Often, this also means lowered throughput and increased latencies between the time an input tuple enters the input port of the operator and the corresponding computed output tuple(s) leave the output port(s). If such an increase in latency or reduction in throughput is transient—lasts no more than a few seconds—then partitioning may not be needed (and may even be detrimental since it causes interruption of processing while existing operators are brought down and new operators are started) since OS and platform buffering will allow the operator to catch up once the spike in input has passed.

However, if the input data rates are likely to remain high for an extended period, partitioning may be needed. In any case, it is advisable to carefully benchmark the operators at the expected input data rates so that the processing limits of a single instance are understood and the need for partitioning is clearly established.

Configuring and triggering partitioning

The simplest way of triggering static partitioning of an operator named, say, OpA, is to add a suitable value for the PARTITIONER attribute in the configuration file (typically an XML file named properties.xml), for example:

```
<property>
    <name>apex.operator.OpA.attr.PARTITIONER</name>
    <value>com.datatorrent.common.partitioner.StatelessPartitioner:2</value>
</property>
```

The number following the colon (2 in this example) is the desired number of partitions. The StatelessPartitioner class is already present in the platform and so can be used directly here. This class is part of Apex core and is discussed further later in this chapter.

Alternatively, this attribute can also be set in Java code within the body of the populateDAG() method; here is an example of setting it for the CsvParser operator:

```
CsvParser csvParser = dag.addOperator("csvParser", CsvParser.class);
StatelessPartitioner<CsvParser> p = new StatelessPartitioner<CsvParser>(2);
dag.setAttribute(csvParser, OperatorContext.PARTITIONER, p);
```

The Apex library provides a dynamic partitioner
(StatelessThroughputBasedPartitioner) that can be used in a similar way to partition
at runtime, based on throughput. The base class for it is
StatsAwareStatelessPartitioner, which can be extended to use latency instead. Here
is a code fragment (there is currently no way to configure a partitioner from the XML
configuration file, so this needs to be done in Java code; the StatsListener interface is
covered in some detail in a later section):

```
CsvParser csvParser = dag.addOperator("csvParser", CsvParser.class);
StatelessThroughputBasedPartitioner<CsvParser> p
  = new StatelessThroughputBasedPartitioner<>();
p.setCooldownMillis(10000);
p.setMaximumEvents(30000);
p.setMinimumEvents(10000);
dag.setAttribute(csvParser, OperatorContext.STATS_LISTENERS,
    Arrays.asList(new StatsListener[]{p}));
dag.setAttribute(csvParser, OperatorContext.PARTITIONER, p);
```

This partitioner needs a couple of properties configured, namely the upper and lower
throughput thresholds; when the throughput rises above the upper threshold, it is an
indication that the partition is reaching the limits of its processing capability, so it will be
replicated to two copies; similarly, when the throughput falls below the lower threshold, it
is an indication that the input rate has diminished considerably, so a pair of adjacent
partitions will be replaced by a single new partition. The cool-down interval is used to
prevent frequent repartitions and allow a period of stability before the next repartition
operation. The dynamic nature of these changes is illustrated by the following diagram,
which shows the number of partitions of operator 2 increasing from 2 to 4 and, later, a
similar increase of the number of partitions of operator 3 from 1 to 2:

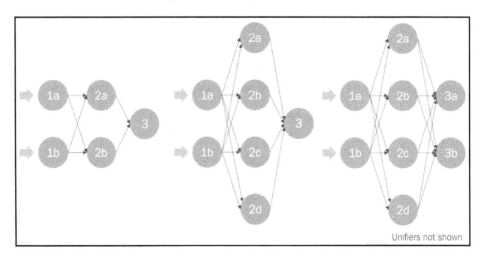

The observant reader will have noticed the Stateless prefix on the names of the preceding built-in partitioners; it indicates the fact that these partitioners are only intended to be used when the operator is stateless. To understand the importance of state, consider an example where an operator is computing a count of input tuples that is periodically emitted on an output port. When it is repartitioned into two instances, suppose the count is N. Clearly, setting the count to N in each new partition is wrong because, when the count is emitted next, the downstream operator would see values $N+K1$ and $N+K2$, where $K1$ and $K2$ are the number of tuples seen by each of the partitions after the repartition. It would then incorrectly assume that a total of $2*N+K1+K2$ tuples had been processed. A correct way to set the count in the two new partitions is to use any two values that sum to N.

Consider a second example where the operator is monitoring an input directory to process any new files that may appear there. As part of its state, it would need to keep track of the set of files already processed to avoid processing them again. When a repartitioning occurs, this set needs to be duplicated *in toto* in each of the new partitions. Thus, state redistribution is closely tied to what the operator does.

StreamCodec

Let us now discuss a couple of concepts that were briefly introduced in the earlier section: StreamCodec and Unifier. A StreamCodec is a simple interface with three methods:

```
Object fromByteArray(Slice fragment);
Slice toByteArray(T o);
int getPartition(T o);
```

Here, a Slice is just a byte array with an associated offset and length indicating the valid part of the array. The first two methods allow the user to provide custom serialization and deserialization code for tuples and the last is used as the first step of the three-step process described above to compute the set of downstream partitions that should receive a tuple. An object implementing this interface should be set as the value of the STREAM_CODEC attribute on the input port of the partitioned operator, for example (opA is the name of the partitioned operator with an input port named in):

```
StreamCodec codec = new MyCodec();
dag.setInputPortAttribute(opA.in, PortContext.STREAM_CODEC, codec);
```

As mentioned briefly earlier in this chapter, the platform will invoke the `getPartition()` method on each tuple to get the discriminant, then iterate over each partition, using its partition mask to mask off the desired bits yielding the partition key and, finally, checking if this key is present in the set of keys of that partition to determine whether to send the tuple to that partition. By appropriately choosing the masks and keys, it is possible to have a tuple sent to a single partition, some set of partitions, all partitions, or even no partition at all. The reader is encouraged to view the source code for the `DefaultPartition` class and the `Partitioner` interface in Apex core alongside this section to gain a better understanding of the concepts discussed here. That interface also declares the `PartitionKeys` inner class and inner interfaces `Partition` and `PartitionContext`.

Let us consider some scenarios to illustrate these steps. Suppose each tuple is a transaction record of some sort with fields for name, amount, date, type, and country wrapped in a Java object called `Record`. Suppose further that we want to ensure all transactions for a particular country are always delivered to the same partition. The default behavior is unlikely to do this, since `Record.hashCode()` will use all the fields of the record. We can define a custom `StreamCodec` that uses only the country field (assuming it is an `Object` such as `String`) and set it on the input port in the `populateDAG()` method, as follows:

```
public class MyCodec extends KryoSerializableStreamCodec<Record> {
  @Override
  public int getPartition(Record tuple) {
    return tuple.country.hashCode();
  }
}

MyCodec codec = new MyCodec();
dag.setInputPortAttribute(opA.in, PortContext.STREAM_CODEC, codec);
```

Here, the base class `KryoSerializableStreamCodec` simplifies things, since it provides suitable implementations for the other two methods of the interface; so, we need only override one of them.

Consider a second example where we have three partitions and we want all deposit records to go to one partition; all small withdrawals to go to the second and all large withdrawals to go to the third. This StreamCodec will do the job:

```
public class MyCodec extends KryoSerializableStreamCodec<Record> {
  @Override
  public int getPartition(Record tuple) {
    return tuple.type.isDeposit() ? 0 : tuple.amount < LARGE ? 1 : 2;
  }
}
```

Consider a third example where we find that the default `hashCode()` is not distributing tuples uniformly; so, we want round-robin dispatch (round-robin cannot guarantee idempotency, but may be appropriate in some situations) to *N* partitions:

```
public class MyCodec extends KryoSerializableStreamCodec<Record> {
  int p = -1;
  @Override
  public int getPartition(Record tuple) {
    ++p;
    if (p == N) p = 0;
    return p;
  }
}
```

Finally, consider a situation where we have four partitions and, similar to the previous example, we are processing transaction records. However, in addition to withdrawals and deposits, we have a third transaction type, which is a balance enquiry. We want all such enquiries to be discarded, all deposits to reach the first partition, all small withdrawals the second, all large withdrawals the third, and finally, all (non-enquiry) records from the US to reach the fourth. Here, we need some tuples to be sent to more than one partitions and some tuples to be ignored; such behavior cannot be achieved with the `StreamCodec` alone and needs masks and keys to be defined as well in the `definePartitions()` method.

We can achieve this distribution by using three low-order bits of the discriminant as follows: the first two bits encode the four types of transactions (0, 1, 2, 3 for balance enquiry, deposit, small and large withdrawal) and the third indicates if the transaction is from the US or not. Then, we can set the masks and key sets for the four partitions, as shown in the following table:

Partition	Mask (binary)	Keys (binary)
1	11	01
2	11	10
3	11	11
4	111	101, 110, 111

The first three partitions mask off the two low-order bits of the discriminant and choose to receive deposits, small withdrawals, and large withdrawals respectively—the country of the transaction (indicated by the third bit) is ignored. Since 0 does not appear as a key, balance enquiries will be discarded. The fourth partition uses all three bits and only selects transactions occurring in the US as desired. The getPartition() method of the StreamCodec interface is simple:

```
public int getPartition(Record tuple) {
  int result = "US".equals(tuple.country) ? 4 : 0;
  return result | (tuple.type.isDeposit() ? 1 : tuple.amount < LARGE ? 2 :
3);
}
```

The definePartitions() method for setting up the masks and key sets is a bit more elaborate:

```
// Assume the operator class is MyOperator with an input port field named
"in":
//    public final transient DefaultInputPort<Record> in = new
DefaultInputPort<>(){ ... }
//
public Collection<Partition<MyOperator>>
definePartitions(Collection<Partition<MyOperator>> partitions,
PartitioningContext context)
{
  final int mask1 = 3, mask2 = 7;

  final Partition<MyOperator>[] newPartitions = new Partition[] {
    new DefaultPartition<MyOperator>(new MyOperator()),
    new DefaultPartition<MyOperator>(new MyOperator()),
    new DefaultPartition<MyOperator>(new MyOperator()),
    new DefaultPartition<MyOperator>(new MyOperator()) };

  final HashSet<Integer>[] set
    = new HashSet[] {new HashSet<>(), new HashSet<>(), new HashSet<>(), new
      HashSet<>()};

  set[0].add(1); set[1].add(2); set[2].add(3);
  set[3].add(5); set[3].add(6); set[3].add(7);

  final PartitionKeys[] keys = {
    new PartitionKeys(mask1, set[0]),
    new PartitionKeys(mask1, set[1]),
    new PartitionKeys(mask1, set[2]),
    new PartitionKeys(mask2, set[3]) };

  for (int i = 0; i < 4; ++i ) {
```

```
      newPartitions[i].partition.getPartitionKeys().put(in, keys[i]);
   }

   return new
ArrayList<Partition<MyOperator>>(Arrays.asList(newPartitions));
}  // definePartitions
```

So, the tripartite scheme of defining discriminants, masks, and keys provides a very flexible mechanism of controlling how tuples are distributed to partitions. Naturally, the situation will be somewhat more involved in the case of dynamic partitions, since the number of existing partitions and the number of desired partitions are both variable.

Unifier

When partitioning is present, each partition receives only a part of the input stream; if it is computing any aggregates, such as means, sums, or counts for example, they need to be combined downstream of all the partitions to yield correct results. That function is performed by a unifier. For example, if the tuples are numbers and each partition is computing the per-window sum and emitting it at the end of each streaming window, the downstream unifier would need to add all the per-partition sums and emit that value at the end of each window. Thus, the results coming out of the unifier would be indistinguishable from the situation where partitioning was not present.

By default, if no unifier is defined, the platform supplies a pass-through unifier. If the partitions are simply performing some per-tuple computations, such as enrichment or filtering, the default unifier may be adequate but, if any aggregation is involved, a custom unifier will be needed to get correct results.

The Unifier interface extends the Operator interface and defines only one additional method:

```
interface Unifier<T> extends Operator {
  void process(T tuple);
}
```

A unifier is, therefore, an operator like any other, but with one big difference: it must not define any input ports. It will automatically be connected by the platform to the output ports of the upstream partitions. It needs at least one output port defined for emitting the unified results.

Once a custom implementation of this interface is defined, say `MyUnifier`, it can be used by returning a new instance of it in the `getUnifier()` override of the output port of the partitioned operator, for example:

```
public final transient DefaultOutputPort<Double> out = new
DefaultOutputPort<Double>() {
  @Override
  public Unifier<Double> getUnifier() { return new MyUnifier(); }
};
```

The custom implementation can be provided in multiple ways:

- The partitioned operator itself may implement the `Unifier` interface
- The implementation can be a standalone class
- The implementation can be an inner static class of the partitioned operator

Here is a sample implementation using the last method; it emits the per-window sum of incoming numbers and is implemented in the `RandomNumberGenerator` operator that is automatically generated by the maven archetype:

```
public class RandomNumberGenerator extends BaseOperator implements
InputOperator {
  private int numTuples = 100;
  private transient int count = 0;

  public final transient DefaultOutputPort<Double> out
      = new DefaultOutputPort<Double>() {
        @Override
      public Unifier<Double> getUnifier() { return new MyUnifier(); }
      };

  @Override
  public void beginWindow(long windowId) { count = 0; }

  @Override
  public void emitTuples() {
   if (count > numTuples) return;
   ++count;
   out.emit(Math.random());
  }

  public int getNumTuples() { return numTuples; }
  public void setNumTuples(int n) { this.numTuples = n; }

  public static class MyUnifier extends BaseOperator implements
Unifier<Double> {
```

```
   double sum;

   public final transient DefaultOutputPort<Double> unified
        = new DefaultOutputPort<Double>();

   @Override
   public void process(Double tuple) { sum += tuple; }

   @Override
   public void beginWindow(long windowId) { sum = 0; }

   @Override
   public void endWindow() { unified.emit(sum); }
 } // MyUnifier
}
```

A unifier will typically run in the same container as its downstream operator to conserve network bandwidth. Attributes for it are specified in the configuration file using a slight variation of the name; for example, to set the timeout window count and the memory allocated for a partitioned operator named opA with an output port name out, the syntax is as follows:

```
<property>
<name>apex.operator.opA.outputport.out.unifier.attr.TIMEOUT_WINDOW_COUNT</n
ame>
   <value>1200</value>
</property>

<property>
   <name>apex.operator.opA.outputport.out.unifier.attr.MEMORY_MB</name>
   <value>4072</value>
</property>
```

Naturally, when the partitioned operator has multiple output ports, each port can have a different custom unifier as appropriate for tuples emitted on that port.

When two consecutive operators are partitioned, a single unifier interposed between them may itself become a bottleneck, so the platform will create as many unifiers as the number of partitions of the second operator. For example, if the upstream operator has three and the downstream two partitions, two unifiers will be created as shown in the earlier diagram in the *Partitioning and how it works* section of this chapter).

Similarly, if the number of partitions of an operator is very large (several hundred), a single downstream unifier can turn into a bottleneck; in such cases, the unification load can be spread across multiple unifiers by setting the UNIFIER_LIMIT attribute. The platform will then create multiple unifiers to ensure that each unifier is connected to no more than this many partitions (this may require unifiers cascading into multiple levels). Here is an example:

```
<property>
  <name>apex.operator.opA.outputport.out.attr.UNIFIER_LIMIT</name>
  <value>4072</value>
</property>
```

Custom dynamic partitioning

Now that we've discussed most of the concepts related to partitioning (distribution of tuples to the partitions, unifying the output of partitions, and use of the built-in stateless partitioners for both static and dynamic partitioning) let us consider an advanced topic: custom dynamic partitioning for potentially stateful operators.

As noted earlier, construction of the new set of partitions is done in the definePartitions() method of the Partitioner interface:

```
Collection<Partition<T>> definePartitions(Collection<Partition<T>>
partitions, PartitioningContext context);
```

It is important to remember that this function is invoked in the Application Master and not in any of the containers running the partitions.

The first argument is the list of currently existing partitions. We've already seen an example implementation of this method earlier in the context of defining partition masks and keys. That example creates a list of new partitions using the built-in DefaultPartition class, customizes each partition as needed, and returns the new list. However, it is possible to reuse some or all of the existing partitions in the new list by simply copying the references from the incoming list to the new list. The platform will kill all existing partitions that are not present in the returned new list, preserve those present in both lists, and create new ones for those in the new list but not in the old.

The state of each existing partition can be retrieved and redistributed among the new list as needed before returning the new list.

When does the Application Master invoke this method? The answer lies in the
`StatsListener` interface mentioned earlier. It defines some inner interfaces and classes as
well as a single method:

```
interface OperatorRequest { ... }
interface OperatorResponse { ... }
interface BatchedOperatorStats { ... }
class Response {
  public boolean repartitionRequired;
  ...
}
Response processStats(BatchedOperatorStats stats);
```

The `processStats()` method can examine various metrics available via the incoming
argument and return a `Response` object with the `repartitionRequired` field set if a
change to the partitioning is required. Just like `definePartitions()`, this method is also
invoked by the Application Master once per second. Here, for example, is the function in its
entirety from the `AbstractFileInputOperator`:

```
@Override
public Response processStats(BatchedOperatorStats batchedOperatorStats)
{
  Response res = new Response();
  res.repartitionRequired = false;
  if (currentPartitions != partitionCount) {
    LOG.info("processStats: trying repartition of input operator current {}
      required {}", currentPartitions, partitionCount);
    res.repartitionRequired = true;
  }
  return res;
}
```

The fields, `currentPartitions` and `partitionCount` represent the current partition
count and the desired new partition count (which may have been dynamically set by the
user); if the two differ, a repartition is requested by setting the field as described earlier.

The `Partitioner` interface also defines a method for letting the operator know when a
repartition operation has occurred:

```
void partitioned(Map<Integer, Partition<T>> partitions);
```

In most cases, this can just be an empty method.

Performance optimizations

In addition to partitioning, there are other aspects of how an Apex application is deployed on the cluster that are under the control of the application writer which can be used to further improve performance.

For example, consider consecutive operators opA and opB in a DAG. If the former generates a large volume of data on its output port and the latter performs some sort of filtering or aggregation operation so that the volume of data leaving its output port is considerably diminished, it may make sense to co-locate them in the same node to conserve network bandwidth; this is called NODE_LOCAL locality.

Additionally, tuple serialization and deserialization overhead (which can be considerable in some cases) can be eliminated if they could be co-located within the same container; this is called CONTAINER_LOCAL locality. The following figure shows different options of co-location of two operators:

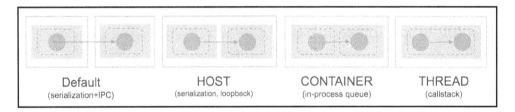

These co-locations can be achieved by setting the locality of the appropriate stream, for example:

```
<property>
  <name>apex.application.MyFirstApp.stream.Events.locality</name>
  <value>CONTAINER_LOCAL</value>
</property>
```

Other available values are THREAD_LOCAL, NODE_LOCAL, and RACK_LOCAL. When the input stream is sparse, it may not be enough to keep even a single thread occupied; in such cases, using THREAD_LOCAL to serialize the callback invocations of both operators in a single thread makes sense. We've already mentioned the benefits of NODE_LOCAL and CONTAINER_LOCAL; RACK_LOCAL is useful to avoid going through a switch to reach a different rack. These values are Java enum constants defined in the DAG class.

The performance characteristics of some of these locality settings are illustrated by this table:

Message size (bytes)	Default locality (bytes/s)	CONTAINER_LOCAL (bytes/s)	THREAD_LOCAL (bytes/s)
64	59,176,512	204,748,032	2,480,432,448
128	89,803,904	395,023,360	3,662,684,672
256	137,019,648	671,409,664	5,218,227,968
512	156,255,744	1255,749,632	4,416,738,304
1024	167,139,328	2,022,868,992	3,423,519,744
2048	182,349,824	3,508,013,056	4,050,688,000
4096	255,229,952	3,732,725,760	3,884,101,632

A couple of points are noteworthy in this table: As expected, the throughput increases with the message size since the fixed per-message overhead becomes a progressively smaller fraction of the total cost. The default locality yields the smallest number, since the full overhead of serializing tuples, sending them across the network interfaces, and finally deserializing them is incurred. The THREAD_LOCAL values are high, since all of this overhead is bypassed, but these are deceptive numbers since, in a real application, the loss of concurrency is likely to have a significant negative impact on throughput.

Affinity and anti-affinity

A related topic is operator **affinity** and **anti-affinity**. There are circumstances when we want a set of operators to run on the same (affinity) or different (anti-affinity) node, container, or thread. For example, suppose we have an upstream operator A and a downstream operator B that is not a direct successor of A in the DAG. If they are both heavy consumers of CPU resources, it makes sense to allocate them on different nodes (anti-affinity). Stream locality cannot achieve this effect, since there is no stream connecting them. Another situation is where the application is computing latencies between operators A and B. Simply looking at the system clock may not be adequate, since the clocks on different nodes may not be exactly synchronized, so requiring them to be allocated on the same node (affinity) will yield more reliable results.

These affinity effects can be achieved by setting a suitable `AffinityRulesSet` object as the value of the `AFFINITY_RULES_SET` attribute of the DAG, for example:

```
AffinityRulesSet ruleSet = new AffinityRulesSet();
List<AffinityRule> rules = new ArrayList<>();
rules.add(new AffinityRule(Type.ANTI_AFFINITY, Locality.NODE_LOCAL, false,
  "rand", "operator1", "operator2"));
rules.add(new AffinityRule(Type.AFFINITY, Locality.CONTAINER_LOCAL, false,
  "console", "rand"));
ruleSet.setAffinityRules(rules);
dag.setAttribute(DAGContext.AFFINITY_RULES_SET, ruleSet);
```

Here, `rand`, `operator1` and `operator2` form a set of named operators that should be allocated on different nodes (`ANTI_AFFINITY`) while console and rand should be in the same container (`AFFINITY`). The operator set can also be specified as a regular expression using a different constructor:

```
rules.add(new AffinityRule(Type.AFFINITY, "*" , Locality.NODE_LOCAL,
false));
```

The Boolean argument indicates that the affinity rule may be ignored if adequate resources are not available to satisfy it.

These rules are also settable from properties files using a JSON string; when the same operator name appears twice in an anti-affinity rule (as done for `operator1` in the following code snippet) it is an indication that partitions of that operator should be allocated on different nodes:

```
<property>
<name>apex.application.AffinityRulesSampleApplication.attr.AFFINITY_RULES_S
ET
  </name>
    <value>
    {
      "affinityRules": [
        {
          "operatorRegex": "console*",
          "locality": "CONTAINER_LOCAL",
          "type": "AFFINITY",
          "relaxLocality": false
        },
        {
         "operatorsList": [
          "rand",
          "passThru"
          ],
          "locality": "NODE_LOCAL",
```

```
            "type": "ANTI_AFFINITY",
            "relaxLocality": false
        },
        {

            "operatorsList": [
            "operator1",
            "operator1"
            ],
            "locality": "NODE_LOCAL",
            "type": "ANTI_AFFINITY",
            "relaxLocality": false
        }
    ]
  }
</property>
```

Low-latency versus throughput

As mentioned in `Chapter 1`, *Introduction to Apex*, Apex is capable of very low-latency processing while also delivering high throughput and fault-tolerance. Processing latency evaluation ultimately depends on the specific use case and end-to-end pipeline functionality. It is nevertheless important to know the platform limits and what is theoretically possible. Resource consumption translates to cost. It is essential that a platform can scale to meet current and future needs at reasonable cost. Complex streaming analytics applications can run on hundreds of processes and consume TBs of memory. At such a scale, it is essential to understand how future growth of business and data volume will translate into cost for the solution.

The Apex user does not have to trade latency for throughput as would be the case in batch systems or a micro-batch architecture. Performance benchmark results and production deployments have shown that Apex can process millions of events per second with low latency and efficient resource utilization. We covered how partitioning enables scalability. The next sections will explain some of the controls available to the user to optimize performance, including the locality aspect. In Apex, data continuously moves through the pipeline, which in the end is a collection of queues that are managed by the engine. How operators are collocated and how these internal queues operate affect the performance limits. Many use cases won't push these limits, but for those that do there are a few more advanced knobs to optimize (queue sizes, wait millis).

Apex clearly illustrates the fact that there need be no tradeoff between low latency and throughput: data can be streamed at network speeds along the DAG, complex computations can be decomposed into smaller units and run in their own containers to better exploit CPU, and memory resources and bottlenecked operators can be dynamically partitioned to eliminate the bottlenecks and restore throughput—all with little or no developer intervention.

The following links discusses specific benchmarks:

- https://www.datatorrent.com/blog/blog-apex-performance-benchmark/

- https://www.datatorrent.com/blog/throughput-latency-and-yahoo/

Sample application for dynamic partitioning

In this section, we will take a detailed look at an example application that illustrates the use of dynamic partitioning of an operator. It uses an input operator that generates random numbers and outputs them to a DevNull library operator (which, as the name suggests, simply discards them). The input operator starts out with two partitions; after some tuples have been processed, a dynamic repartition is triggered via the StatsListener interface discussed above to increase the number of partitions to four. The source code is available at the following link: https://github.com/apache/apex-malhar/tree/master/examples/dynamic-partition.

The populateDAG() method is, as expected, very simple:

```
@Override
public void populateDAG(DAG dag, Configuration conf)
{
  Gen gen          = dag.addOperator("gen",     Gen.class);
  DevNull devNull = dag.addOperator("devNull", DevNull.class);
  dag.addStream("data", gen.out, devNull.data);
}
```

The interesting code is in the input operator `Gen` which looks like the following:

```
public class Gen extends BaseOperator implements InputOperator,
Partitioner<Gen>, StatsListener
{
  ....
  private static final int MAX_PARTITIONS = 4; // maximum number of
partitions
  private int partitions = 2;
  ....
}
```

Notice that it implements the two interfaces discussed above: `Partitioner` and `StatsListener`.

The two variables `MAX_PARTITIONS` and `partitions` are used by the partitioning code: the first is the number of partitions that will be created by the dynamic repartition step and the second is the desired number of partitions; they are discussed up next.

The implementation of the `StatsListener.processStats()` of the latter interface is a minor variation of the sample discussed earlier:

```
@Override
public Response processStats(BatchedOperatorStats batchedOperatorStats)
{
  final long emittedCount = batchedOperatorStats.getTuplesEmittedPSMA();

  // we only perform a single dynamic repartition
  Response res = new Response();
  res.repartitionRequired = false;
  if (emittedCount > 500 && partitions < MAX_PARTITIONS) {
    LOG.info("processStats: trying repartition of input operator current {}
      required {}",
        partitions, MAX_PARTITIONS);
    LOG.info("**** operator id = {}, window id = {}, tuplesProcessedPSMA =
{},
tuplesEmittedPSMA = {}",
      batchedOperatorStats.getOperatorId(),
batchedOperatorStats.getCurrentWindowId(),
      batchedOperatorStats.getTuplesProcessedPSMA(), emittedCount);
    partitions = MAX_PARTITIONS;
    res.repartitionRequired = true;
  }

  return res;
} // processStats
```

It is important to keep in mind that, even though the method is part of the operator code, it is never invoked by the operator process; instead, it is invoked by the Application Master (AM).

The method first retrieves one of the built-in operator metrics—the moving average of the number of tuples emitted per second—from the incoming argument. Initially, while the operator is warming up, the number will be small; when the number reaches an arbitrarily chosen threshold (500 in this case), a repartition is triggered to create MAX_PARTITIONS partitions. Only a single repartition occurs (done via the condition partitions < MAX_PARTITIONS), since the purpose of the example is to show how to exercise the dynamic repartitioning functionality. The log messages illustrate how to retrieve other, potentially useful information from the argument such as the current operator id, window id, and so on.

If the repartitionRequired field of the response is true, the AM will then invoke the definePartitions method of the Partitioner interface.

```
@Override
public Collection<Partition<Gen>> definePartitions(
  Collection<Partition<Gen>> list, PartitioningContext context)
{
  if (partitions < 0) {      // error
    String msg = String.format("Error: Bad value: partitions = %d%n",
      partitions);
    LOG.error(msg);
    throw new RuntimeException(msg);
  }

  final int prevCount = list.size();
  if (1 == prevCount) {      // initial call
    LOG.info("definePartitions: First call, prevCount = {}, partitions =
{}",
    prevCount, partitions);
  }

  if (prevCount == partitions) {
    LOG.info("definePartitions: Nothing to do in definePartitions");
    return list;      // nothing to do
  }

  LOG.debug("definePartitions: Repartitioning from {} to {}", prevCount,
    partitions);
  Kryo kryo = new Kryo();
  List<Partition<Gen>> newPartitions =
    Lists.newArrayListWithExpectedSize(partitions);
  for (int i = 0; i < partitions; i++) {
```

```
      Gen oper = cloneObject(kryo, this);
      newPartitions.add(new DefaultPartition<>(oper));
    }
    LOG.info("definePartition: returning {} partitions",
  newPartitions.size());
    return newPartitions;
  }
```

The very first call to this function happens before the operator starts running and, for that call, the argument collection is always a singleton. If the current number (`prevCount`) equals the desired number, there is nothing to do, so the argument is simply returned. Otherwise, we must create a new list of partitions with the desired number of elements (value of the `partitions` field in this case). Each element is created as a new instance of the `DefaultPartition` object which is initialized with a copy of the current operator object; the copy is created via a single instance of Kryo which is created outside the loop and passed to the `cloneObject()` function inside the loop; this method is defined as a static method of the `KryoCloneUtils` library class.

At this stage, if we wanted to preserve some or all of the existing partitions, we could have simply copied them from incoming argument collection into the new list; such partitions will continue to run unmolested. The remaining partitions of the argument collection however will be killed. If the operator is stateful, the desired state transfer from the old to the new partitions must be done before this function returns.

The only other method of the `Partitioner` interface is as follows:

```
@Override
public void partitioned(Map<Integer, Partition<Gen>> map)
{
  if (partitions != map.size()) {
    String msg = String.format("partitions = %d, map.size = %d%n",
  partitions,
      map.size());
    throw new RuntimeException(msg);
  }
}
```

As mentioned earlier, this method can simply be empty but a simple sanity check has been added for illustrative purposes. The argument is a *partition id* → *Partition* map of the current set of partitions immediately after the repartition step; clearly the size of this map should equal the number of desired partitions.

This concludes our discussion of this example. Many operators in the library utilize this powerful feature to provide smooth dynamic scalability capabilities transparently to Apex applications.

Performance – other aspects for custom operators

When tuning an application with custom operators, some common Java coding practices can act as hidden performance drains so developers should avoid them as far as possible. We've already mentioned one earlier, in passing—inadvertently including a large number of fields (or fields whose values are large) of an operator in the state by not adding the `transient` modifier. As the size of the state increases, serializing it for every checkpoint can become a hidden bottleneck. Generally speaking, if a field is cleared for every streaming or application window, it does not need to be part of the state.

A second practice is the per-tuple use of reflection (or the use of Maps and other Java collections) which is an expensive operation; this is often done when the type of the tuple is not known at compile time, so just `Object` is used. For such cases, Apex provides a utility class called `PojoUtils` which can be used to create custom getter and setter methods for an object at runtime; these methods are generated as bytecode and run at the same speed as normal methods, thus obviating the need for reflection.

For example, we could declare a field for a getter method, as follows:

```
private transient Getter<Object, String> keyGetter;
```

Then, we could initialize it lazily using the above utility class when tuples are processed:

```
if (null == keyGetter) {  // NOTE: executed only once
  Class<?> tupleClass = tuple.getClass();
  keyGetter = PojoUtils.createGetter(tupleClass, expressions.get(0),
String.class);
}
```

Here, expressions is a list retrieved from the configuration properties file; each expression can simply be a field name of the tuple or an expression involving multiple fields such as `{$.id} + {$.id1}` indicating that fields `id` and `id1` of the tuple need to be added.

Finally, we could use the getter method on each tuple to retrieve fields of the object:

```
String key = keyGetter.get(tuple);
```

Examples of such use can be seen in many operators in the Apex library, for instance, the `CouchbasePOJOSetOperator`.

A third practice is the superfluous creation new objects when a single object could be reused; object reuse can substantially reduce the number of GC calls, resulting in a beneficial impact on performance. Of course, as is well known, object reuse introduces additional risks of incorrect operation if the object is not properly cleared before each reuse or if appropriate synchronization is not in place when multiple threads are present, but if maximizing performance is a primary goal, the risks may be worth taking.

Summary

In this chapter, we discussed the partitioning of operators and how it is the key platform feature that provides both static scalability and adaptive dynamic scalability to Apex applications with minimal required effort on the part of the application writer. We discussed related concepts such as shuffled partitioning, parallel partitioning, unifiers, and stream codecs, how these features can be configured either in code or in properties files and how the interplay of these features results in unparalleled flexibility and outstanding run-time performance. Finally, we concluded by discussing a sample application that illustrates some of these features.

In the next chapter, we will cover another key strength of Apex: fault tolerance and reliability with check-pointing and processing guarantees.

5
Fault Tolerance and Reliability

Apex was built from the ground up for enabling data processing pipelines that are highly available and providing strong processing guarantees for accurate results. From its first release in 2013, Apex has supported exactly-once semantics based on distributed checkpointing and full fault-tolerance, including the application master. In this chapter, we will look at how these important properties are achieved, and what different components in the stack contribute to it:

- The need for the distributed data processing platform to be resilient
- Failure scenarios in Apex and how they are handled
- Consistent, distributed checkpointing and how it works
- Efficient, incremental, and large-scale state saving
- Why the accuracy of the processing is important, and what guarantees does Apex provide
- An example application for end-to-end exactly-once results

Distributed systems need to be resilient

As discussed in `Chapter 2`, *Getting Started with Application Development*, Apex applications run on a cluster as a distributed set of processes. Distribution enables scalability, and with the correct architecture, adding more resources to a compute cluster (such as YARN) allows applications to scale horizontally (refer to `Chapter 4`, *Scalability, Low Latency, and Performance*). At the same time, growing number of processes and machines also increases the likelihood of failure. Hardware or software failures cannot be avoided.

In order to prevent failure resulting in downtime or incorrect results, the system has to be resilient. Fault-tolerance mechanisms should cover high availability (HA) as well as provide with processing correctness guarantee to the user. For a production-quality and business-critical system, these aspects should be important evaluation criteria. A stream data processing platform should provide fault-tolerance along with scalability and high performance, and where necessary, low-latency processing support.

The evolution of large scale data processing tools and frameworks surprisingly reveals that it took long for platforms (such as Apex, Flink, and Kafka) to emerge that not only overcome processing paradigm restrictions of early frameworks, such as MapReduce, but also consider the nonfunctional and operational requirements as foundational to their architecture. Part of the reason may be the growing awareness among users, who typically will focus on functionality in the early stages of project design and implementation and only later on operability. However, addressing these aspects as an afterthought is often difficult, resulting in expensive rework or failed projects. Such symptoms are not uncommon in the Hadoop ecosystem.

Fault-tolerance components and mechanism in Apex

In `Chapter 2`, *Getting Started with Application Development*, we looked at the deployment of an Apex application when it is executing on a YARN cluster. Let's revisit the diagram to see which type of failures may occur and how they are handled by the system:

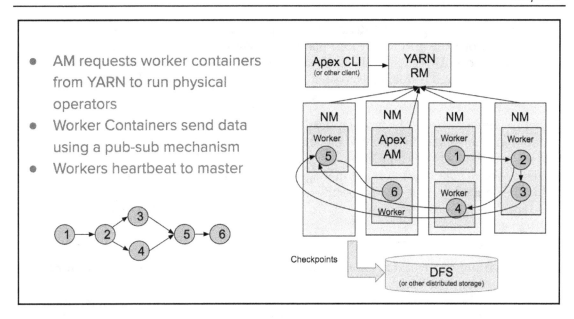

- AM requests worker containers from YARN to run physical operators
- Worker Containers send data using a pub-sub mechanism
- Workers heartbeat to master

The client is only required for launching the application; it is not involved in the execution of the DAG on the cluster, and failure of the client node does not affect the pipeline. Since Apex is running on YARN, let's first see how YARN supports resilient applications (from a user's perspective).

YARN consists of a resource manager (RM) and node managers (NM). Each YARN cluster node has a node manager service running, which communicates with the resource manager.

- **Failure of an NM**: When a node manager fails (regardless of software or hardware failure), the RM will detect this and ensure that the affected containers can be allocated on different machines. The RM itself cannot recover those containers, but it can inform the application master (AM), which then can take action and request a new container. YARN provides the notification, and the application framework needs to handle it. Therefore, the occurrence and implementation of failover ultimately depends on the AM.
- **Failure of the RM**: When installed in a HA setup, the RM has a standby instance. Clients (including applications) will automatically failover, and running applications incur no downtime (except that they will not be able to allocate new containers until the failover completes).

An appropriately configured YARN cluster will provide failover for its services. It will also allow application state restoration after planned downtime such as rolling upgrade or other maintenance work. This enables the application framework running on YARN to provide HA support, although it still needs to do its part to be resilient. We will now look at how that works in Apex.

Apex (like any other YARN-based application) has an application master and one or multiple worker containers. The AM manages the workers, and this relationship is roughly analogous to that between an RM and NMs or that between the name node and data nodes in HDFS. The worker containers are managed by the AM through a "heartbeat" protocol. The implementation of the AM is specific to the framework, and we already discussed the function of the Apex AM in `Chapter 2`, *Getting Started with Application Development*.

The following are the recovery scenarios:

- **Failure of a worker container (unexpected process termination or machine failure)**: The AM will receive a notice from YARN that a container process failed (or discovered a heartbeat timeout). The Apex AM will at this point request a replacement container from YARN and once the resource is allocated, redeploy the affected operators. In order to do so, the state of the operators needs to be restored. How the state is saved and how recovery for individual operators works will be explained in the *Checkpointing* section, later in the chapter.
- **Hung worker container due to internal issues**: Sometimes the JVM process runs, but it can actually be unresponsive. Examples include JVM stuck in garbage collection due to resource leaks and user code deadlock. This isn't a failure from the YARN perspective, but is one from the application perspective since data is not flowing into or out of the operators in that container. The Apex AM can detect such conditions based on timeouts (heartbeat or lack of operator processing progress), and kill and recover the worker container. As long as the issue is transient and not a functional problem with processing the data, the container can be recovered and processing can continue. The recovery handling can be controlled by the user through configuration attributes.

- **Failure of the AM**: When the **main** container fails, the Apex application will continue to execute, and data will continue to flow through the DAG (worker containers can continue to run; this feature is known in YARN as work preserving restart). While the master is gone, monitoring, recovery of worker containers, autoscaling, and other centrally controlled application behavior is unavailable. The YARN resource manager will be notified of the failure by the NM and restart the AM in a new container. The application attempt ID will tell Apex that it needs to recover the state of the AM. Like for worker containers, the AM state needs to be checkpointed to support this. An example of such state is the DAG (logical and physical plan), which may change at runtime. Once the AM is recovered, worker containers will locate the new address through a file stored in HDFS and resume the heartbeat protocol.

These recovery scenarios are handled by Apex automatically, the user does not need to do anything special for it. There is no need for manual intervention. Later, we will look at some of the underlying mechanics. When everything works as intended, the Apex application will run, as long as the YARN cluster is sufficiently functional to provide the resources required by the application. When the cluster itself fails there is obviously no way for Apex to run.

However, it is possible to resume an application from its previous state, even when the YARN RM does not remember it. This is called a stateful restart, where the user can specify the previous application ID and the new application will continue where the previous instance left off. Apex has its automated distributed state snapshot that recovers the entire DAG. It is therefore possible to kill the application, perform disruptive maintenance on a cluster, and resume, as long as the state snapshot (by default, stored in HDFS) is not removed.

There is one problem that Apex and any other reliable platform cannot handle, and that's incorrect user code that leads to deterministic failure. For instance, a parsing exception that is not handled won't go away no matter how many times Apex recovers the worker. Whenever the record is replayed, it will fail again. This isn't a problem of the Apex engine, but rather a functional defect in the operator code that needs to be considered at design time. A recoverable failure on the flipside would be a database or another external system that isn't fully reliable and is intermittently unavailable. The Apex worker may fail, but it will eventually be able to resume when the external problem is fixed.

What can be done about the bad record that wasn't considered when the code was written, which now stops the pipeline? One way is to remove the record from the source system to allow processing to continue. But eventually, the problem can surface again. It is possible, though, to use the stateful restart mechanism that we just discussed to update the user code—the JAR file with the operator code can be updated in HDFS, and on restart the bug fix will be online. This works as long as the operator code isn't modified in a way that is incompatible with the checkpointed state previously saved. An example of such incompatibility is the removal of non-transient fields or methods involved in the serialization or deserialization of the operator.

Checkpointing

Checkpointing is the mechanism to save the state of the application to make it recoverable in the event of failure. Apex saves snapshots of the state periodically, and can use them for recovery. Checkpointing state is not a new concept; many systems have the concept of state saving that can be used for recovery.

However, since Apex executes as a distributed system with operators in different worker containers, the mechanics of state saving involves subtleties that go well beyond conventional checkpointing so that it results in a consistent snapshot that allows the application to continue after some or all of those containers have failed. This bookkeeping complexity is not something that the application developer should have to deal with; it should be handled by the platform behind the scenes. So, what is the magic of checkpointing in Apex?

There are several pieces to this, and before we come to the actual details of how data is saved to a durable storage, we will look at the key ingredient to achieve a distributed state snapshot: each operator in the execution layer should know that state needs to be saved at a particular point in time. To illustrate why this is not trivial, let's consider how Apache Storm (an early streaming processing platform) left management of application state completely to the user. In earlier versions, it would attempt to guarantee that in-flight data tuples or records are not lost when a failure occurs and also recover the workers, but not the state that was possibly accumulated in the application.

Let's revisit the example of counting words. Storm will ensure that none of the words are lost, but will not maintain accuracy of counts post-failure, so after recovery, the counts are back to 0 when the word stream resumes. At this point, we have data loss; one could say the application has lost its memory. Therefore, finding a way to mitigate this was left to the application developer.

Of course, one could write code to save the counters to a database, but when to save? Saving on every change does not scale, and it will overwhelm the database on a high-throughput stream. Saving periodically can still lead to undercounting for up to one interval. Once there are multiple stateful operations in different workers, how do we synchronize the interval boundaries? And this is just scratching the surface. Moving down the path of writing custom state saving code for a distributed stream processor quickly turns out to be peeling the onion to discover ever more challenges.

Application developers are not tasked and are typically not equipped to solve such problems. The issue is not related to application functionality and should be solved by the platform. So here is how Apex does it.

When to checkpoint

Let's start with how Apex determines when state needs to be saved. Instrumental to the process of consistent state saving is the streaming window, which was briefly introduced in Chapter 1, *Introduction to Apex*. Every streaming window (processing time interval) has a timestamp ID (assigned at the source) and traverses the entire DAG, embedded in the data flow. The engine is aware of these windows and has an opportunity to ask each operator to perform state saving at the same consistent boundary:

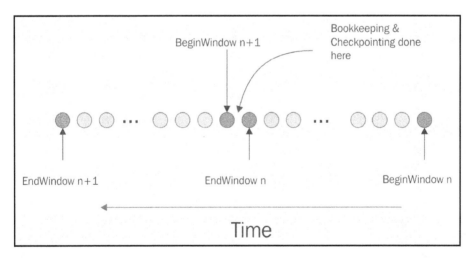

The preceding diagram shows how the window markers flow with the data and how checkpoints occur between streaming windows. Normally, checkpointing does not need to occur at every streaming window. By default, a streaming window is 500 ms, and the interval between checkpoints is 60 windows (30 seconds).

The user can influence how often checkpointing occurs by configuring the `CHECKPOINT_WINDOW_COUNT` attribute. Compared to typical in-memory processing, state saving is an expensive operation, so frequent checkpointing is detrimental to the overall application performance. The other extreme is a very large checkpoint interval, which makes application recovery expensive because a large amount of state needs to be restored.

The following configuration sets the checkpoint interval count to 20, resulting in a 10-second time interval (20×500 ms streaming window size):

```
<property>
  <name>apex.attr.CHECKPOINT_WINDOW_COUNT</name>
  <value>20</value>
</property>
```

If a failure occurs during window $n + 1$, Apex will restore affected operators to the nearest recovery checkpoint. To be used for recovery, a checkpoint was not only created by the worker container, but its existence was also communicated to the master as part of the worker-to-master heartbeat protocol. Because checkpointing is decentralized and asynchronous in the distributed workers, only the master knows which checkpoints were completed by each operator in the DAG.

There can be multiple checkpoints tracked for each operator (they will be purged once when they are *committed*, that is, processed throughout the entire DAG). The master will determine which of the available checkpointed states needs to be used for recovery. In this example, the checkpoint was taken after window n, and assuming that the master knows about it and the downstream operators had also reached this checkpoint, then the operator will be restored to the state as of the completion of window n and start processing window $n + 1$ from the beginning.

When an operator fails, we cannot simply restore that operator alone to the saved checkpoint; we need to restart all downstream operators. To understand why, consider the following scenario: Operator A (upstream) is connected to Operator B (downstream), which is a sink—it has no operators downstream of it. Suppose A and B are processing windows $n + 10$ and n, and their latest respective checkpoints were performed on windows $n + 5$ and $n - 5$. If A fails and is restored to $n + 5$, the data between n and $n + 5$ would be lost since B does not have it yet and A will not retransmit it. Both operators need to be restored from the checkpoint for the same window. In this example, the smallest k such that both operators were last checkpointed at $n - k$ is chosen as the restoration checkpoint by the platform. The logic is similar when multiple downstream operators are present.

In order for the AM to make this determination, it must be aware of what checkpoints are available for all the operators of the DAG. So each operator, whenever it successfully completes a checkpoint, communicates the relevant metadata to the master via the worker-to-master heartbeat protocol. When all operators of a DAG have checkpointed a particular window, we have an important synchronization point—all checkpoints prior to this one for all operators can now be removed since no operator will ever be restored from any of those checkpoints and this is, in fact, how checkpoint purging is performed. Checkpoints that are purged are committed and operators may also choose to be notified (the `CheckpointNotificationListener` interface) to perform operations such as finalizing the state that became immutable.

How to checkpoint

The state of the operator needs to be extracted and saved to a durable storage. The `StorageAgent` interface makes this pluggable behavior. The default implementation uses the Kryo serialization framework to turn the operator state into bytes and relies on HDFS to save the serialized state to files. HDFS is already part of the Hadoop installation, and so no additional external system dependency is required by default. Any alternative FS implementation supporting the same interface could optionally be used.

The default storage agent performs a checkpoint as follows:

- Kryo serializes the operator object into an in-memory buffer. During this operation, the operator cannot process any data, as the serialization is blocking. The rest of the state saving process is asynchronous. As soon as Kryo has done its work, the operator will start processing the next streaming window.
- A background thread will copy the serialized in-memory state to HDFS. It does so by creating a temporary file, and once writing is complete, renames the file so that it can be identified with the window ID, should it be required for recovery. The rename operation is needed for two reasons:
  - The master must see only completed checkpoint files when listing the directory.
  - HDFS creates an exclusive lease for the file and assigns it to the writer. So, if the writer fails, a dangling lease stays behind and prevent writing the rest of the checkpoint after recovery. The temporary file (along with its attached lease) is simply abandoned and a new one is created upon recovery.
- Once the file is written, the worker propagates the checkpoint information to the master using the heartbeat protocol mentioned earlier.

The `StorageAgent` interface has four methods (`save`, `load`, `delete`, and `list`) and is easy to implement for a different method of extracting data from the operator or saving to a different storage backend. For example, a custom implementation can contain highly optimized serialization code that is specific to the operator implementation. Or, it can use an in-memory data grid to save the state (an implementation for Apache Geode is available in the Apex library's `contrib` module).

What to checkpoint

As described, checkpointing is costly and when writing custom operators, it is important to consider what data needs to be part of the saved state.

Some operators are stateless; their computation does not depend on the previous state. Application developers can skip the checkpointing for such operations using the `STATELESS` attribute, or if it is a custom operator, by annotating the operator with `@Stateless`. Examples include stateless transformations such as filtering or parsing or a connector that writes to JDBC (refer to `Chapter 3`, *The Apex Library*).

Stateful operators, such as the counter discussed previously, depend for their computation on state from previous streaming windows and need to be checkpointed. If there are any fields that don't need to be saved (such as a cache that can be rebuilt), they should be declared `transient` to be excluded from checkpointing. For the nontransient fields, careful consideration should be given to the size of the state that needs to be externalized at every checkpoint.

Connectors are often stateful. For example, the Kafka consumer needs to remember the offsets for each partition. It does not need to remember the messages though, since those are already stored in Kafka and can be replayed.

WindowedOperator accumulates state to implement the various user-level windowing concepts (refer to `Chapter 3`, *The Apex Library*). That state can potentially grow very large and needs to be checkpointed. A naïve approach would be to store all data in a HashMap and have the field serialized at every checkpoint. This may work for a few hundred keys, but performance will quickly degrade with high key cardinality. Instead, operators that accumulate large state can use incremental state saving, which will be discussed in the next section.

Incremental state saving

Operators can hold a large amount of state in memory to facilitate fast access for low-latency processing. At the same time, this state also needs to be recoverable in the event of failure. With the growing state, the time to checkpoint increases, leading to larger pauses in processing, and eventually, certain processing time thresholds are exceeded, to the crash of the operator. To overcome this and achieve the twin goals of fault tolerance and fast processing, state needs be saved in an efficient manner, such that the size of the checkpointed state is capped.

For this purpose, the Apex library has `Managed State`, a fault-tolerant, scalable bucketing mechanism that uses files to persist the data (the Hadoop distributed file system is used by default). State is keyed and stored in buckets; a bucket is an abstraction for a collection of tuples, all of which share a common key (which could be derived from any combination of fields in a tuple, including time, similar to the hash code of Java objects). `Managed State` has the following features:

- Checkpoints key/value state incrementally. Only state deltas are included in a given checkpoint, instead of a full snapshot (state in the operator is mutable, but the bucket storage files are not—at least in HDFS).
- `Managed State` allows setting a threshold on the size of data in heap memory. Data that has been persisted is off-loaded from memory when the threshold is reached.
- Keys can be partitioned in user-defined buckets, which helps with operator partitioning and efficient off-loading from memory.
- Key/values are persisted in HDFS in a block structured file format that is optimized for querying. A read cache that keeps blocks of frequently accessed data in memory is also present (it would not be acceptable to incur disk I/O whenever the keyed state needs to be retrieved).
- Purges state that is no longer needed from disk (in a streaming scenario with unbounded data). Based on the bucket structure this is done by simply discarding segments of data without having to look at individual keys, similar to how topic data is expired by Kafka brokers.

Consider this example of how the operator developer would use this component to delegate state saving:

```
// write
managedState.put(1L, key, value)

// read
managedState.getSync(1L, key)
managedState.getAsync(1L, key)
```

The following diagram shows what occurs under the hood to handle state saving, so that on checkpoint only relevant portions of state are processed, for a sequence of streaming windows (**W**) with key-value pairs (**key, value**):

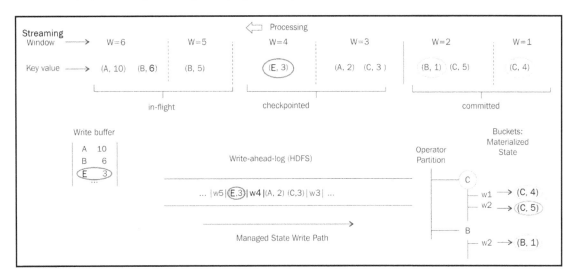

The **write path** of Managed State is comprised of an in-memory write buffer for streaming windows until they are checkpointed. The modified data resides in memory after the operator code has called put(). At the time of checkpoint, the operator needs to ensure that data is durable (for potential recovery), hence the changes are written to a write-ahead-log (set of files that contain all tuples for the checkpointed streaming windows).

Once a checkpoint is committed (which signals to the operator that no replay will occur), the data is materialized into buckets. The buckets are a two-level structure. In this example, the first level is derived from the key, and the second level from the streaming window time. The time component is simplified; typically, buckets represent larger time intervals than individual streaming windows, and the time is often derived from the event. Also, while in the figure state, buckets are shown to have a single key, a real-world setup would have many keys in a bucket. The granularity of buckets determines the maximum parallelism. The mapping between operator partitions and buckets could also change dynamically, but a bucket can only belong to a single operator partition.

The **read path** involves data that was materialized in bucket files, data that may still be in the write-buffer, and in addition to that, a block cache that keeps previously accessed data from bucket files in memory (beneficial for repeated access to a particular key range). A read will first check the write buffer. If the element isn't present, then lookup continues in the buckets. This may involve multiple bucket files, depending on whether the read is constrained by key and time or not. In the preceding diagram, key C has values for W1 and W2, and possibly other time buckets. A lookup would need to inspect these files in reverse chronological order until a match is found, within the given time range. With event time windowing, this would typically be a single candidate time bucket, identified by the window timestamp.

The mapping of keys and time to the bucket structure varies for different transformations. This is why `Managed State` provides three different bucket implementations that result in different storage layouts on disk, and different ways to get and put values by key and/or time.

 Details are available from the following javadoc:
https://ci.apache.org/projects/apex-malhar/apex-malhar-javadoc-r
elease-3.8/org/apache/apex/malhar/lib/state/managed/AbstractMana
gedStateImpl.html.

The data access pattern and choice of bucketing scheme is critically important for the performance of the stateful operator. For example, the window operator uses the window time (and key) to access state. It assumes that typically the arrival order of tuples and updates for the window state will occur on "hot data" (while the state is held in the write buffer) and not involve frequent file rewrites and read-cache invalidations. Under the typical access pattern, `Managed State` can achieve high throughput per partition, which exceeds the limits of an external database system. `Managed State` relies on the distributed file system that is already present in the cluster and does not require additional stack components, which is an advantage from an operability perspective.

Let's look at how recovery works with this structure. The first diagram here shows the failure of an operator after the committed checkpoint 120, which means that changes that occur in the streaming window 130 need to be replayed:

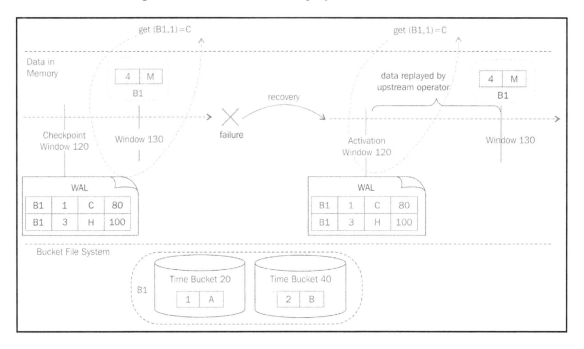

As discussed in the *Checkpointing* section, the operator is restored to the checkpointed state (that does not include the in-flight changes), and a replay will restore the transient state. Effectively, this is at-least-once processing with the exactly-once effect on the state, something that we will further examine in the *Processing guarantees* section.

The next diagram illustrates the scenario of a failure that occurs after the checkpoint (data was written to the WAL), and before the transfer and write to the bucket files are completed:

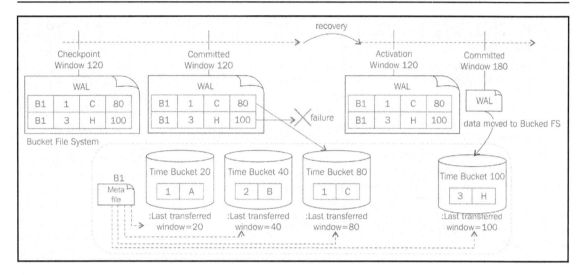

The last entry in the WAL is **(3, H)**, which eventually needs to be written to bucket **100** (in this, the setup bucket and streaming window are the same, but different mappings are possible). The failure occurs before bucket 100 was written. Recovery happens at streaming window 120, and during activation, the write will be completed.

When using `Managed State`, the developer works with an API that is flexible and exposes serialization, synchronous versus asynchronous reads, and other lower-level details that may be required in special cases. For other operator implementations though, this flexibility translates to extra complexity. To address this, Spillable Data Structures provide an API that is familiar to the Java developer used to working with collections such as Maps, Lists, and Sets, but cannot use the standard collection implementations due to the checkpoint size constraints discussed earlier. Spillable Data Structures provide the same interface with an implementation that wraps away the Managed State complexities.

For more information about Managed State and Spillable Data Structures refer to this document: `http://events.linuxfoundation.org/sites/events/files/slides/Stateful%20streaming%20data%20pipelines.pdf`.

Incremental recovery

Incremental recovery refers to the ability of Apex to handle a failure of an operator by only recovering the affected operator and its downstream dependencies versus resetting the entire DAG.

Let's consider how the failure of an operator affects the processing in the following two topologies:

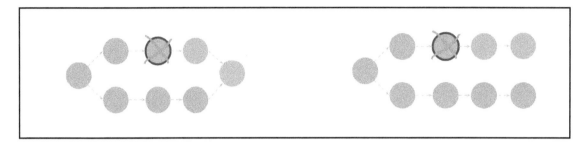

The pipeline upstream of the failed operator is identical, downstream is different. Operators affected by the failure are in gray.

On the left-hand side, the stream merges with another branch. In this case, processing in the output operator is blocked and no results can be emitted until the failed operator recovers. On the right-hand side, processing in the lower branch can continue, while the upper branch is blocked.

 Why is this important? Depending on the topology, this capability can reduce or even eliminate downtime. Apex already has a very efficient recovery mechanism that can bring the DAG back to operation within a few seconds (a single digit, depending on how fast the cluster manager can provide the replacement resource). However, if the use case requires a processing time SLA, just relying on the recovery may not be possible. Let's say the use case was real-time fraud prevention, and it is important that a result is available within milliseconds. Downtime of any one operator will block the processing path and the latency SLA cannot be met. The ability of Apex to restore only affected operators in conjunction with a suitable DAG layout, can be used to guarantee the SLA by implementing redundant processing (similar to speculative task execution in MapReduce).

If we modify the preceding DAG to eliminate the branch after the source, so that each path has its own source and processes the same data, then any failure in one branch (including the input operator) no longer affects the other. This is analogous to running two separate applications, except that it can be done with synchronized streaming windows so that results of any computation in one path of the DAG can be guaranteed to be the same as that in the other, as long as both complete.

The component in the Apex data flow that enables incremental recovery is the buffer server. It is an in-memory pub/sub mechanism that is essentially invisible to the user and allows looser coupling of the upstream and downstream operators.

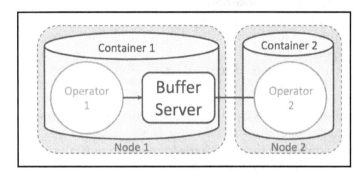

The buffer server resides in the same container as the operator that emits data (upstream). It buffers data in memory for one or multiple subscribers (depending on the partitioning) that will ultimately consume it. Similar to the offset in a Kafka partition, the Apex streaming window ID allows the subscriber to specify exactly where to start processing the stream. When, after a container failure, the replacement downstream operator starts to replay, it will provide the streaming window ID that corresponds to the checkpoint at which it was restored to resubscribe and resume processing.

This exact mechanism also enables dynamic scaling of an operator without having to reset the entire DAG: old partitions and their downstream operators are undeployed by the platform, the set of new partitions of the dynamically scaled operator is derived from the old partitions and then deployed along with the downstream operators. Upon deployment, these operators resume processing by subscribing to the upstream buffer servers, starting from the checkpointed window ID.

Processing guarantees

The Apex engine by default guarantees that data is processed at-least-once and that state updates within the DAG occur exactly-once. With respect to state mutation through interaction with external systems, the results depend on the connector (refer to Chapter 3, *The Apex Library*). Connectors that support the exactly-once results include Files, Kafka, JDBC, Cassandra, and all others where the write operations are, or can be made, idempotent. We will look at an example application in the next section.

In distributed systems, a guarantee of the exactly-once processing is not really possible since nodes may go down at any time and when they are restored, some reprocessing of prior data, however minimal, must occur in order to guarantee correctness (or we have to accept data loss, which yields at-most-once processing). So, when we see exactly-once in published feature matrices of stream processors, it really means at-least-once along with the often implicit assumption of idempotency of state updates. This is because in the presence of idempotency, a repeated update is indistinguishable from the original. There are, however, techniques used by Apex (discussed later in this chapter) to avoid duplicate state updates irrespective of idempotency.

The application developer in Apex can influence processing semantics by choosing the processing mode on a per-operator basis through the PROCESSING_MODE attribute. The modes may also look familiar to those with the knowledge of RPC and other distributed systems, so let's see what the options are and what they mean in this context:

- AT_LEAST_ONCE: On recovery, state will be restored to a checkpoint and the input stream rewound to the corresponding streaming window, as previously discussed. This is the default mode; it ensures that no messages are lost and it forms the basis for the exactly-once output that will be covered later.
- AT_MOST_ONCE: Data is not processed more than once, but it is possible that some of it won't be processed at all and therefore some data can be lost. This is normally not acceptable. This mode has faster recovery time, since processing will resume from the latest available streaming window instead of rewinding the stream to the checkpoint window. This is potentially suitable for use cases that require only the latest data.
- EXACTLY_ONCE: This processing mode is really a misnomer and should not be confused with effective-once or end-to-end exactly-once, which we will cover later. This processing mode means that an operator will be checkpointed after every streaming window (which is very inefficient), and it still has a very small possibility of incorrect results when the engine fails to complete the checkpoint write after the operator endWindow() callback was completed (it is not a distributed transaction). In short, this mode should be avoided as it comes at high cost for questionable benefit. Hopefully, it will be removed in a future Apex version. Practical exactly-once options will be covered here.

With this inventory of available modes, it is almost always best to go with the default (at-least-once)! Having the guarantee of no data loss, we can complement at-least-once processing with two more ingredients to achieve the exactly-once results. Combined with idempotency and consistent state, it is possible to guarantee that ultimately the result is end-to-end exactly-once, even when after a recovery some reprocessing has to occur. Apex was first among the stream processors to support the end-to-end exactly-once results guarantee through several of its connectors.

This guarantee is supported by three features of the Apex platform:

- The distributed checkpointing discussed earlier
- Specific capabilities of certain connectors to external systems
- The repeatable processing order guarantees within the DAG (not related to and not to be confused with the out of order input from sources)

Example – exactly-once counting

The following example is again a variation of the word count that will further illustrate the concepts in this chapter. Incorporating the interaction with external systems, it will be closer to the requirements of real-world streaming applications:

- Read from a source (in this case Kafka)
- A transformation (counting words) that emits incremental aggregates
- A JDBC sink that will maintain totals accumulating the incremental aggregates

The source code for the example can be found at the following link:
`https://github.com/apache/apex-malhar/tree/master/examples/exactly-once`

This scenario will allow us to examine in more detail how the end-to-end exactly-once processing guarantee is supported by Apex and its connectors. The following diagram shows the logical layout of the application:

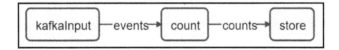

With Kafka as the streaming source, the data flow is unbounded. However, the computation is stateful, and we need a window to update the aggregate count. Windowing was explained in Chapter 3, *The Apex Library*. For this example, the count operator will be very simple and aggregate over a streaming window in processing time. It retains the aggregates as state for the duration of the window, emits them at the end of the window, and clears the state.

The final state is held in the database table, which is used to illustrate how the exactly-once output can be done. The store operator incrementally updates the database with partial counts it receives. This needs to occur in such a way that neither undercounting due to lost events nor overcounting due to reprocessing after recovery from failure is possible. Having this accuracy is necessary more often than not, as in the case of use cases that involve counting money. The Java code for the DAG looks like this (ExactlyOnceJdbcOutputApp):

```
KafkaSinglePortStringInputOperator kafkaInput =
dag.addOperator("kafkaInput",
  new KafkaSinglePortStringInputOperator());
kafkaInput.setWindowDataManager(new FSWindowDataManager());
UniqueCounterFlat count = dag.addOperator("count", new
UniqueCounterFlat());
CountStoreOperator store = dag.addOperator("store", new
CountStoreOperator());
store.setStore(new JdbcTransactionalStore());
ConsoleOutputOperator cons = dag.addOperator("console", new
  ConsoleOutputOperator());
dag.addStream("words", kafkaInput.outputPort, count.data);
dag.addStream("counts", count.counts, store.input, cons.input);
```

Let's see how the three key ingredients for exactly-once are provided:

- **At-least-once processing**: It is guaranteed by the Apex engine and its checkpointing, as explained in the previous sections.
- **Idempotency**: The Kafka input operator remembers which events were consumed in which streaming window, and will replay them in the same streaming windows should recovery occur. Replay in this way allows downstream processing to repeat the computations for streaming windows with identical results. Kafka preserves the data, and the operator tracks the offset ranges.
- **Consistent state in an external system**: The JDBC operator writes to the database in transactions. Every partial count is added to the current count. This operation is not idempotent and would lead to overcounting when repeated during replay. The JDBC operator therefore tracks which streaming window was committed as part of the transaction so that a duplicate write can be detected and skipped.

How is state managed to ensure that no duplication in the external system depends on the specific connector? The example project contains another application that writes to files. Instead of transactions, the file writer uses atomic rename to ensure no duplicate output. In contrast to JDBC, file output does not support incremental updates and needs to wait for final data to be available, which implies higher latency. Another example is the exactly-once output to Kafka, which Apex actually supports even for pre 0.11 Kafka (this version introduces support for the exactly-once delivery). An example can be found here: `https://github.com/apache/apex-malhar/tree/master/examples/kafka/src/main/java/org/apache/apex/examples/kafka/exactlyonceoutput`

The exactly-once output to JDBC

The JDBC output for this example extends the base transactional JDBC output operator from the Apex library. This operator contains all the plumbing for JDBC connection and transaction handling, so that we can focus on what's required to update the counts:

```
public static class CountStoreOperator
  extends AbstractJdbcTransactionableOutputOperator<KeyValPair<String,
    Integer>>
  {
    public static final String SQL =
        "MERGE INTO words USING (VALUES ?, ?) I (word, wcount)"
      + " ON (words.word=I.word)"
      + " WHEN MATCHED THEN UPDATE SET words.wcount = words.wcount +
I.wcount"
      + " WHEN NOT MATCHED THEN INSERT (word, wcount) VALUES (I.word,
        I.wcount)";

    @Override
    protected String getUpdateCommand()
    {
      return SQL;
    }

    @Override
    protected void setStatementParameters(PreparedStatement statement,
      KeyValPair<String, Integer> tuple) throws SQLException
    {
      statement.setString(1, tuple.getKey());
      statement.setInt(2, tuple.getValue());
    }
  }
```

The count update is an incremental UPSERT operation; partial counts emitted upstream are added to the previously stored value. This operation isn't idempotent, unlike a put into a key-value store. We could, of course, accumulate the state upstream (using the window operator and accumulation instead of discarding when triggering the output), and then, instead of incrementing, just set the new total to make it idempotent. However, here the goal is to explore how state can be correctly handled in the external system when required.

The JDBC output will, as part of every transaction that updates the word count, also record the last-processed streaming window in an extra metadata table. By comparing the current window ID with the one last stored, the operator will know whether the update has already happened or not. Remember that this technique works because on replay, events are presented in the same order and window sequence, guaranteed by the input operator and the engine.

The JDBC output can also make use of the streaming window to optimize for fewer JDBC operations—multiple updates can be batched and committed as larger transactions. Aggregation at the window boundary reduces data sent through the stream, and thus the number of database updates.

Finally, the test case (ExactlyOnceJdbcOutputTest) shows how the application can run as an integration test. It creates the embedded Kafka cluster and HSQL instance, and initializes the topic and tables. Part of this setup is the creation of the metadata table that tracks the committed streaming window ID (the base JDBC output operator expects this table to exist in the target database):

```
@Before
public void beforeTest() throws Exception
{
  // setup hsqldb
  Class.forName(DB_DRIVER).newInstance();
  Connection con = DriverManager.getConnection(DB_URL);
  Statement stmt = con.createStatement();
  String createMetaTable = "CREATE TABLE IF NOT EXISTS "
      + JdbcTransactionalStore.DEFAULT_META_TABLE + " ( "
      + JdbcTransactionalStore.DEFAULT_APP_ID_COL + " VARCHAR(100) NOT
        NULL, "
      + JdbcTransactionalStore.DEFAULT_OPERATOR_ID_COL + " INT NOT
NULL, "
      + JdbcTransactionalStore.DEFAULT_WINDOW_COL + " BIGINT NOT
NULL, "
      + "UNIQUE (" + JdbcTransactionalStore.DEFAULT_APP_ID_COL + ", "
      + JdbcTransactionalStore.DEFAULT_OPERATOR_ID_COL + ", "
      + JdbcTransactionalStore.DEFAULT_WINDOW_COL + ") "
      + ")";
```

```
        stmt.executeUpdate(createMetaTable);
        String createTable = "CREATE TABLE IF NOT EXISTS " + TABLE_NAME
            + "(word VARCHAR(255) not NULL, wcount INTEGER, PRIMARY KEY (
word
            ))";
        stmt.executeUpdate(createTable);
    }
```

Summary

This chapter covered how Apex is a reliable platform for stream processing that is highly available and provides accuracy of results. Two of the most important aspects for production-quality stream data processing are fault tolerance and end-to-end exactly-once guarantees, and these turn out to be strong points of Apex and key differentiators.

Up to this point, the book has emphasized Apex as a platform and framework overall. The next few chapters will be examples and focus on application development.

6
Example Project – Real-Time Aggregation and Visualization

In the previous chapters, we introduced the API to develop Apex applications and the library of connectors and transformations that are available out of the box. We also covered the scalability, performance, and fault tolerance of the Apex platform. This chapter is the first of three example project chapters that are dedicated to developing applications that are representative for scenarios and use cases readers may find in various verticals.

This chapter will cover the following topics:

- Streaming ETL and beyond
- The application pattern in a real-world use case
- Analyzing Twitter feed
- Running the application
- The Pub/Sub server
- Grafana Visualization

Streaming ETL and beyond

This first application will be an example of processing live streaming data with windowing and real-time visualization. The data source will be Twitter, processing of the tweet stream will compute the top hashtags in a time window as well as some counts that can be visualized as time series. The pattern is applicable to many similar use cases: data is continuously consumed from a streaming source and aggregated. Traditionally, results of such computation will land in a storage system (files, databases, and so on). Such processing can be broadly categorized as **extract-transform-load** (**ETL**) in streaming fashion. However, the focus here will be on stream processing that goes beyond the realm of general purpose ETL tools and can support streaming analytics use cases.

Stream processing needs a source of data, so every pipeline will involve the *E* of ETL with connector(s) to *extract* or *ingest* data (with Kafka being a common streaming source and files for batch use cases). As for the *T* part, Apex is more suited for pipelines that need to go beyond a restricted set of simple transforms (such as parsing, filtering, enrichment, and so on).

The applications are built by developers and use cases will demand more complex processing logic, such as stateful transformations with aggregations and windowing, pattern detection, alerts, and so on. These applications typically also involve custom development for specific business logic that cannot be adequately mapped to a generic library of building blocks.

The final *L* of ETL is actually something that we will skip (or replace) in this example. Instead of loading the results into a storage system, we will use them directly for real-time visualization. The broader idea is that when the stream processing pipeline already has all the data (the **in-memory state** of the **stateful** application), we can directly make use of it, without having to first write to a datastore and then consume the data from there. With stateful streaming platforms, this pattern is termed **queryable state** or **stream processor as database**.

The application pattern in a real-world use case

One of the case studies mentioned in the introductory chapter was an ad-tech use case. The Apex-based system powering that use case went into production in 2014 and fits the same pattern of the example that we will build in this chapter. Summarized at a high level, the system consumes log records from Apache Kafka, then aggregates these records into a dimensional model and provides the aggregates to a real-time dashboard that users can use to gain actionable insights into the performance of advertising campaigns. Time to insight is critical, as the ability to perform timely adjustments often translates to incremental revenue or reduced cost (or both) for the business:

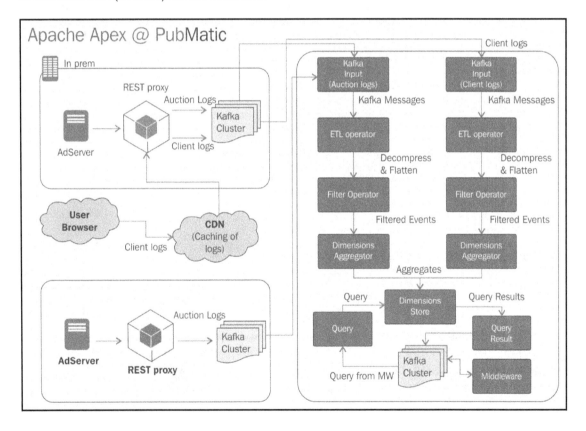

The Apex-based implementation replaced a batch system that involved several hours of latency with a streaming pipeline that reduced latency to seconds (end-to-end, including data collection and ingestion). The dimension store holds the aggregated data in memory (conceptually, a table with dimension keys such as advertiser and publisher for metrics such as revenue and cost). The operator is partitioned based on the same dimension keys and the state checkpointed for fault tolerance. This leads to the question of how the metrics that are held in the operator heap memory and continuously being updated from incoming ad-server log records reach the users' real-time dashboard.

The dashboard server (**Middleware**) sends queries and retrieves results through a Kafka based Pub/Sub mechanism. Queries are keyed to reach the dimension store partition that holds the corresponding aggregates and will send a response Kafka message. At first, this looked complicated: three years ago and from a traditional web application developer perspective, it was exotic to **query data** via Kafka! The outcome was convincing: a robust and scalable system (since the partitioning of queries follows the partitioning of the aggregation) and low query result latency (< 50ms).

More information can be found at:

- https://www.slideshare.net/ashishtadose1/realtime-adtech-reporting-targeting-with-apache-apex
- https://www.slideshare.net/ApacheApex/actionable-insights-with-apache-apex-at-apache-big-data-2017-by-devendra-tagare

Analyzing Twitter feed

The example we are going to build will show how an application similar to the ad-tech use case can be built using the Apex library. Instead of processing a stream of ad-impression events from Kafka clusters, we will use a stream of tweets retrieved via the Twitter developer API. Instead of a dimensional model, we will compute windowed aggregates for selected metrics. The data visualization will take advantage of **Grafana** with a Pub/Sub plugin instead of a custom portal and frontend server. The goal will be to introduce the relevant building blocks and enable the reader to derive a similar application for their domain or use case.

The following sections will walk through the application functionality, its components, and a few selected implementation details. The full code, ready to run is available at the following link: `https://github.com/tweise/apex-samples/tree/master/twitter`.

The following is the DAG of the example application:

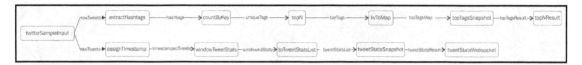

The input operator reads tweets from the Twitter streaming API (`https://dev.twitter.com/streaming/overview`). This API gives access to the tweet stream in real time, although by default Twitter makes only 1% of the tweets, randomly sampled, available through this API. To use the API, you need to have a Twitter API account to create access tokens that will need to be configured (explained next).

The Tweet sampler is a connector from the Apex library (`https://github.com/apache/apex-malhar/tree/master/contrib/src/main/java/com/datatorrent/contrib/twitter`) that emits `Status` objects that contain all the information available in a tweet, such as author, URLs, hashtags, location, created date, and so on. When serialized as JSON, the data can be rather bulky (1K per tweet is not uncommon). Most of this data also isn't required for our application, and instead of having to serialize the `Status` objects in order to transfer them to the downstream operators (where extra information is essentially discarded), we define the stream as `CONTAINER_LOCAL`.

 Recall from earlier chapters that this setting collocates the downstream operators in the same JVM process as the upstream, thereby avoiding both serialization and network transmission.

The pipeline branches at this point. One path will compute top hashtags for a sliding window, the other path will aggregate tweet counts for time series.

Before we look at the Apex application in detail, let's have a look at the final visualization in Grafana:

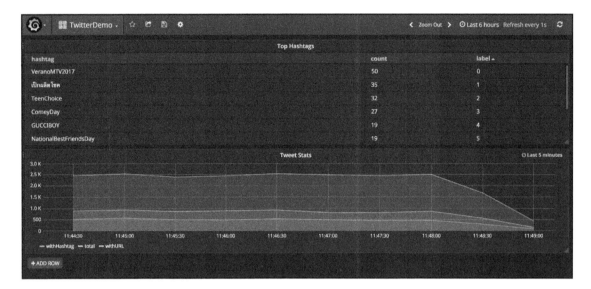

The dashboard shows the most frequent hashtags in the top panel, which is a table with hashtag and count columns (the extra row number column isn't of interest for display but could be used to to build a pie chart, for example). The second panel is for the time series showing three count metrics.

How does data flow from the Apex application to Grafana? There needs to be an endpoint for Grafana to connect to. It would be possible to use one of the out-of-the-box Grafana data sources, but this would require to first write from Apex to an external store and incur additional latency. The goal here is to query the state of the Apex application directly. Since the client is JavaScript code running in Node.js, it is preferably an HTTP-based protocol. The Apex application, although it ultimately serves the data, isn't the most suitable candidate to provide this HTTP endpoint. An operator could act as the HTTP server, but it isn't known beforehand on which host and port in the cluster it will be deployed. A simple solution is to use a Pub/Sub mechanism to solve this.

There are several options for a Pub/Sub mechanism, such as using Kafka topics as shown in the introductory use case earlier in this chapter (especially when a Kafka cluster is already available in the existing infrastructure). Here, we will be using a WebSocket to HTTP Pub/Sub server (it can be found at `https://github.com/atrato/pubsub-server`). WebSocket is not a general recommendation but it is convenient in this case, since the Apex library provides the connector and there is no need to write integration code for a different sink.

The following diagram illustrates the setup for the top hashtags results; it will be identical for any other streams that need to be published:

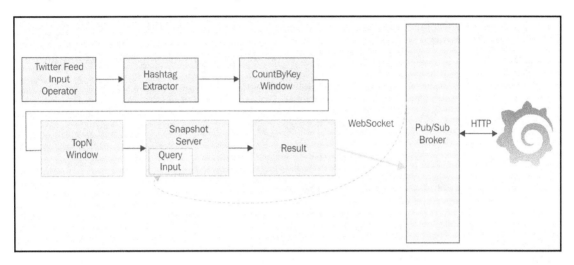

The Apex application as the publisher sends result data via WebSocket to the Pub/Sub broker, and Grafana is the subscriber using HTTP to pull the data (and visualize it). The green line (the arrow towards the **Pub/Sub Broker**) is for publishing the results and the dotted orange line (the dotted line from **Query Input** to **Pub/Sub Broker**) for the flow for queries. Queries are submitted from the frontend to tailor the results to the visualization needs, for example, specific keys as filter criteria for a widget.

Note that queryable state as shown is implemented by using existing connectors and the streaming data flow, and not a special interface or protocol for queryable state. In the DAG this is reflected by the presence of the **Snapshot Server**, which will collect the state for the visualization. The upstream window operator has state about current windows, but the UI may also require completed windows. Compared to a generic mechanism that exposes state of all operators this requires upfront planning, but also ensures that the data delivered is tailored to the visualization needs (the developer may decide to combine data from multiple logical operators or partitions into a single streaming output).

Now that the overall setup is covered, let's examine the functionality of the Apex application in more detail. Each branch is discussed in a separate subsection up next.

Top Hashtags

The top hashtags computation is, essentially, a windowed word count that only outputs the *n* largest counts for each window. As shown in the DAG figure graph, the operation is split into `countByKey` and `topN` and both transforms use existing operators and accumulations. `countByKey` is implemented as a key based window operator with `SumLong` accumulation:

```
KeyedWindowedOperatorImpl<String, Long, MutableLong, Long> countByKey =
    new KeyedWindowedOperatorImpl<>();
countByKey.setAccumulation(new SumLong());
countByKey.setDataStorage(new InMemoryWindowedKeyedStorage<String,
    MutableLong>());
countByKey.setWindowOption(new
    WindowOption.TimeWindows(Duration.standardMinutes(5)));
countByKey.setWindowStateStorage(new
    InMemoryWindowedStorage<WindowState>());
countByKey.setTriggerOption(TriggerOption.AtWatermark().
    withEarlyFiringsAtEvery(25).accumulatingFiredPanes());
```

Counts are emitted as key value pairs—the key is the hashtag and the value is the number of occurrences in the window. Since the window is five minutes and results should be shown early to reflect them in the visualization as updates occur, we set a count based trigger that will fire as changes occur. This will ensure that updates are only triggered for active windows (as opposed to time-based triggering) and inactive windows will not propagate results downstream.

The `topN` is a non-keyed window operator with prebuilt `topN` accumulation. This operator collects all counts emitted by potentially multiple upstream partitions and retains the *n* highest counts. The result of `topN` is a list of `KeyValPair` objects.

```
TopNByKey<String, Long> topNByKey = new TopNByKey<>();
topNByKey.setN(10);
WindowedOperatorImpl<KeyValPair<String, Long>, Map<String, Long>,
  List<KeyValPair<String, Long>>>
topN = new WindowedOperatorImpl<>();
topN.setAccumulation(topNByKey);
topN.setDataStorage(new InMemoryWindowedStorage<Map<String, Long>>());
topN.setWindowStateStorage(new InMemoryWindowedStorage<WindowState>());
topN.setTriggerOption(TriggerOption.AtWatermark().withEarlyFiringsAtEvery(2
)
  .accumulatingFiredPanes());
```

The next operator is just a simple map transform that converts the list of `KeyValPair` (key-value pairs) to a `Map`. Though this may look counter-intuitive, since the `Map` does not retain order, this conversion is required for the next operator that provides the integration for state query.

```
static class KeyValPairToMap implements
Function.MapFunction<Tuple.WindowedTuple<List<KeyValPair<String, Long>>>,
  List<Map<String, Object>>>
  {
    @Override
    public List<Map<String, Object>>
f(Tuple.WindowedTuple<List<KeyValPair<String, Long>>> input)
    {
      List<Map<String, Object>> result = new ArrayList<>();
      int rowNum = 0;
      for (KeyValPair<String, Long> kv : input.getValue()) {
        Map<String, Object> row = new HashMap<>();
        row.put("hashtag", kv.getKey());
        row.put("count", kv.getValue());
        row.put("label", Integer.toString(rowNum++));
        result.add(row);
      }
      return result;
    }
  }
```

The `topTagsSnapshot` operator is responsible for the queryable state. It is an extension of `AppDataSnapshotServerMap` that accepts input data as `Map` and transforms it into the JSON format and emits it to the downstream operator when a query is received.

```
TopNSnapshotServer topTagsSnapshot = new TopNSnapshotServer();
String JSON = SchemaUtils.jarResourceFileToString(TOPN_SCHEMA);
topTagsSnapshot.setSnapshotSchemaJSON(JSON);
```

The schema for the input data is the list of keys in the `Map` and the schema of the result determined by the query:

```
{
  "values": [
    {"name": "hashtag",   "type": "string"},
    {"name": "count",     "type": "long"},
    {"name": "label",     "type": "string"}
  ]
}
```

Alternatively, we could have used the base class that accepts any object as input and implemented our own `convert` function, thus eliminating the need for conversion in a separate, preceding operator.

The snapshot server operator can accept queries from any source that implements the `EmbeddableQueryInfoProvider` or the data can come from an upstream connector that is attached to the query port. Examples would be Kafka or WebSocket input operators, which may receive queries from the frontend with specific parameters. In this simplified example, we publish the latest data regardless of whether there is a subscriber or not.

This is done through an **automatic query** that is generated for every streaming window and includes all the field names of the input schema:

```
public class TopNSnapshotServer extends AppDataSnapshotServerMap
{
  @Override
  public void beginWindow(long windowId)
  {
    super.beginWindow(windowId);
    Fields fields = (super.getTableFieldToMapField() != null) ?
        new Fields(super.getTableFieldToMapField().values())
        : super.schema.getValuesDescriptor().getFields();
    DataQuerySnapshot query = new DataQuerySnapshot("topHashtags", fields);
    queryProcessor.enqueue(query, null, null);
  }
}
```

The output is in JSON format, suitable for consumption by the table panel in Grafana:

```
{
    "id": "topHashtags",
    "type": "dataResult",
    "data": [
      {
        "count": "24",
        "label": "0",
        "hashtag": "BTSBBMAs"
      },
      {
        "count": "14",
        "label": "1",
        "hashtag": "PREMIOSMTVMIAW"
      },
      ...
    }
```

The final operator in this branch is responsible to emit the results via WebSocket to the Pub/Sub server and this connector requires the WebSocket address to write to (for example, `ws://localhost:8890/pubsub`):

```
PubSubWebSocketAppDataResult wsResult = dag.addOperator("topNResult",
    new PubSubWebSocketAppDataResult());
wsResult.setUri(uri);
wsResult.setTopic(topic);
```

The address needs to be configured; by default the example will write to the console.

Please note that the following paragraphs will refer to event time windowing and related concepts that were introduced in `Chapter 3`, *Apex Library*.

TweetStats

In this branch, we compute aggregate metrics over a sliding window in event time that can be used for time series visualization. The metrics are simple counts: total tweets, number of tweets with hashtags, and number of tweets with URLs. The result will contain these metrics along with the window timestamp for visualization.

The first operation is to assign the timestamp to the incoming event. This is necessary because the window operator currently requires the input tuple time to implement a tuple interface and the Twitter status object needs to be wrapped to accomplish this. While we're at it, we can also extract the event time (when the tweet actually occurred) from the status object and make it available under `TimestampedTuple`.

```
FunctionOperator.MapFunctionOperator<Status, TimestampedTuple<Status>>
    assignTimestamp =
        new FunctionOperator.MapFunctionOperator<>(
            new Function.MapFunction<Status, TimestampedTuple<Status>>()
            {
              @Override
              public TimestampedTuple<Status> f(Status input)
              {
                long timestamp = input.getCreatedAt().getTime();
                return new TimestampedTuple<>(timestamp, input);
              }
            }
        );
```

The next operator is the window operator that is configured to compute TweetStats aggregates over one minute windows, with a sliding interval of 30 seconds. Since we want to see updates in near real time, we trigger early results every two seconds, before the watermark (and because in this case no watermark is generated by the source, output is exclusively generated through early triggering):

```
WindowedOperatorImpl<Status, TweetStats, TweetStats> windowTweetStats = new
WindowedOperatorImpl<>();
    windowTweetStats.setAccumulation(new TweetStatsAccumulation());
    windowTweetStats.setDataStorage(new
InMemoryWindowedStorage<TweetStats>());
    windowTweetStats.setWindowStateStorage(new
      InMemoryWindowedStorage<WindowState>());
    windowTweetStats.setWindowOption(new
      WindowOption.SlidingTimeWindows(Duration.standardMinutes(1),
      Duration.standardSeconds(30)));
    windowTweetStats.setTriggerOption(TriggerOption.AtWatermark()
        .withEarlyFiringsAtEvery(Duration.standardSeconds(2))
        .accumulatingFiredPanes());
```

We are using in-memory heap storage for the window state since, in this case, it is minimal; there are only three non-keyed counts. Of course, the application could theoretically still run out of memory due to the absence of watermarks that discard the window state and it is something that needs to be considered in a real use case scenario: The watermark aspect is important for a real use case, as it is the only way for the window operator to output final results and purge state that otherwise can grow without limit.

The accumulation defines how incoming tuples are aggregated and how aggregates are merged. In this case, the accumulation is custom, it takes Twitter Status as input and uses the TweetStats class for accumulation and result:

```
public class TweetStatsAccumulation implements Accumulation<Status,
TweetStats,
  TweetStats>
 {
   @Override
   public TweetStats defaultAccumulatedValue()
   {
     return new TweetStats();
   }

   @Override
   public TweetStats accumulate(TweetStats accumulatedValue, Status input)
   {
     accumulatedValue.total++;
     if (input.getHashtagEntities().length > 0) {
```

```
      accumulatedValue.withHashtag++;
    }
    if (input.getURLEntities().length > 0) {
      accumulatedValue.withURL++;
    }
    return accumulatedValue;
  }

  @Override
  public TweetStats merge(TweetStats accumulatedValue1, TweetStats
    accumulatedValue2)
  {
    accumulatedValue1.total += accumulatedValue2.total;
    accumulatedValue1.withHashtag += accumulatedValue2.withHashtag;
    accumulatedValue1.withURL += accumulatedValue2.withURL;
    return accumulatedValue1;
  }

  @Override
  public TweetStats getOutput(TweetStats accumulatedValue)
  {
    return accumulatedValue;
  }

  @Override
  public TweetStats getRetraction(TweetStats value)
  {
    throw new UnsupportedOperationException();
  }
}
```

There is no need for any state handling code since that is taken care of by the window operator itself. The window operator emits `WindowedTuple<TweetStats>` objects. Although `TweetStats` already has a timestamp field, we cannot populate the field in our accumulation code because we don't have access to the window (see `getOutput(...)`). We do this in a downstream map transform that will also produce a single element list required by the snapshot operator:

```
FunctionOperator.MapFunctionOperator<WindowedTuple<TweetStats>,
List<Object>>
      toTweetStatsList =
          new FunctionOperator.MapFunctionOperator<>(
              new Function.MapFunction<WindowedTuple<TweetStats>,
List<Object>>()
                {
                  @Override
                  public List<Object> f(WindowedTuple<TweetStats> input)
```

```
                    {
                        input.getValue().timestamp = input.getTimestamp();
                        return
    Collections.<Object>singletonList(input.getValue());
                    }
                }
            );
```

Different from the top hashtags path, the snapshot server is an extension of `AppDataSnapshotServerPOJO` because the inputs are `TweetStats` objects. It also implements additional logic to not just serve the latest received (single element) list, but a configurable number of most recent data points (based on the timestamps), suitable for time series output.

This is done by merging previous output with new tuples to retain the most recent data points. This is necessary, since there can be multiple open windows that can trigger updates due to tweets that arrive out of order with respect to their creation time. It therefore cannot be assumed that every data point received by the snapshot server has a timestamp equal or more recent than existing state. The following is a snippet of the output:

```
{
    "id": "tweetStats",
    "type": "dataResult",
    "data": [
      {
        "withHashtag": "162",
        "total": "812",
        "withURL": "289",
        "timestamp": "1495601970000"
      },
      {
        "withHashtag": "342",
        "total": "1973",
        "withURL": "679",
        "timestamp": "1495602000000"
      },
      {
        "withHashtag": "391",
        "total": "2325",
        "withURL": "781",
        "timestamp": "1495602030000"
      },
      ...
    }
}
```

Compared to top hashtags the format is different (contains timestamp) but delivery via WebSocket output operator to the Pub/Sub server for visualization remains the same.

Running the application

This section assumes that you have already set up the development environment as explained in the Chapter 2, *Getting Started with Application Development*. All components of the Twitter example can run on the host OS. There is no need for a Hadoop cluster, although it would also be possible to run the Apex application in the Docker container. We will instead run it as a JUnit test, as it is easier to modify and experiment with.

1. Check out the code using the following command:

```
git clone https://github.com/tweise/apex-samples.git
```

2. Then, import the Twitter project into your IDE and run JUnit test:

```
TwitterStatsAppTest.testApplication
```

Alternatively, you can run it from the command line:

```
cd twitter; mvn test -Dtest=TwitterStatsAppTest
```

By default the test runs the application with a file source of sample tweets (instead of connecting to the Twitter API) and writes results to the console (instead of WebSocket).

1. To configure the application for live input and visualization of results, start by copying the template file:

```
cp ./twitterDemoProperties_template.xml ./twitterDemoProperties.xml
```

2. Then, modify ./twitterDemoProperties.xml with the editor of your choice.

Configuring Twitter API access

Before enabling the Twitter API connector, you need to obtain tokens for authentication. See the following:

- https://dev.twitter.com/oauth
- https://dev.twitter.com/oauth/overview
- https://dev.twitter.com/oauth/overview/application-owner-access-tokens

You need a Twitter API account and OAuth access tokens. Go to `https://apps.twitter.com/` to create an application in your Twitter account and obtain the access tokens:

- Consumer Key
- Consumer Secret
- Access Token
- Access Token Secret

Update the corresponding properties in `./twitterDemoProperties.xml`:

```
<property>
    <name>apex.operator.twitterSampleInput.prop.consumerKey</name>
    <value>...</value>
</property>
<property>
    <name>apex.operator.twitterSampleInput.prop.consumerSecret</name>
    <value>...</value>
</property>
<property>
    <name>apex.operator.twitterSampleInput.prop.accessToken</name>
    <value>...</value>
</property>
<property>
    <name>apex.operator.twitterSampleInput.prop.accessTokenSecret</name>
    <value>...</value>
</property>
<property>
    <name>twitterDemo.isTwitterSampleInput</name>
    <value>true</value>
</property>
```

Enabling WebSocket output

By default, results will be output to the console and this is good to test the application in isolation. Once that's done and we know that tweets are consumed and processed, our goal will be to visualize the results with a frontend. To do that, we enable output to WebSocket instead of console.

```
<property>
    <name>twitterDemo.isWebsocketOutput</name>
    <value>true</value>
</property>
```

The Pub/Sub server

Once the WebSocket output is enabled and the application is running, you will see connect exceptions trying to reach the Pub/Sub server (`java.net.ConnectException: Connection refused: localhost/127.0.0.1:8890`). To launch the server, open a new terminal window and run the following commands to fetch the source code and run the server:

```
git clone https://github.com/atrato/pubsub-server.git
cd pubsub-server
mvn compile exec:java
```

The console will show in the first log lines the listening address of the server:

```
[INFO] --- exec-maven-plugin:1.5.0:java (default-cli) @ atrato-pubsub-
server ---
 2017-06-16 14:18:29,408 [io.atrato.pubsubserver.PubsubServer.main()] INFO
util.log initialized - Logging initialized @4190ms
 2017-06-16 14:18:29,487 [io.atrato.pubsubserver.PubsubServer.main()] INFO
server.Server doStart - jetty-9.1.6.v20160112
 2017-06-16 14:18:30,055 [io.atrato.pubsubserver.PubsubServer.main()] INFO
handler.ContextHandler doStart - Started
o.e.j.s.ServletContextHandler@3f681a5a{/,null,AVAILABLE}
 2017-06-16 14:18:30,072 [io.atrato.pubsubserver.PubsubServer.main()] INFO
server.ServerConnector doStart - Started
ServerConnector@4ef01f3c{HTTP/1.1}{0.0.0.0:8890}
 2017-06-16 14:18:30,073 [io.atrato.pubsubserver.PubsubServer.main()] INFO
server.Server doStart - Started @4857ms
```

No further log will be output until a subscriber connects via HTTP to consume data from a topic. To test the subscriber side outside of Grafana, use the `curl` utility:

```
curl http://localhost:8890/ws/v1/pubsub/topics/twitter.topHashtags
curl http://localhost:8890/ws/v1/pubsub/topics/twitter.tweetStats
```

Another way to simulate the Pub/Sub client to inspect the topic data is the *Simple Websocket Client browser extension* (`https://chrome.google.com/webstore/detail/simple-websocket-client/pfdhoblngboilpfeibdedpjgfnlcodoo?hl=en`). The steps to connect and send or receive messages are in `README.md` in the project directory.

Here is an example that shows the continuous updates from the `topHashtags` topic (matching the query name in `TopNSnapshotServer.java`):

The client sends the `subscribe` message and subsequently receives periodic updates until the connection is closed.

Following the instructions, it would also be possible to test the Pub/Sub server without an Apex application, by sending test data to the topic and collecting it either vial WebSocket or HTTP.

At this point, we have validated that the application runs and publishes data as expected and that we are able to consume the data under the expected topic names. Let's look at visualization with Grafana.

Grafana visualization

Grafana is an open source metric visualization suite that can be used to build dashboards from various widgets and data sources. Grafana is traditionally used for visualizing time series data for infrastructure and application monitoring, but it is generic and can be used with pretty much any data source that produces time series and tabular data. Thanks to its monitoring orientation Grafana is suitable for low-latency visualization of frequently changing data. We will use this capability to display the top hashtags and counts, and have them updated as changes occur in the application (with perhaps one to two seconds of end-to-end latency).

In order to use Grafana, we need to tap into the data that is available from the Pub/Sub server. The Pub/Sub server has an HTTP interface, but the data format of the queryable state protocol of the Apex application needs to be adapted to what Grafana requires.

There are two options to accomplish this:

- Implementing a new datasource that can be added to the Grafana installation
- Using an existing datasource
  (http://docs.grafana.org/datasources/overview/)

It would be possible, for example, to write the result data into one of the supported backends instead of using WebSocket output. For a real application, if one of these systems were part of the infrastructure (and Apex has a matching connector), that may be a good option.

In this case, we will use Grafana's Simple JSON Datasource
(https://github.com/grafana/simple-json-datasource) and implement the adapter that pulls the data from the Pub/Sub server.

We will install Grafana, then add the JSON datasource to it, and finally setup the adapter for the JSON datasource to talk to the Pub/Sub server:

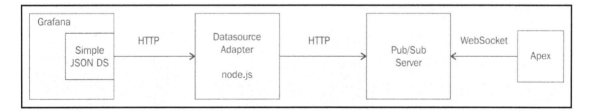

Installing Grafana

First, let's install Grafana. There are various ways to install Grafana and they may differ between operating systems. Please refer to Grafana documentation for details (http://docs.grafana.org/). The following instructions are for macOS and use Homebrew:

```
brew install
brew install grafana
```

This will install Grafana at /usr/local/share/grafana. At the time of writing, the Grafana version is 4.1.1.

Installing Grafana Simple JSON Datasource

To install Grafana Simple JSON Datasource follow these steps:

1. First, clone or download the Simple JSON Datasource repo into a directory of your choice:

```
$ git clone https://github.com/grafana/simple-json-datasource
```

2. Next, copy the Simple JSON Datasource plugin's /dist directory into the Grafana plugins datasource directory:

```
$ cp -r simple-json-datasource/dist \
/usr/local/share/grafana/public/app/plugins/datasource
```

3. Now, rename the copied /dist folder to grafana-simple-json-datasource so that it matches the id attribute in the Simple JSON Datasource's plugin.json file:

```
$ cd /usr/local/share/grafana/public/app/plugins/datasource
$ mv dist grafana-simple-json-datasource
```

4. We are now ready to launch Grafana and read from a JSON datasource:

```
$ brew services start grafana
```

5. Open Grafana in your browser at the following address: http://localhost:3000.

6. Log in to Grafana with the default username (admin) and password (admin).

There is still one piece missing which is needed to fetch data from the Pub/Sub server, and that's the HTTP endpoint that will provide the expected data format to the JSON datasource. It would be possible to modify the Pub/Sub server to do just that, but instead we keep the Grafana specifics in a separate service.

The Grafana Pub/Sub adapter server

Get the source code:

```
git clone https://github.com/atrato/apex-grafana-datasource-server.git
```

This component is very simple, it only implements the /search and /query endpoints to convert the JSON responses from the Pub/Sub server into the format expected by Grafana. If you are interested, have a look at the single source file (https://github.com/atrato/apex-grafana-datasource-server/blob/master/index.js) that contains this logic.

Build and start the Apex Grafana Datasource server.

```
$ cd apex-grafana-datasource-server
$ npm install
$ node index.js
```

The server should now be running at http://localhost:3333 to connect Grafana with Apex. We are now ready to create the dashboard to visualize the data.

Setting up the dashboard

To set up the dashboard, follow the steps:

1. Navigate to the **Data Sources** page from the home screen or the left navigation and select **Add data source**.
2. Select SimpleJson as type and give it a name that will later be the reference when creating the dashboard.
3. Set the **Url** to http://localhost:3333 and **Access** to direct.

4. Click on **Add** to save the new data source and you should see the **Success** message as shown in the screen below:

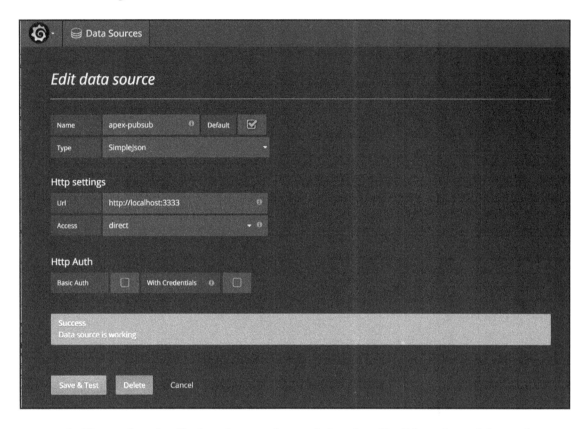

4. Next, select the Grafana logo at the top-left, select **Dashboards** and then select + **New**.
5. A selection of widget appears; select **Graph**.
6. Click on the **Panel Title** and then **edit**.

At this point, make sure that the Apex application is running as otherwise we cannot see the available metrics.

1. Under the **Metrics** tab, select `twitter.tweetStats` — it will provide data suitable for the graph panel:

2. Then on the top of the page, click on **Refresh every 5s** and a settings panel will appear that allows you to set the time range and refresh interval:

3. Select **Last 5 minutes** for the time range and a small refresh interval to allow for the visualization to update frequently.

The smallest setting available by default is five seconds. You can click on the wheel and then **Time Picker** to create a smaller **1s** refresh interval that is suitable for the frequency at which updates are provided by the Apex application.

After these settings are applied you should see the graph populated with data points with the two rightmost data points updating every second as per the `tweetStats` operator windows settings discussed earlier (1 minute window with 30 second sliding interval):

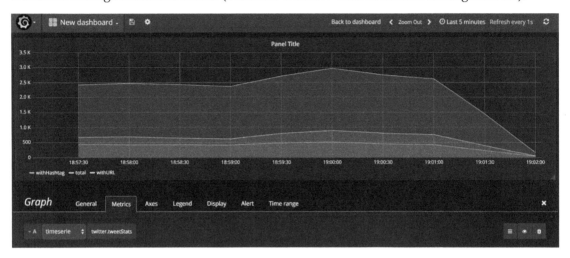

Similarly, you can visualize the top hashtags: instead of **Graph**, select **Table** and the `twitter.topHashtag` as the metric.

Summary

The project that we developed in this chapter is an example for streaming analytics. The incoming tweet stream is processed to compute aggregates which are visualized in real time with a Grafana dashboard. It shows how continuously generated data (in this case, tweets) can be analyzed and used to generate immediate insights. We have seen how existing building blocks from the Apex library (connectors, windowing) are used to accelerate application development and how integration with other infrastructure for data visualization can be accomplished.

The pipeline pattern is broadly applicable. Similar to the introductory ad-tech use case, it can be applied to other domains with data streams such as mobile, sensor, or financial transaction data. Instead of simple functionality (top words and counters), real-world applications may perform sentiment analysis, fraud detection, device health monitoring, and other complex processing.

The next chapter will go into more depth with windowing and event-time processing using taxi ride data from files as data source.

7
Example Project – Real-Time Ride Service Data Processing

In this chapter, we will discuss an example that demonstrates how Apache Apex can be used for processing real-time ride service data. We don't have live access to such data; however, a historical Yellow Cab trip data is freely available on the website of the New York City government, which we will use in this example to simulate real-time ride service data processing.

We will use some important concepts in stream processing and Apache Apex in this example, including event-time windowing, out-of-order processing, and streaming windows. In this chapter we'll cover following topics:

- The goal
- Datasource
- The pipeline
- Simulation of real-time feed using historical data
- Running the application

The goal

The goal of this example is to process the historical New York City Yellow Cab trip data and simulate it as a real-time feed. Each entry of the source data contains the pickup time, pickup latitude-longitude coordinate, passenger count, trip distance, drop-off time, drop-off latitude-longitude coordinate, total fare amount, and many other fields.

We want to implement a simple pipeline that processes this data, and advises a taxi driver looking for passengers (the user of this application), to drive toward a direction, while maximizing the chance of passenger pickup and the fare they will get, based on the data in real time.

Datasource

The historical Yellow Cab trip data can be downloaded from `http://www.nyc.gov/html/tlc/html/about/trip_record_data.shtml`. The data is present as CSV files with the following fields:

- VendorID
- Pickup Date Time
- Dropoff Date Time
- Passenger Count
- Trip Distance
- Pickup Longitude
- Pickup Latitude
- Rate Code ID
- Store and Forward flag
- Dropoff Longitude
- Dropoff Latitude
- Payment Type
- Fare Amount
- Extra Fee
- MTA Tax
- Improvement Surcharge
- Tip Amount
- Tolls Amount
- Total Payment

For the purpose of this example and to keep it simple, we are only looking at the **Pickup Date Time**, **Pickup Longitude**, **Pickup Latitude**, and **Total Payment**.

Also, the trip data file is not sorted, and you may see lines that can be up to 30 days ahead of the next entry.

You can find the code for this example by going to the `examples/nyctaxi` directory under the `apex-malhar` GitHub repository, at the following link: `https://github.com/apache/apex-malhar/tree/master/examples/nyctaxi`.

The pipeline

The application pipeline consists of six operators as shown in the following diagram:

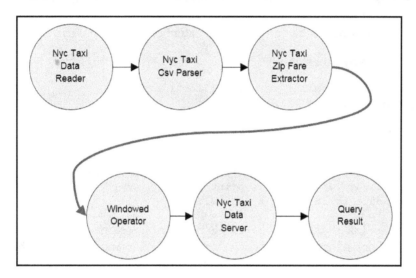

The first operator, `NycTaxiDataReader`, reads from the source file(s). The second operator, `NycTaxiCsvParser`, reads the raw lines from `NycTaxiDataReader`, parses the data, and passes it to the third operator, `NycTaxiZipFareExtractor`.

The `NycTaxiZipFareExtractor` operator extracts the zip code from the lat-lon information in the data and prepares the output for `WindowedOperator` to consume. It also produces watermarks for `WindowedOperator`. `NycTaxiDataServer` takes the output from `WindowedOperator` and serves the data by WebSocket by passing the data to `QueryResult`. `QueryResult` is `PubSubWebSocketOutputOperator`, which delivers results via WebSocket.

Simulation of a real-time feed using historical data

Before you run this example, download some Yellow Cab trip data CSV files from the aforementioned website at `nyc.gov`. At the time of writing, this example is compatible with the data format used in the CSV files between 2015-01 and 2016-06. Let's say you have chosen2016-01 and saved the data as `yellow_tripdata_2016-01.csv`.

We want to simulate a real-time feed. However, because the trip data source is wildly unordered, we want to sort the data with some random deviation. A real-time feed usually contains some out-of-order data, but not to the extent of the original trip data files.

So, let's sort the data by timestamp:

```
bash> sort -t, -k2 yellow_tripdata_2016-01.csv >
yellow_tripdata_sorted_2016-01.csv
```

Next, add some random deviation to the sorted data:

```
bash> cat yellow_tripdata_sorted_2016-01.csv | perl -e '@lines = (); while
(<>) { if (@lines && rand(10) < 1) { print shift @lines;  } if (rand(20) <
1) { push @lines, $_; } else { print $_; } }' >
yellow_tripdata_sorted_random_2016-01.csv
```

This bash command, with the help of a simple perl script, assigns each entry with a 5% chance of delay. For each subsequent entry, there is a 10% chance the one of the delayed entries will appear, in effect introducing an out-of-order sequence of the entries while keeping the entries mostly sorted.

Then, create an HDFS directory and copy the CSV file there:

```
bash> hdfs dfs -mkdir nyctaxidata
bash> hdfs dfs -copyFromLocal yellow_tripdata_sorted_random_2016-01.csv
nyctaxidata/
```

The `NycTaxiDataReader` operator reads in the CSV files in the specified HDFS directory and emits the CSV line by line. Each output tuple represents one line in the CSV file. The operator is a subclass of `LineByLineInputOperator` provided by the Apex Malhar library, which just scans the specified directory and outputs the files in the directory, line by line.

We could theoratically read the data live from the website, but in practice it is generally not a good idea to hit a website with freely available data programmatically because doing so could result in having your IP banned from the website.

In order to simulate a real-time feed, we cannot read the CSV lines and pump those lines to downstream as fast as possible, which LineByLineInputOperator does. The data rate should approximately follow the real-world arrival rate, which can be simulated with streaming windows. In Chapter 1, *Introduction to Apex*, section, *Windowing and time*, we described the streaming windows as a wall-clock heartbeat. The streaming window is the processing time quantum of WindowedOperator, which we introduced in Chapter 3, *The Apex Library*. Also, because the lowest time unit in the trip data is 1 second, let's assume that each streaming window represents 1 second of wall-clock time, and in Application.java, we set the streaming window size to be 1 second:

```
dag.setAttribute(DAG.STREAMING_WINDOW_SIZE_MILLIS, 1000);
```

In this example, within a streaming window, we stop emitting lines from the CSV file if the time unit changes until the next streaming window.

In order to achieve this behavior, we create a class called NycTaxiDataReader, which extends LineByLineFileInputOperator to override the readEntity method so that it will suspend emitting the lines if we see a timestamp that is different from the previous line in the feed. Note, in the code, the manipulation of the suspendEmit Boolean member variable, and the emitBatchSize member set to be Integer.MAX_VALUE:

```java
public class NycTaxiDataReader extends LineByLineFileInputOperator
{
  private String currentTimestamp;
  private transient boolean suspendEmit = false;

  public NycTaxiDataReader()
  {
    // Whether or not to advance the window does not depend on the
    // size. It solely depends on the timestamp of the data. See below
    // for "suspendEmit".
    emitBatchSize = Integer.MAX_VALUE;
  }

  @Override
  protected boolean suspendEmit()
  {
    return suspendEmit;
  }
```

```
@Override
protected String readEntity() throws IOException
{
  String line = super.readEntity();
  String[] fields = line.split(",");
  if (fields.length > 1) {
    String timestamp = fields[1];
    if (currentTimestamp == null) {
      currentTimestamp = timestamp;
    } else if (timestamp != currentTimestamp) {
      // suspends the emit of data in the current streaming window
      // when timestamp is different from the current timestamp.
      suspendEmit = true;
      currentTimestamp = timestamp;
    }
  }
  return line;
}

@Override
public void beginWindow(long windowId)
{
  super.beginWindow(windowId);
  suspendEmit = false;
}
}
```

Also note that in the case of NYC taxi trip data, the fare is not known until the trip has concluded. However, for ride-sharing services, such as Uber and Lyft, the fare is usually known at the pickup time. We are assuming that this is the case when simulating our real-time feed.

Parsing the data

NycTaxiCsvParser takes in the data from NycTaxiDataReader. It simply splits each line by a comma and outputs Map<String, String> containing individual fields. This is the definition of the input port of the NycTaxiCsvParser operator:

```
public final transient DefaultInputPort<String> input = new
DefaultInputPort<String>()
{
 @Override
 public void process(String tuple)
 {
   String[] values = tuple.split(",");
```

```
      Map<String, String> outputTuple = new HashMap<>();
      if (values.length > 18 && StringUtils.isNumeric(values[0])) {
        outputTuple.put("pickup_time", values[1]);
        outputTuple.put("pickup_lon", values[5]);
        outputTuple.put("pickup_lat", values[6]);
        outputTuple.put("total_fare", values[18]);
        output.emit(outputTuple);
      }
    }
  };
```

As mentioned previously, we are only interested in the pickup time (Key `pickup time`), pickup lat-lon coordinate (Keys `pickup lon` and `pickup lat`), and total payment (Key `total fare`), so we are only emitting those fields in the operator.

Looking up of the zip code and preparing for the windowing operation

The `NycTaxiZipFareExtractor` operator is the operator that is immediate downstream of the `NycTaxiCsvParser` explained above. It looks at the pickup latitude-longitude coordinate, looks up the zip code given the latitude-longitude coordinate, and prepares a `TimestampedTuple` for the `KeyedWindowedOperatorImpl` operator downstream. The output tuple is of the `TimestampedTuple<KeyValPair<String, Double>>` type, with the key being the zip code, and the value being the total payment amount.

Here's the definition of the input port of the `NycTaxiZipFareExtractor` operator:

```
public final transient DefaultInputPort<Map<String, String>> input = new
DefaultInputPort<Map<String, String>>()
{
 @Override
 public void process(Map<String, String> tuple)
 {
   try {
     String zip =
       NycLocationUtils.getZip(Double.valueOf(tuple.get("pickup_lat")),
       Double.valueOf(tuple.get("pickup_lon")));
     Date date = dateFormat.parse(tuple.get("pickup_time"));
     long timestamp = date.getTime();
     double fare = Double.valueOf(tuple.get("total_fare"));
     output.emit(new Tuple.TimestampedTuple<>(timestamp, new
KeyValPair<>(zip,
       fare)));
```

```
      if (timestamp > currentTimestamp) {
        currentTimestamp = timestamp;
        watermarkOutput.emit(new Watermark(timestamp - 60 * 1000));
      }
    } catch (ParseException ex) {
      LOG.warn("Ignoring tuple with bad timestamp {}",
  tuple.get("pickup_time"));
    }
  }
};
```

Since we are only talking about dozens of zip codes in New York City, we just store the geographical information of all NYC zip code in memory. Again, for simplicity sake, for each data point, we assign the zip code by looking for the shortest distance to the centroids of all zip codes by brute force. This is done in the `NycLocationUtils` class.

 Note that if we need to deal with much more geographical data than this, we'll need to do this differently.

As one might notice in the code, `NycTaxiZipFareExtractor` also produces watermarks for the downstream `KeyedWindowedOperatorImpl` operator to consume. These watermarks, along with the output data of this operator, allow us to do event-time windowing on the data, which we will discuss in the next section.

Windowed operator configuration

Because we are developing an application for a taxi driver looking for passengers, we are only interested in the last few minutes of data, to have a good advice for the driver where to look. We are accumulating the data in 5-minute sliding windows that slide by 1 minute so that we always use the data from the past 5 minutes for our service. In `Application.java`:

```
KeyedWindowedOperatorImpl<String, Double, MutableDouble, Double>
windowedOperator
  = new KeyedWindowedOperatorImpl<>();
// 5-minute windows slide by 1 minute
windowedOperator.setWindowOption(new
WindowOption.TimeWindows(Duration.standardMinutes(5)).slideBy(Duration
  .standardMinutes(1)));
// Because we only care about the last 5 minutes, lateness horizon
// is set to 4 minutes since the watermark is set to one minute before
// the latest timestamp.
windowedOperator.setAllowedLateness(Duration.standardMinutes(4));
```

We are now setting the accumulation to be a `SumDouble`, which sums the total payment of each tuple, keyed by the zip code:

```
windowedOperator.setAccumulation(new SumDouble());
```

We then set the operator to trigger at watermark. This means that a tuple is fired downstream with the data for windows that completely lie beyond the watermark timestamp.

A watermark is an indicator to the pipeline downstream that all tuples with an earlier timestamp are late:

```
windowedOperator.setTriggerOption(TriggerOption.AtWatermark());
```

Also, since we only care about the data from the past 5 minutes, and the slide-by duration is 1 minute, we want the trigger to be fired if a sliding window has totally gotten out of the latest timestamp. Therefore, we have the upstream `NycTaxiZipFareExtractor` operator generate a watermark, which has a timestamp of the incoming data timestamp, 1 minute lesser. Along with allowed lateness being 4 minutes, the information of all windows that are more than 5 minutes before the incoming data tuple is discarded.

Also, since we have introduced some random delay for some events in the data, data that is more than 5 minutes late will be discarded entirely.

Note that we are also using the checkpointed in-memory implementation for both the window state storage and the data storage for the window operator. In a real-world application, when we are dealing with much more data, we will need the storage to be spillable to disk. In the Apex Malhar library, there is an option to use the spillable implementation of windowed storage (refer to `Chapter 3`, *The Apex Library*):

```
windowedOperator.setDataStorage(new InMemoryWindowedKeyedStorage<String,
    MutableDouble>());
windowedOperator.setWindowStateStorage(new InMemoryWindowedStorage
    <WindowState>());
```

Serving the data with WebSocket

We have just finished the aggregation of real-time ride data, and now we have the dollar amount for each zip code with sliding data in real time. We have to make use of this data in real time as well. Let's do that!

`NycTaxiDataServer` is an operator that listens to the triggers from the aforementioned `WindowedOperator`. It also listens for incoming query messages via WebSocket, processes the queries according to the real-time state, and sends back the results, again via WebSocket.

In order to do that, `NycTaxiDataServer` extends from the `AbstractAppDataServer` class, which provides the embedded query listening capability. This allows an input operator to be embedded in the operator so that message from the input operator can be sent immediately to the operator. If the input operator is part of the pipeline, the messages from the input operator could be delayed due to lag of the rest of the pipeline.

Note that the triggers from the upstream `WindowedOperator` are sent with the zip code, and the total payment of the window as individual `KeyValPair` tuples. We have to collect all these tuples and insert them to a map:

```
private transient Map<String, Double> currentData = new HashMap<>();
...
public final transient
DefaultInputPort<Tuple.WindowedTuple<KeyValPair<String, Double>>> input =
new DefaultInputPort<Tuple.WindowedTuple<KeyValPair<String, Double>>>()
{
  @Override
  public void process(Tuple.WindowedTuple<KeyValPair<String, Double>>
tuple)
  {
    if (!currentWindowHasData) {
      currentData = new HashMap<>();
      currentWindowHasData = true;
    }
    KeyValPair<String, Double> tupleValue = tuple.getValue();
    currentData.put(tupleValue.getKey(), tupleValue.getValue());
  }
};

@AppData.ResultPort
public final transient DefaultOutputPort<String> queryResult = new
DefaultOutputPort<>();

private Map<String, Double> servingData = new HashMap<>();
private transient Map<String, Double> currentData = new HashMap<>();
private transient ArrayDeque<String> resultQueue = new ArrayDeque<>();
private boolean currentWindowHasData = false;

@Override
public void beginWindow(long l)
{
```

```
    super.beginWindow(l);
    currentWindowHasData = false;
}

@Override
public void endWindow()
{
    while (!resultQueue.isEmpty()) {
        String result = resultQueue.remove();
        queryResult.emit(result);
    }
    servingData = currentData;
    super.endWindow();
}
```

Since the triggers for one window are sent all at once during one streaming window, every time we receive the first tuple during a streaming window, we start a new map to record the data for this window. This is done in the process method of the input port.

At the end of each streaming window, we go through all the results in the queue and emit them one by one to the downstream QueryResult operator. resultQueue is populated by the processQuery method:

```
@Override
protected void processQuery(String queryStr)
{
 try {
    JSONObject query = new JSONObject(queryStr);
    JSONObject result = new JSONObject();
    double lat = query.getDouble("lat");
    double lon = query.getDouble("lon");
    Pair<String, String> zips = recommendZip(lat, lon);
    result.put("currentZip", zips.getLeft());
    result.put("driveToZip", zips.getRight());
    resultQueue.add(result.toString());
 } catch (JSONException e) {
    // query does not contain lat and lon.
    LOG.error("Unrecognized query: {}", queryStr);
 }
}
```

The processQuery method is invoked when there is a query coming in from the embedded input operator. In this example, the query string is a JSON object that has the latitude (lat) and the longitude (lon). Then it looks up the zip code of the given coordinate with its neighboring zip codes, and finds out the maximum total payment amount. The zip code that corresponds to the maximum total payment amount is the result, and it will be added to the queue, which, in turn will be emitted in the endWindow() method.

Note that because the input operator that provides the query is embedded, the callback processQuery() is run by the main thread of the input operator, not the main thread of the NycTaxiDataServer operator. In Apex, only the main thread of the operator is allowed to emit to its output ports. This is the reason why we need the result queue and have the endWindow() method emit to the output port of NycTaxiDataServer.

In the populateDag method of the Application class, we hook up a PubSubWebSocketAppDataQuery operator as the embedded query info provider and set the listening topic and the broker URL:

```
PubSubWebSocketAppDataQuery wsQuery = new PubSubWebSocketAppDataQuery();
wsQuery.enableEmbeddedMode();
wsQuery.setTopic("nyctaxi.query");
  try {
    wsQuery.setUri(new URI("ws://localhost:8890/pubsub"));
  } catch (URISyntaxException ex) {
    throw Throwables.propagate(ex);
  }
dataServer.setEmbeddableQueryInfoProvider(wsQuery);
```

The query topic here is nyctaxi.query, and the broker URL is ws://localhost:8890/pubsub. In order to issue a query, the message has to be sent to the "nyctaxi.query" topic. As mentioned in Chapter 6, *Example Project - Real-Time Aggregation and Visualization* the WebSocket communication requires a broker to deliver the messages to the subscribers. We will talk about how to run the message broker in the next section.

The results of queries are delivered to the downstream `PubSubWebSocketAppDataResult` operator named `QueryResult`, which sends the results to WebSocket with the specified topic:

```
PubSubWebSocketAppDataResult wsResult = dag.addOperator("QueryResult", new
PubSubWebSocketAppDataResult());
  wsResult.setTopic("nyctaxi.result");
  try {
    wsResult.setUri(new URI("ws://localhost:8890/pubsub"));
  } catch (URISyntaxException ex) {
    throw Throwables.propagate(ex);
  }
dag.addStream("server_to_query_output", dataServer.queryResult,
wsResult.input);
```

The result topic is `nyctaxi.result`. The broker URL is the same as before. The entity that issues the query needs to subscribe to this topic before it can receive any results.

Running the application

As mentioned in the previous section, we need to run the Pub/Sub server for the WebSocket communication to happen. Let's do that:

```
bash> git clone https://github.com/atrato/pubsub-server
```

Then build and run the pub/sub server (the message broker):

```
bash> cd pubsub-server; mvn compile exec:java
```

The pub/sub server is now running, listening to the default port 8890 on localhost.

Now that the server is all set up, let's open the Apex CLI command prompt (refer back to `Chapter 2`, *Getting Started with Application Development*, for instructions on setting up Apache Apex, if necessary) and actually run the application:

```
bash> apex
apex> launch target/malhar-examples-nyc-taxi-3.8.0-SNAPSHOT.apa
```

After the application runs for one minute, we can start querying the data. The reason why we need to wait for one minute is that we need to wait for the first window to pass the watermark for the triggers to be fired by `WindowedOperator`.

Note that since we are using sliding windows, the first window is the 5 minute window with the last minute containing the first event not discarded as a result of lateness horizon (Refer to `Chapter 3`, *The Apex Library* on how sliding windows work).

Subsequent triggers will also be fired every 1 minute, since the `slideBy` is 1 minute. If you're not yet familiar with the pub-sub format, now is the time to go back to `Chapter 6`, *Example Project - Real-Time Aggregation and Visualization* to review the WebSocket pub/sub format.

In order to query the data, we need a websocket client. As mentioned in `Chapter 6`, *Example Project - Real-Time Aggregation and Visualization* we can use the Simple WebSocket Client Chrome extension. Open the extension and connect to `ws://localhost:8890/pubsub`. Let's subscribe to the query result topic first because results to any query will be delivered to this topic by sending this to the WebSocket connection:

```
{"type":"subscribe","topic":"nyctaxi.result"}
```

Now, let's issue a query with the `40.731829` latitude and `-73.989181` longitude. This is somewhere in the East Village neighborhood in Manhattan:

```
{"type":"publish","topic":"nyctaxi.query","data":{"lat":40.731829,
    "lon":-73.989181}}
```

You should get back something like the following:

```
{"type":"data","topic":"nyctaxi.result","data":{"currentZip":"10003","drive
ToZip":"10011"},"timestamp":1500769034523}
```

This result tells the driver to drive toward the zip code `10011`, the Chelsea neighborhood, in order to maximize the amount of dollars the driver will get.

The result to the same query changes as time goes by since we have real-time ride data coming in:

```
{"type":"publish","topic":"nyctaxi.query","data":{"lat":40.731829,
  "lon":-73.989181}}
{"type":"data","topic":"nyctaxi.result","data":
{"currentZip":"10003","driveToZip":"10003"},"timestamp":1500769158530}
{"type":"publish","topic":"nyctaxi.query","data":{"lat":40.731829,
  "lon":-73.989181}}
{"type":"data","topic":"nyctaxi.result","data":{"currentZip":"10003","drive
ToZip":"10011"},"timestamp":1500769827538}
{"type":"publish","topic":"nyctaxi.query","data":{"lat":40.731829,
  "lon":-73.989181}}
{"type":"data","topic":"nyctaxi.result","data":{"currentZip":"10003","drive
ToZip":"10012"},"timestamp":1500770540527}
```

One can build on top of this kind of data exchange and write a mobile app for drivers of a ride-sharing service.

Running the application on GCP Dataproc

This section will provide a tutorial on how to run the Apex application on a real Hadoop cluster in the cloud. Dataproc (`https://cloud.google.com/dataproc/`) is one of several options that exist (Amazon EMR is another one, and the instructions here can be easily adapted to EMR as well).

The general instructions on how to work on a cluster were already covered in `Chapter 2`, *Getting Started with Application Development*, where a Docker container was used. This section will focus on the differences of adding Apex to an existing multi-node cluster.

To start with, we are heading over to the GCP console (`https://console.cloud.google.com/dataproc/clusters`) to create a new cluster.

For better illustration we will use the UI, but these steps can be fully automated using the REST API or command line as well:

1. The first step is to decide what size of cluster and what type of machines we want. For this example, 3 worker nodes of a small machine type will suffice (for larger applications, the input for this would come from benchmarking with production workload).
2. After clicking on the **Create** button, the cluster will be created. This can take several minutes during which an **in progress** message is shown, and once the cluster is ready, we see this:

On the details page, we can see the individual cluster nodes, along with the instructions on how to use SSH to login to the master. The master node is **apex-cluster-m**. We will refer to this name in subsequent commands to connect to it:

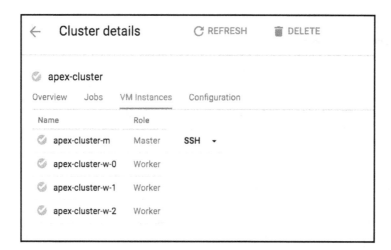

We will later also cover how to access the Hadoop UI (which requires extra configuration for the browser, since it is internal to the cluster nodes in the cloud). Here is the cluster overview page from the YARN resource manager:

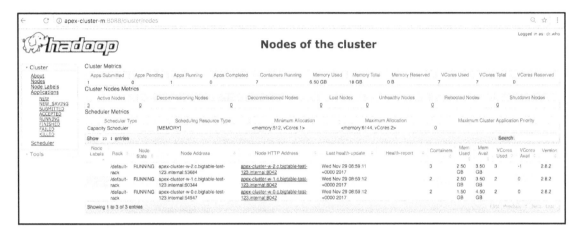

3. Next, login to the master node to set up Apex (we need to add the Apex CLI):

```
gcloud compute ssh --zone "us-west1-a" "apex-cluster-m"
```

4. On being prompted, download, extract and run (just for testing) the Apex CLI:

```
thomas@apex-cluster-m:~$ curl -LSO
https://github.com/atrato/apex-cli-
    package/releases/download/v3.6.0/apex-cli-package-3.6.0-bin.zip
thomas@apex-cluster-m:~$ unzip apex-cli-package-3.6.0-bin.zip
thomas@apex-cluster-m:~$ ./apex-cli-package-3.6.0/bin/apex
Apex CLI 3.6.0 01.05.2017 @ 13:40:03 IST rev: 5a51734 branch:
    5a517348ae497c06150f32ce39b6915588e92510
apex> exit
```

That's everything we need to start Apex pipelines that are packaged as .apa files. Now, a few more things need to be set up that are specific to the nyctaxi example.

The Pub/Sub server is running on the local machine (see instructions earlier in the chapter) but the worker nodes that need to connect to it are in the cloud. We will use SSH to open a connection from the cluster back to the local machine, this technique is called reverse tunneling. It allows us to turn the local laptop into a server that can be accessed from the cluster, without opening it to the public.

We are still on the master node and need to enable remote connections (from other cluster nodes) to the reverse tunnel:

```
echo "GatewayPorts clientspecified" | sudo tee -a /etc/ssh/sshd_config
sudo /etc/init.d/ssh restart
```

Then type `exit` to get back to the local machine.

Now it is time to copy the locally built `.apa` file to the master node, we will need it to actually launch the pipeline. This is done using `scp`:

```
gcloud compute scp ~/devel/apex-malhar/examples/nyctaxi/target/malhar-
examples-nyc-taxi-3.8.0.apa apex-cluster-m:   --zone "us-west1-a"
malhar-examples-nyc-taxi-3.8.0.apa
```

Now we want to get back to the master node, using SSH, and with additional options for the reverse tunnel as well as dynamic port forwarding on port 1080 to access the web UI:

```
gcloud compute ssh --zone "us-west1-a" "apex-cluster-m" -- -R
\*:8890:localhost:8890 -D 1080
```

Verify that the Pub/Sub connection works using `curl http://apex-cluster-m:8890`.

The final preparation step before we can actually run the example is to provision the input file to the Hadoop File System. Unless you have a really fast internet connection, it is best to repeat the data preparation steps on the cluster instead of copying > 1GB of data to it:

```
curl -LSO
https://s3.amazonaws.com/nyc-tlc/trip+data/yellow_tripdata_2016-01.csv
```

1. Run sort and randomization as shown earlier:

```
hdfs dfs -mkdir -p nyctaxidata
hdfs dfs -copyFromLocal yellow_tripdata_sorted_random_2016-01.csv
nyctaxidata/
```

2. Now finally it is time to start the Apex application:

```
./apex-cli-package-3.6.0/bin/apex

launch malhar-examples-nyc-taxi-3.8.0.apa -D
apex.operator.*.attr.MEMORY_MB=256 -D
apex.stream.input_to_parser.prop.locality=CONTAINER_LOCAL
```

The -D options are passed to optimize the resource usage and serve as an example how parameters can be changed at launch without having to rebuild the package or edit a local config file. We are reducing the default memory allocation for operators and the locality of one stream to fit the application with the cluster resource constraints. (On the Apex Docker container, this would be required to work with the minimum containers size of 1024 MB for yarn.scheduler.minimum-allocation-mb.)

It would also be possible to run the application in embedded mode using launch -local, if you wanted to try it on the edge node first.

3. After the application runs, check for activity in the Pub/Sub server log. We should see the connection from the cluster in the cloud in the local Pub/Sub server console:

```
2017-11-29 00:24:31,072 [qtp1915976306-865] DEBUG
pubsubserver.PubsubBroker subscribe - Client
io.atrato.pubsubserver.PubsubSocket@22bff9d4 subscribes to topic
nyctaxi.query
```

Within the Apex CLI, there are a few commands that you can use to check the application. Here are just a few examples.

Example 1:

```
apex (application_1511939727270_0001) > list-apps
 {"apps": [{
   "startTime": "2017-11-29 08:28:44 +0000",
   "id": 1,
   "name": "NycTaxiExample",
   "state": "RUNNING",
   "trackingUrl": "http:\/\/apex-cluster-
     :8088\/proxy\/application_1511939727270_0001\/",
   "finalStatus": "UNDEFINED",
   "tags": []
}]}
```

Example 2:

```
apex (application_1511939727270_0001) > list-containers
 {"containers": [
    {
      "id": "container_1511939727270_0001_01_000001",
      "host": "apex-cluster-w-2.c.bigtable-test-123.internal:53684",
      "state": "ACTIVE",
      "jvmName": "3467@apex-cluster-w-2",
      "lastHeartbeat": "-1",
      "numOperators": "0",
      "operators": null,
      "memoryMBAllocated": "1024",
      "memoryMBFree": "182",
      "gcCollectionTime": "0",
      "gcCollectionCount": "0",
      "containerLogsUrl":
"http:\/\/apex-cluster-w-2.c.bigtable-test-
        123.internal:8042\/node\/containerlogs\
        /container_1511939727270_0001_01_000001\/thomas",
      "startedTime": "1511944131881",
      "finishedTime": "-1",
      "rawContainerLogsUrl":
"http:\/\/apex-cluster-w-2.c.bigtable-test-
        123.internal:8042\/logs\/userlogs\
/application_1511939727270_0001\/container_1511939727270_0001_01_00
0001"
    },
...
```

Example 3:

```
apex (application_1511939727270_0001) > list-operators PubSub
 {"operators": [{
    "id": "6",
    "name": "QueryResult",
    "className":
"com.datatorrent.lib.io.PubSubWebSocketAppDataResult",
    "container": "container_1511939727270_0001_01_000006",
    "host": "apex-cluster-w-0.c.bigtable-test-123.internal:54947",
    "totalTuplesProcessed": "0",
    "totalTuplesEmitted": "0",
    "tuplesProcessedPSMA": "0",
    "tuplesEmittedPSMA": "0",
    "cpuPercentageMA": "0.3127337855061908",
    "latencyMA": "10",
    "status": "ACTIVE",
    "lastHeartbeat": "1511944431099",
```

```
                  "failureCount": "0",
                  "recoveryWindowId": "6493750596024140075",
                  "currentWindowId": "6493750596024140076",
                  "ports": [{
                    "name": "input",
                    "type": "input",
                    "totalTuples": "0",
                    "tuplesPSMA": "0",
                    "bufferServerBytesPSMA": "8",
                    "queueSizeMA": "1",
                    "recordingId": null
                  }],
                  "unifierClass": null,
                  "logicalName": "QueryResult",
                  "recordingId": null,
                  "counters": null,
                  "metrics": {},
                  "checkpointStartTime": "1511944429501",
                  "checkpointTime": "64",
                  "checkpointTimeMA": "77"
              }]}
```

14. After the application has run for at least 5 minutes, we can check results with the Simple WebSocket Client (refer to earlier instructions for details):

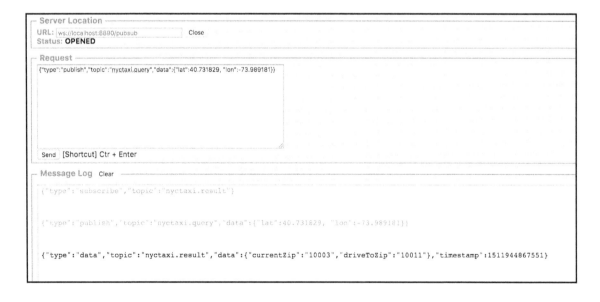

15. Finally, let's access the YARN web UI, as that will show how to use the dynamic port we had defined in the SSH command. For details, refer to `https://cloud.google.com/dataproc/docs/concepts/accessing/cluster-web-interfaces`.

16. Start the browser using the SOCKS proxy to connect to the cluster machines:

```
Google Chrome executable path \
    --proxy-server="socks5://localhost:1080" \
    --host-resolver-rules="MAP * 0.0.0.0 , EXCLUDE localhost" \
    --user-data-dir=/tmp/master-host-name
```

(On macOS the executable would be `/Applications/Google\ Chrome.app/Contents/MacOS/Google\ Chrome`).

17. Then navigate in the newly opened browser window to the master node: `http://apex-cluster-m:8088/cluster`:

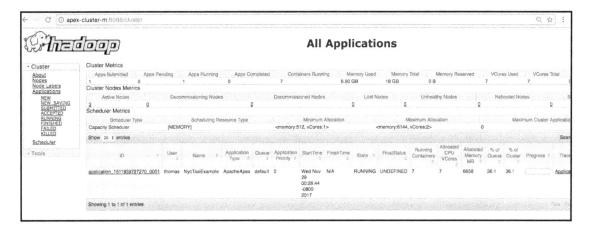

Summary

In this chapter, we have applied the concepts of event-time and out-of-order processing to analyze trip data. In only about 500 lines of Java code, we have developed an example application that processes and makes use of real-time ride service data using Apache Apex. Though this is a simplistic application, this example demonstrates how easy it is to set up a real-time ride data processing pipeline using Apache Apex.

In the next chapter, we will work through an example project for an ETL application and constructing a pipeline using SQL.

8
Example Project – ETL Using SQL

Classic ETL (short for, **Extract**, **Transform**, **Load**) applications are common in the big data world. They typically extract data from one or more external sources, such as message queues, databases, and file systems; process them to perform some common operations, such as filtering, transforming, and enriching; and finally load the results to some data sinks, such as relational databases, files, or NoSQL datastores, where analytics queries can be run against them.

In this chapter, we will examine a sample ETL application in detail and illustrate how easy it is to construct such a pipeline using Apex and its library of operators, along with the built-in support for the SQL query planning and optimizing engine, Apache Calcite. Specifically, we will cover these topics:

- The operators that constitute the application pipeline
- Building the application and running the integration test
- Configuring the application
- Testing the application
- Understanding the logs
- Classes used for integration with Calcite

The application pipeline

The application pipeline of operators and streams is illustrated by the following diagram:

Operators and streams in the application pipeline

The application reads records of phone calls, and parses, filters, and enriches them, and finally writes them out to a destination file. This application is modeled on some of the examples in the Apex Library in the `examples/sql` directory. I encourage you to study these examples to gain a broader understanding of the capabilities of the Apex SQL API.

The input source is a Kafka message broker from where data in the form of CDRs (short for, Call Detail Records) is fetched by the `KafkaInput` operator. The data is in the CSV format and looks like this:

```
13/10/2017 11:45:30 +0000,1,v,111-123-4567,222-987-6543,120
```

Here, the first field is a UTC timestamp, the second a unique record id, the third is v (voice) or d (data), denoting the type of call, the fourth and fifth fields are the origin and destination numbers, and the final field is the duration in seconds.

The data is then parsed by `CSVParser`, filtered by `LogicalFilter_1`, projected to the desired fields (or *columns*) by `LogicalProject_2`, formatted for output by `CSVFormatter`, and finally written to the output file by the `FileOutput_4` output operator (these names are automatically generated when the SQL query is parsed and transformed into the necessary set of operators and streams; they can be used in the XML configuration elements just like user-specified names).

Of these, the first two operators are explicitly created by the application code and the remainder are automatically generated by the configured SQL query.

The output records are also in the CSV format, and they look like this:

```
12/10/2017 05:25:30 -0700,Voice,111-123-4567,999-987-6543,$120.00
```

The format is similar, but includes a final **cost** field, which is computed from the **duration** field and replaces it.

The full source code for this application is available at `https://github.com/amberarrow/samples/tree/master/etl`.

Building and running the application

You can build the application using the usual Maven command:

```
mvn clean package -DskipTests
```

The first time you do this, it may take a few minutes to complete, as it downloads all the dependency artifacts, but subsequent builds should go much faster. When the build completes, you should see a directory called `target` and a file called `et1-1.0-SNAPSHOT.apa` within it.

This is the application archive file that needs to be deployed to run the application on an actual Hadoop cluster.

The application includes a test file that can be used to run the entire application in your favorite IDE (such as Eclipse or IntelliJ) without the need for an external cluster as described in `Chapter 2`, *Getting Started with Application Development*. You can also run the test from the command line using the following command:

```
mvn -Dtest=SampleApplicationTest#test test
```

On modern machines, this should complete successfully in about 40 seconds; if something is wrong, it will fail with a timeout in about 50 seconds. The details of the test are discussed later in this chapter.

To run the application on a cluster, you can use the docker sandbox as described in `Chapter 2`, *Getting Started with Application Development*, or use one of the methods described in the Beginner's Guide at `http://apex.apache.org/docs.html`.

Application configuration

The application is configured via the `properties.xml` file, in the `resources/META-INF` directory, and includes the following elements:

- The Kafka input topic
- The Kafka broker address and port
- A schema of input records and its name
- A schema of output records and its name
- The SQL query used to filter and project
- The output filename
- The output directory

The first two are straightforward:

```
<property>
    <name>apex.operator.KafkaInput.prop.topics</name>
    <value>ETLTopic</value>
</property><property>
    <name>apex.operator.KafkaInput.prop.clusters</name>
    <value>localhost:9092</value>  <!-- broker (NOT zookeeper) address -->
</property>
```

The `topics` property of the `KafkaInput` operator defines the topic for input records, and the `clusters` property defines the address and port of the Kafka broker (it is important to ensure that this is the address and port of the actual broker and not of the ZooKeeper).

Likewise, the last two elements for configuring the output file and directory names via the `outputDir` and `fileName` properties are as follows:

```
<property>
  <name>outputDir</name>
  <value>/tmp/ETLOutput</value>
</property><property>
  <name>fileName</name>
  <value>calls.txt</value>
</property>
```

With this configuration, when the application is run on a cluster, the output file will be `/tmp/ETLOutput/calls.txt` on HDFS.

The remaining properties are a little more involved. The input record schema is defined via the `schema` property of the `CSVParser` operator:

```
<property>
  <name>apex.operator.CSVParser.prop.schema</name>
    <value>{
      "separator":",",
      "quoteChar":"\"",
      "fields": [{
        "name":"tstamp",
        "type":"Date",
        "constraints":{"format":"dd/MM/yyyy hh:mm:ss Z"}
      },{
        "name":"id",
        "type":"Integer"
      },{
        "name":"type",
        "type":"String"
      },{
```

```
        "name":"origin",
        "type":"String"
      },{
        "name":"destination",
        "type":"String"
      },{
        "name":"duration",
        "type":"Integer"
      }]}
    </value>
  </property>
```

The value is a JSON object that defines the **type**, **name**, and any applicable **constraints** for each field via an array called `fields`. In this case, we have five fields, namely **id**, **type**, **origin**, **destination**, and **duration**. Also defined are some global characteristics such as the separator character (comma in this example) and the quote character—used to surround the key and value strings.

The `constraints` property of each field is very flexible and allows early detection of errors or other unexpected values in the input stream. In addition to specifying the format of dates, it can also specify whether a field is required or optional, impose minimum and maximum limits on the length of string fields, and impose similar limits on the values of numeric fields or patterns that string fields must conform to. The full list of such constraints is documented in the CSVParser documentation at http://apex.apache.org/docs/malhar/operators/csvParserOperator/.

The schema name is defined by the value of the `inSchemaName` property, which, in this case, is InputSchema:

```
  <property>
    <name>inSchemaName</name>
    <value>InputSchema</value>
  </property>
```

The value of this property is used in the SQL query as well as in the code to create an input table. Similarly, the name of the output schema is defined by the value of the `outSchemaName` property, which, in this case, is OutputSchema:

```
  </property>
    <name>outSchemaName</name>
    <value>OutputSchema</value>
  </property>
```

This schema name is also used in the SQL query and in the application code. Similar to the schema for input records shown earlier, the schema for output records is defined as the value of the `outputSchema` property:

```
<property>
  <name>outputSchema</name>
  <value>{
    "separator":",",
    "quoteChar":"\"",
    "fields": [{
      "name":"tstamp",
      "type":"Date",
      "constraints":{"format":"dd/MM/yyyy hh:mm:ss Z"}
    },{
      "name":"type",
      "type":"String",
    },{
      "name":"origin",
      "type":"String",
    },{
      "name":"destination",
      "type":"String",
    },{
      "name":"cost",
      "type":"String"
    }]}
    </value>
  </property>
```

Here, again we see a similar pattern, where some global characteristics, such as the field separator and the quote character, are defined followed by an array that defines each output field.

Finally, the central element of this application—the SQL query—is defined as the value of the `query` property:

```
<property>
  <name>query</name>
  <value>
    INSERT INTO OutputSchema
      SELECT STREAM TSTAMP, CALLTYPE(type), origin, destination,
COST(origin,
      destination, duration)
        FROM InputSchema WHERE origin like '111-%' AND destination LIKE
'999-%'
  </value>
</property>
```

Notice that the output schema name is used as the target for INSERT, whereas the input schema name is used by the FROM clause as the source. This query also uses custom user-defined functions, namely CALLTYPE and COST, which are discussed in the next section.

The configuration file also sets a couple of attributes to limit the amount of memory used for each operator, so that the example can run on memory-limited systems such as sandboxes and single-node test clusters:

```
<property>
    <name>apex.operator.*.attr.MEMORY_MB</name>
    <value>200</value>
</property> <property>
    <name>apex.operator.*.port.*.attr.BUFFER_MEMORY_MB</name>
    <value>128</value>
</property>
```

To set these attributes for specific operators (rather than a wildcard that affects all operators), the asterisk in the property name can be replaced with the name of the desired operator, as shown in this example:

```
<name>apex.operator.LogicalFilter_1.attr.MEMORY_MB</name>
```

Recall that we saw similar examples for setting the PARTITIONER attribute in Chapter 4, *Scalability, Low Latency, and Performance*.

When running on a well-configured cluster, these options should be increased or the options should be removed to use the larger defaults to get good performance. They are part of the platform configuration options that were discussed in various contexts in the preceding chapters.

The application code

Now we will discuss the application code, how it uses these properties, and how custom functions can be defined for use in the SQL queries. The application comprises just a single source file, SampleApplication.java. As discussed in Chapter 2, *Getting Started with Application Development*, the entry point of an Apex application is a class that implements the StreamingApplication interface and, in particular, the populateDAG() method of that interface. The first part of this method looks like this:

```
@ApplicationAnnotation(name = "ETLExample")
public class SampleApplication implements StreamingApplication
{
  @Override
```

```
public void populateDAG(DAG dag, Configuration conf)
{
  try {
    // without this, the application fails at launch with this error:
    //   java.sql.SQLException: No suitable driver found for jdbc:calcite
    //
    Class.forName("org.apache.calcite.jdbc.Driver");
  } catch (ClassNotFoundException e) {
    throw new RuntimeException(e);
  }
  // register custom user defined functions (UDFs)
  final SQLExecEnvironment env = SQLExecEnvironment.getEnvironment();
  env.registerFunction("CALLTYPE", this.getClass(), "callType");
  env.registerFunction("COST", this.getClass(), "cost");
  final Map<String, Class> fieldMap = new HashMap<String, Class>(6);
  fieldMap.put("tstamp",      Date.class);
  fieldMap.put("id",          Integer.class);
  fieldMap.put("type",        String.class);
  fieldMap.put("origin",      String.class);
  fieldMap.put("destination", String.class);
  fieldMap.put("duration",    Integer.class);
  .........
}
```

To begin with, we will load the Calcite JDBC driver; this is necessary to retrieve the necessary classes. We will then create an SQLExecEnvironment object, which is the key entry-point to much of the SQL functionality. Next, we'll register the two functions cost and callType that we use in our SQL statement. These functions are defined as simple static methods in our application class:

```
public static String callType(String s) {
    if ("v".equals(s)) return "Voice";
    if ("d".equals(s)) return "Data";
    throw new RuntimeException(String.format("Error: Bad call type: %s",
s));
}
public static String cost(String origin, String dest, int duration) {
    final double centsPerSec = 0.2;
    return String.format("$%.2f", duration * centsPerSec);
}
```

The callType function is used to convert the cryptic single letter code present in the input records and denoting the type of call, to a more understandable string such as *Voice* or *Data*; other enrichment functions can be added similarly as and when needed. The cost function is used to convert the duration of the call to an actual monetary cost based on the origin and destination numbers.

The next step is to create a map that describes each field of the input record by associating it with an implementing class: the timestamp field tstamp is mapped to the Date class (**timestamp** is an SQL function name in some systems and can cause odd and difficult-to-diagnose errors if used here, so we choose the abbreviated form); the origin and destination fields are mapped to the String class, and so on. This map will be passed to the input endpoint of the SQL stream later.

The next part of the function forms the core of the application. It creates the input and parser operators, and registers the input and output tables (notice that they are not true tables in the traditional database sense, but rather a table-like view of the stream of input records). Finally, it executes the configured SQL query using the executeSQL() function:

```
// Add Kafka Input
KafkaSinglePortInputOperator input = dag.addOperator("KafkaInput",
  KafkaSinglePortInputOperator.class);
input.setInitialOffset("EARLIEST");
// Add CSVParser
CsvParser parser = dag.addOperator("CSVParser", CsvParser.class);
dag.addStream("KafkaToParser", input.outputPort, parser.in);
// Register CSV Parser output as input table for SQL input endpoint
env.registerTable(conf.get("inSchemaName"), new StreamEndpoint(parser.out,
  fieldMap));
// Register FileEndpoint as output table for SQL output endpoint
env.registerTable(conf.get("outSchemaName"), new
  FileEndpoint(conf.get("outputDir"),
  conf.get("fileName"), new CSVMessageFormat(conf.get("outputSchema"))));
// Convert query to operators and streams and add to DAG
env.executeSQL(dag, conf.get("query"));
```

The KafkaSinglePortInputOperator is a simple subclass of AbstractKafkaInputOperator, with much of the functionality present in the base class. Since there are multiple versions of the Kafka consumer API, there are matching versions of this operator in these directories: kafka/kafka09, kafka/kafka010, and so on. Each directory there has its own pom.xml, which defines the corresponding artifact with the matching API version number. The earliest API version supported is 0.8, and the corresponding code is in the contrib subdirectory. Each version of the subclass uses the appropriate version of the consumer, KafkaConsumer09, KafkaConsumer010, and so on.

The base class is in kafka/kafka-common and defines no output ports, leaving that to the subclasses; the preceding subclass, as the name suggests, defines a single output port in a field named outputPort. This field is used as argument of the addStream() call when defining the stream connecting the input operator to the parser. If you need to write output to multiple ports, you can simply extend the base class and define the necessary ports in your subclass.

We set the initial offset for this input operator to `EARLIEST` so that all available messages from the queue are read. This property can, as with most other properties and attributes of Apex operators, also be configured in the properties file if desired. Several additional properties of this operator are documented at the following link:
`http://apex.apache.org/docs/malhar/operators/kafkaInputOperator/`.

Next, the parser operator is created and its input port is hooked up to the output port of the Kafka operator via a stream called `KafkaToParser` using the `addstream()` method. Then, the SQL streaming input endpoint is created and connected to the output port of the parser, and the field map created earlier is passed as a parameter. Finally, this endpoint and the input schema are provided as arguments to the `registerTable()` call, thus completing the input side of things. The output side is configured similarly by the next `registerTable()` call, but the difference is that, instead of `StreamEndpoint`, we create `FileEndpoint`; if you wanted the output of the SQL to be further processed by some streaming operators, you would create `StreamEndpoint` instead.

The final step is to retrieve and process the query from the configuration (which eventually comes from the `properties.xml` file) via the `executeQuery()` method.

Partitioning

As discussed in `Chapter 4`, *Scalability, Low Latency, and Performance*, stateless partitioning of a single operator can be accomplished by setting the `PARTITIONER` attribute. For the current example, we could partition `CSVParser` using the following configuration stanza:

```
<property>
  <name>apex.operator.CSVParser.attr.PARTITIONER</name>
  <value>com.datatorrent.common.partitioner.StatelessPartitioner:2</value>
</property>
```

If we want some section of the SQL pipeline to be partitioned in parallel, we can set the `PARTITION_PARALLEL` attribute on the input ports of the downstream operators in that section, as shown in this example:

```
<property>
<name>apex.operator.LogicalFilter_1.inputport.input.attr.PARTITION_PARALLEL
    </name>
  <value>true</value>
</property>
```

With these changes, the physical DAG of our application would look like this:

The application's physical DAG

Application testing

In addition to the normal unit tests for individual functions or other small units of behavior, Apex simplifies the task of *integration testing* of the entire application directly on the command line of your development machine, or within your IDE without the need to set up an entire Hadoop cluster, which can be a tedious process. When developing Apex applications, it is very important to use this mechanism so that bugs can be discovered and corrected early in the development process.

As described in `Chapter 2`, *Getting Started with Application Development*, a single JUnit test is encapsulated in a method of the test class (`SampleApplicationTest` in this case), which is annotated with `@Test`. But there is a bit more to this test due to its dependence on external servers, namely, ZooKeeper and Kafka. To facilitate this, we use the testing library from `https://github.com/chbatey/kafka-unit`, specifically the `KafkaUnit` and `KafkaUnitRule` classes:

```
private final String testTopicData = "dataTopic";
private TimeZone defaultTZ;
private final int brokerPort = NetUtils.getFreeSocketPort();
private final int zkPort = NetUtils.getFreeSocketPort();
@Rule
public KafkaUnitRule kafkaUnitRule = new KafkaUnitRule(zkPort, brokerPort);
{
  // required to avoid 50 partitions auto creation
  this.kafkaUnitRule.getKafkaUnit().setKafkaBrokerConfig("num.partitions",
"1");

  this.kafkaUnitRule.getKafkaUnit().setKafkaBrokerConfig(
    "offsets.topic.num.partitions", "1");
}
private static String outputFolder = "target/output/";
@Rule
public TestName testName = new TestName();
```

```
@Before
public void setUp() throws Exception
{
  defaultTZ = TimeZone.getDefault();
  TimeZone.setDefault(TimeZone.getTimeZone("GMT"));
  KafkaUnit ku = kafkaUnitRule.getKafkaUnit();
  // topic creation is async and the producer may also auto-create it
  ku.createTopic(testTopicData, 1);
  outputFolder += testName.getMethodName() + "/";
}
```

The class begins by initializing the `brokerPort` and `zkPort` local variables to a couple of available ports, to avoid interfering with applications that may already be using the default ports.

The `KafkaUnitRule` class does all the work behind the scenes of starting up a ZooKeeper or Kafka broker (refer to `KafkaUnit.startup()` for details) to listen on these ports. The initial anonymous code block ensures that sane default values are configured for the broker. The output directory is then set to a subdirectory of `target` because that directory will be deleted and recreated each time maven is invoked with `mvn clean ....` , thereby ensuring that any clutter from running tests gets cleaned up as part of the routine build process.

The `setup()` method sets the time zone to be GMT (also known as UTC). This is important since we compare the input and output strings, and if the output uses the timezone of the user running the test, they will not match, resulting in a failed test. It then creates the needed topic.

The `test()` method contains the core of the test:

```
@Test
public void test() throws Exception
{
  Configuration conf = new Configuration(false);
  conf.addResource(this.getClass().getResourceAsStream
    ("/META-INF/properties.xml"));
  conf.set("apex.operator.KafkaInput.prop.topics", testTopicData);
  conf.set("apex.operator.KafkaInput.prop.clusters",
"localhost:"+brokerPort);
  conf.set("apex.operator.KafkaInput.prop.initialOffset", "EARLIEST");
  conf.set("outputDir", outputFolder);
  conf.set("fileName", "out.tmp");
  SampleApplication app = new SampleApplication();
  EmbeddedAppLauncher<?> launcher =
Launcher.getLauncher(LaunchMode.EMBEDDED);
  Attribute.AttributeMap launchAttributes = new
```

```
    Attribute.AttributeMap.DefaultAttributeMap();
  launchAttributes.put(EmbeddedAppLauncher.RUN_ASYNC, true); // terminate
after
    results are available
  AppHandle appHandle = launcher.launchApp(app, conf, launchAttributes);
  String[] messages = {
      "13/10/2017 11:45:30 +0000,1,v,111-123-4567,222-987-6543,120",
      "13/10/2017 12:25:30 +0000,2,v,111-123-4567,999-987-6543,600",
      "14/10/2017  9:15:00 +0000,3,d,444-823-4864,555-381-7241,300",
      "15/10/2017 10:15:00 +0000,4,d,111-222-3333,999-187-7654,1845"
  };
  KafkaUnit ku = kafkaUnitRule.getKafkaUnit();
  for (String msg : messages) {
    ku.sendMessages(new KeyedMessage<String, String>(testTopicData, msg));
  }
  // timeout after 50 seconds
  final File output = waitForFile(outputFolder, 50 * 1000);
  assertNotNull(output);
  appHandle.shutdown(ShutdownMode.KILL);
  // compare actual and expected output
  final String[] actualLines = FileUtils.readLines(output).toArray
    (new String[0]);
  final String[] expectedLines = new String[] {
      "13/10/2017 12:25:30 +0000,Voice,111-123-4567,999-987-6543,$120.00",
      "",
      "15/10/2017 10:15:00 +0000,Data,111-222-3333,999-187-7654,$369.00",
      ""
  };
  assertArrayEquals(expectedLines, actualLines);
} // test
```

When this test function runs, KafkaUnitRule has, as noted earlier, already started the ZooKeeper and Kafka servers and the setup function has created the topic. We first create a configuration object that is initialized with the values defined in the default configuration file, properties.xml, and then overwrite some properties to reflect the current test environment.

This includes redefining the topic name to dataTopic (this step illustrates the capability, but is actually superfluous here since the test uses a newly created Kafka broker), and redefining the broker address and port to avoid clashes with other servers that may be using the hardcoded ports, as well as the initial offset, output directory, and file.

Next, we create an application object and a launcher that can launch an application in embedded mode, set the RUN_ASYNC attribute to true to run the application asynchronously (that is, not on the current thread), and launch the application using launcher.launchApp(); the returned handle will be used to shutdown the application after it has processed the input records and generated the output.

Then, we retrieve the KafkaUnit object from the rule and use it to send messages to the Kafka topic. The sendMessages() method is used because it greatly simplifies the process by abstracting away all the boilerplate setup needed to send messages. The waitForFile() function is then invoked (with a timeout of 50 seconds) to monitor the output directory for any output; upon return, the output file is read, and the test succeeds or fails depending on whether the contents of the output file equal or differ from the expected output.

The output directory is monitored in a loop, waiting for the output file to appear; if the file appears within the timeout interval, the corresponding File object is returned; otherwise null is returned:

```
// Helper routine to wait for output file to be created; arguments:
//    dest    : destination directory in which output file is created
//    timeout : milliseconds to wait before giving up
//
// Returns true if the destination file was detected with nonempty content
within
   the timeout
// interval, false otherwise.
//
static File waitForFile(final String dest, final int timeout) throws
IOException,
    InterruptedException {
  final long start = System.currentTimeMillis();
  final File dir = new File(dest);
  do {
    if (dir.exists()) {
      final File[] list = dir.listFiles();
      if (list.length > 0 && 0 != FileUtils.readLines(list[0]).size()) {
          return list[0];
      }
    }
    Thread.sleep(500);
  } while (System.currentTimeMillis() - start < timeout);

  return null;
} // waitForFile
```

To avoid consuming CPU cycles needlessly, it sleeps for 500 milliseconds on each iteration.

Understanding application logs

When the test is run, it generates a copious amount of log messages. Understanding this output is invaluable for debugging and troubleshooting purposes, we will discuss some important elements of these messages next. This section is, unavoidably, rather dense since it delves into the content of log files generated by the application, but it will be invaluable for developers since they will need to understand these log files for troubleshooting and optimization.

Early in the message output you will see ZooKeeper starting up:

```
2017-10-29 07:49:40,878 [main] INFO  server.ZooKeeperServer <init> -
Created server with tickTime 500 minSessionTimeout 1000 maxSessionTimeout
10000 datadir /tmp/zookeeper-snapshot2513970348898676323/version-2 snapdir
/tmp/zookeeper-logs2532702519793579042/version-2
2017-10-29 07:49:40,951 [main] INFO  server.NIOServerCnxnFactory configure
- binding to port localhost/127.0.0.1:39429
```

This will be followed by a long list of Kafka configuration values, as shown in this example:

```
offsets.topic.num.partitions = 1
auto.create.topics.enable = true
zookeeper.connect = localhost:39429
port = 38461
broker.id = 1
inter.broker.protocol.version = 0.9.0.X
....
```

This list should be examined to ensure that Kafka is configured as expected. There will then be many messages from various Kafka threads as they initialize components of the system followed by messages showing our operators getting initialized:

> However, note that these messages may not appear together; the order depends on how the output of different threads get interleaved during a particular run.

```
2017-10-29 07:49:44,492 [main] DEBUG logical.LogicalPlan <init> -
Initializing KafkaInput as
org.apache.apex.malhar.kafka.KafkaSinglePortInputOperator
2017-10-29 07:49:44,528 [main] DEBUG logical.LogicalPlan <init> -
Initializing CSVParser as com.datatorrent.contrib.parser.CsvParser
2017-10-29 07:49:46,079 [main] DEBUG logical.LogicalPlan <init> -
Initializing LogicalFilter_1 as
org.apache.apex.malhar.sql.operators.FilterTransformOperator
2017-10-29 07:49:46,245 [main] DEBUG logical.LogicalPlan <init> -
```

```
Initializing LogicalProject_2 as
org.apache.apex.malhar.sql.operators.FilterTransformOperator
2017-10-29 07:49:46,271 [main] DEBUG logical.LogicalPlan <init> -
Initializing CSVFormatter_3 as
com.datatorrent.contrib.formatter.CsvFormatter
2017-10-29 07:49:46,284 [main] DEBUG logical.LogicalPlan <init> -
Initializing FileOutput_4 as
org.apache.apex.malhar.lib.fs.GenericFileOutputOperator$StringFileOutputOpe
rator
```

We should see our SQL statement being parsed, and the resulting relational algebra tree with something like this:

```
2017-10-29 07:49:44,719 [main] INFO  sql.SQLExecEnvironment executeSQL -
Parsing SQL statement:
    INSERT INTO OutputSchema
        SELECT STREAM TSTAMP, CALLTYPE(type), origin, destination,
COST(origin,
            destination, duration)
          FROM InputSchema WHERE origin like '111-%' AND destination LIKE
'999-%'
2017-10-29 07:49:46,029 [main] INFO  sql.SQLExecEnvironment executeSQL -
RelNode relationalTree generate from SQL statement is:
LogicalTableModify(table=[[OutputSchema]], operation=[INSERT],
updateColumnList=[[]], flattened=[true])
  LogicalProject(tstamp=[$2], type=[CALLTYPE($4)], origin=[$5],
destination=[$0],
      cost=[COST($5, $0, $1)])
    LogicalFilter(condition=[AND(LIKE($5, '111-%'), LIKE($0, '999-%'))])
      LogicalTableScan(table=[[InputSchema]])
```

Notice the correspondence between the pair of SQL generated operators `LogicalFilter_1` and `LogicalProject_2`, and the pair of nodes of the tree. Both operators are implemented as instances of the same class, namely, `FilterTransformOperator`.

A little later, we see the six containers (these will be individual JVMs on a true cluster, but threads in the local mode used for testing) for the six operators initializing:

```
2017-10-29 07:49:48,267 [container-0] INFO  stram.StramLocalCluster log -
container-0 msg: [container-0] Entering heartbeat loop..
2017-10-29 07:49:48,269 [container-3] INFO  stram.StramLocalCluster log -
container-3 msg: [container-3] Entering heartbeat loop..
2017-10-29 07:49:48,270 [container-2] INFO  stram.StramLocalCluster log -
container-2 msg: [container-2] Entering heartbeat loop..
2017-10-29 07:49:48,269 [container-1] INFO  stram.StramLocalCluster log -
container-1 msg: [container-1] Entering heartbeat loop..
```

```
2017-10-29 07:49:48,270 [container-4] INFO   stram.StramLocalCluster log -
container-4 msg: [container-4] Entering heartbeat loop..
2017-10-29 07:49:48,270 [container-5] INFO   stram.StramLocalCluster log -
container-5 msg: [container-5] Entering heartbeat loop..
```

Eventually, we should see the operators being deployed into the containers. These messages are very useful when trying to track down failures, whether you're running on a true cluster or a simulated local one, because they represent critical life cycle events:

```
2017-10-29 07:49:49,288 [container-5] INFO   engine.StreamingContainer
processHeartbeatResponse - Deploy request:
[OperatorDeployInfo[id=1,name=KafkaInput,type=INPUT,checkpoint={fffffffffff
fffff, 0,
0},inputs=[],outputs=[OperatorDeployInfo.OutputDeployInfo[portName=outputPo
rt,streamId=KafkaToParser,bufferServer=localhost]]]]
2017-10-29 07:49:49,288 [container-4] INFO   engine.StreamingContainer
processHeartbeatResponse - Deploy request:
[OperatorDeployInfo[id=6,name=FileOutput_4,type=GENERIC,checkpoint={fffffff
fffffffff, 0,
0},inputs=[OperatorDeployInfo.InputDeployInfo[portName=input,streamId=Forma
tter_File_3,sourceNodeId=5,sourcePortName=out,locality=<null>,partitionMask
=0,partitionKeys=<null>]],outputs=[]]]
2017-10-29 07:49:49,289 [container-2] INFO   engine.StreamingContainer
processHeartbeatResponse - Deploy request:
[OperatorDeployInfo[id=5,name=CSVFormatter_3,type=GENERIC,checkpoint={fffff
fffffffffff, 0,
0},inputs=[OperatorDeployInfo.InputDeployInfo[portName=in,streamId=Project_
Output_4,sourceNodeId=4,sourcePortName=output,locality=<null>,partitionMask
=0,partitionKeys=<null>]],outputs=[OperatorDeployInfo.OutputDeployInfo[port
Name=out,streamId=Formatter_File_3,bufferServer=localhost]]]]
2017-10-29 07:49:49,290 [container-0] INFO   engine.StreamingContainer
processHeartbeatResponse - Deploy request:
[OperatorDeployInfo[id=4,name=LogicalProject_2,type=GENERIC,checkpoint={fff
fffffffffffff, 0,
0},inputs=[OperatorDeployInfo.InputDeployInfo[portName=input,streamId=Filte
r_Project_2,sourceNodeId=3,sourcePortName=output,locality=<null>,partitionM
ask=0,partitionKeys=<null>]],outputs=[OperatorDeployInfo.OutputDeployInfo[p
ortName=output,streamId=Project_Output_4,bufferServer=localhost]]]]
2017-10-29 07:49:49,290 [container-3] INFO   engine.StreamingContainer
processHeartbeatResponse - Deploy request:
[OperatorDeployInfo[id=2,name=CSVParser,type=GENERIC,checkpoint={fffffffffff
ffffff, 0,
0},inputs=[OperatorDeployInfo.InputDeployInfo[portName=in,streamId=KafkaToP
arser,sourceNodeId=1,sourcePortName=outputPort,locality=<null>,partitionMas
k=0,partitionKeys=<null>]],outputs=[OperatorDeployInfo.OutputDeployInfo[por
tName=out,streamId=StreamInput_Filter_1,bufferServer=localhost]]]]
2017-10-29 07:49:49,292 [container-1] INFO   engine.StreamingContainer
processHeartbeatResponse - Deploy request:
```

```
[OperatorDeployInfo[id=3,name=LogicalFilter_1,type=GENERIC,checkpoint={ffff
ffffffffffff, 0,
0},inputs=[OperatorDeployInfo.InputDeployInfo[portName=input,streamId=Strea
mInput_Filter_1,sourceNodeId=2,sourcePortName=out,locality=<null>,partition
Mask=0,partitionKeys=<null>]],outputs=[OperatorDeployInfo.OutputDeployInfo[
portName=output,streamId=Filter_Project_2,bufferServer=localhost]]]]
```

This is a rather dense output, so we'll examine it carefully and learn how to make sense of the various elements. Each message provides a wealth of important information about the operator being deployed, its ports, and streams. Using the preceding last message as an example, we can see the following:

1. The operator name is `LogicalFilter_1` with ID as 3. This name is internally generated, but if we look at the operators that we explicitly create in the application code, we see that the names shown here match the names provided as the first argument to the `addOperator()` call, namely, `KafkaInput` and `CSVParser`.

2. The container into which it is deployed is `container-1`.

3. The type is `GENERIC` (input operators will instead have `INPUT` here as we see for `KafkaInput`).

4. The initial checkpoint at which it started will be -1 (as shown) for an initial deployment, but if the operator was restarted after a failure, the specific checkpoint at which it resumes would appear here.

5. The inputs to this operator (if any; notice that the `KafkaInput` operator has, as expected, none):

   The name of the input port is `input`; since we know that the implementing class for this operator is `FilterTransformOperator`, we can verify this in the source code of that operator, where we see that it is a subclass of `TransformOperator`, which does indeed have the expected input port:

   ```
   public final transient DefaultInputPort<Object> input = new
     DefaultInputPort<Object>() ....
   ```

   The ID of the upstream operator (`sourceNodeId`) is 2, the name of the output port in that operator is `out`, and the name of the stream (`streamId`) connecting the two is `StreamInput_Filter_1`. Notice, again, that this matches the information printed for `CSVParser` and its outputs; the ID is 2, the stream name is the same, and the `Parser` base class has an output port with the expected name:

   ```
   public transient DefaultOutputPort<Object> out = new
     DefaultOutputPort<Object>() .....
   ```

The outputs from this operator (if any; notice that the file output operator, FileOutput_4, has, as expected, no outputs) are as follows:

The name of the output port is output; here again, we can verify that TransformOperator has an output port with the required name.

The name of the stream is Filter_Project_2, which matches the data for the LogicalProject_2 operator, which is the downstream operator (the ID of the downstream operator is not printed since a stream can have multiple downstream operators).

Much later, we see the file output operator opening the output file:

```
2017-10-29 07:49:49,713 [6/FileOutput_4:StringFileOutputOperator] INFO
fs.AbstractFileOutputOperator load - opened out.tmp_6.0, active
target/output/test/out.tmp_6.0.1509288589711.tmp
```

We then see shutdown messages from various components followed by the expected success message:

```
Tests run: 1, Failures: 0, Errors: 0, Skipped: 0
[INFO] ------------------------------------------------------------
----
[INFO] BUILD SUCCESS
[INFO] ------------------------------------------------------------
----
```

Calcite integration

For readers who are curious about how the integration with Calcite is implemented, we cover the relevant classes briefly in this section.

Calcite is a rather substantial project with a large and complex API, so in this short section we will merely touch upon its capabilities; the reader is encouraged to review the Calcite docs and source code to gain deeper insights into the API.

Here is a (very) high-level summary of how things work. After the desired custom functions and pseudo-tables are registered with the `SQLExecEnvironment` class (typically, in the `populateDAG()` method), the `executeSQL()` method is invoked to kick off all the hard work of parsing the SQL query, creating the necessary operators and adding them to the DAG, generating Java classes for the columns, wrapping them in a JAR file and finally adding the JAR file to the appropriate DAG attribute, so that they can be found and used at runtime. The bulk of the work starts with the `RelNodeVisitor.traverse()` call near the end of that method. Some of the important call sequences are illustrated by the following diagram:

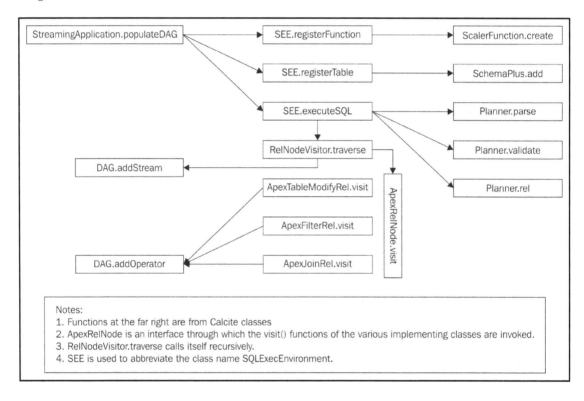

A few Calcite classes relevant to the Apex integration are summarized in the following table:

Class	Description
`Delta`	This is the abstract class representing a relational operator that converts a relation to a stream.
`RelNode`	This encapsulates a relational expression; concrete implementing classes are typically verbs indicating how data is processed, such as **Sort**, **Join**, and **Project**.
`RelDataType`	This is the interface that represents the type of result (typically a row) yielded by a relational expression. It has several methods for retrieving row metadata such as the type of keys, type of values, and list of field names.
`RelDataTypeFactory`	This is the factory for datatype descriptors. It is used in the various `Endpoint` classes and also in the `CSVMessageFormat` class to create type descriptors for the various core SQL types such as Boolean, Date, and String.

The main entry point in our application is the `SQLExecEnvironment` class in the `sql` directory of the Apex library code. It includes the `registerTable()`, `registerFunction()` and `executeSQL()` methods we've seen in our application along with a couple of supporting methods.

The rest of the code is logically divided into four groups in the corresponding subdirectories of **SQL**: **codegen**, **operators**, **planner**, **schema** and **table**, which are summarized in the following tables.

The classes under `codegen` relate to compiling Calcite expressions into fast bytecode:

Class	Description
`BeanClassGenerator`	This dynamically generates Java bean classes for the column types of all the registered pseudo tables that are registered. It is used by `TupleSchemaRegistry` discussed next.
`ExpressionCompiler`	This converts the internal Calcite expressions that are created when Calcite parses the SQL query, to something resembling Java expressions, which can then be processed by `PojoUtils` to generate corresponding bytecode for fast runtime evaluation.

The classes under `operators` are operator implementations along with some utilities for generating synthetic names for them:

Class	Description
`FilterTransformOperator`	This extends `TransformOperator` in the Apex library; it is configured with a Boolean expression in string form. The `activate()` method compiles this string into Java bytecode using the `PojoUtils` class (discussed in `Chapter 4`, *Scalability, Low Latency, and Performance*) for high performance. The `processTuple()` method evaluates this compiled expression in the context of each incoming tuple, filtering out those that yield a false result.
`InnerJoinOperator`	This extends `POJOInnerJoinOperator` in the Apex library to simply change a few configuration parameters. Since doing a join requires tuples to be stored, the base class has somewhat elaborate mechanisms for storing tuples from both input streams, retrieving them at high speed, performing various types of joins, and expiring them, so that they don't consume all available space. There are also a number of configuration options related to these mechanisms that are beyond the scope of the current document.
`LineReader`	This is a simple extension of `AbstractFileInputOperator` with trivial implementations of the abstract methods. It is used to read input files, a line at a time.
`OperatorUtils`	This has a few utility methods for, for example, generating names of operators that get created automatically from SQL.

The classes under `planner` relate to traversing the relational algebra associated with the query:

Class	Description
ApexRelNode	This is an abstract class that works as a visitor for relational nodes of Calcite SQL. The single `visit()` abstract method encapsulates the Apex DAG augmentation for each node. It also has a static inner class named `RelContext`, which wraps the DAG, `JavaTypeFactory` and `TupleSchemaRegistry`, and is passed as the first argument to the `visit()` function. The following concrete extensions of this class are present in the same file: `ApexDeltaRel`, `ApexTableScanRel`, `ApexTableModifyRel`, `ApexProjectRel`, `ApexProjectRel`, and `ApexJoinRel`. The concrete implementation of the `visit()` method in these classes retrieves the `Endpoint` from the node and invokes either the `populateInputDAG()` or `populateOutputDag()` methods to add the appropriate operator to the DAG.
RelInfo	This concrete class is used to communicate connection and type information of an Apex stream across stages of the relational algebra. This includes the sole input port and the set of output ports.
RelNodeVisitor	This is a visitor class that traverses the entire relational algebra, augmenting the DAG with the appropriate operator at each node via the `visit()` method discussed earlier. It is invoked from the `executeSQL()` method of `SQLExecEnvironment`.

The classes under **schema** relate to handling the table schema registered by the user:

Class	Description
ApexSQLTableFactory	This is the factory class for creating `ApexSQLTable` objects.
ApexSQLTable	This is the class that acts as a shim between the table types that Calcite needs and the schema that are passed to the `registerTable()` method of `SQLExecEnvironment`. They are created by the `create()` method of `ApexSQLTableFactory`.

TupleSchemaRegistry	This class handles some of the core plumbing work to ensure that the various custom classes for processing tuples are accessible at runtime. It creates a new package, whose name is the value of the static field FQCN_PACKAGE, creates custom Java bean classes within this package for all the table column types, creates a jar file containing these classes and finally, in the traverse() method of RelNodeVisitor (mentioned earlier), adds it to the LIBRARY_JARS attribute of DagContext.

The classes under **table** relate to the various endpoints and how operators and streams are generated:

Class	Description
CSVMessageFormat	This is the concrete implementation of the MessageFormat interface; the constructor is initialized with a schema string. The getRowType() method uses a couple of helper classes to convert this schema to a RelDataType object and returns it. The populateInputDAG and populateOutputDAG methods respectively create instances of the CsvParser and CsvFormatter operators, configure them, and add them to the DAG. Both return a newly created RelInfo object, which wraps the operator, its name, and stream metadata such as the input and output ports of the operator.
Endpoint	This is the interface that defines an endpoint; it has the EndPointType enum, which defines the types of supported endpoints that currently include FILE, KAFKA, and PORT, corresponding to the implementing classes FileEndpoint, KafkaEndpoint, and StreamEndpoint. These implementations have a MessageFormat field, which is used for conversion into and out of the appropriate format. The key methods here are populateInputDAG and populateOutputDAG.
FileEndpoint	This is a concrete implementation of the Endpoint interface for files. The populateInputDAG and populateOutputDAG methods respectively create instances of LineReader and StringFileOutputOperator, configure them, create suitable streams connecting them to the rest of the DAG, and finally, return a newly created RelInfo object that wraps the metadata of the newly created operator and stream.

`KafkaEndpoint`	This is a concrete implementation of the `Endpoint` interface for files. The `populateInputDAG` and `populateOutputDAG` methods respectively create instances of `KafkaSinglePortInputOperator` and `KafkaSinglePortOutputOperator`, configure them, create suitable streams connecting them to the rest of the DAG, and finally, return a newly created `RelInfo` object that wraps the metadata of the newly created operator and stream.
`MessageFormat`	This is the interface that defines how messages (that is, tuples) are parsed. Analogous to `Endpoint`, it has a `MessageFormatType` enum with CSV as its sole member, for which the `CSVMessageFormat` class provides a concrete implementation. The key methods here are `getRowType`, `populateInputDAG`, and `populateOutputDAG`.
`StreamEndpoint`	This is a concrete implementation of the `Endpoint` interface for streams. The `populateInputDAG` and `populateOutputDAG` methods differ from the implementations of other endpoints, since there is no need to create an operator or stream. They simply return a newly created `RelInfo` object that wraps the port metadata.

Summary

In this chapter, we examined a powerful tool in Apex library—the SQL API (Calcite integration)—and how it enables us to build classical ETL applications using SQL to automatically create many operators and link them into the DAG. We also covered how to build the application to produce the application archive (`.apa`) file which can be deployed in a cluster.

We also saw how to run the integration test locally, on our development machine, to enable detection of bugs, configuration errors, and other defects early in the development process, without the need to install Hadoop, ZooKeeper, or Kafka. We then took a detailed look at the application log messages and saw how to interpret them.

We rounded out the chapter by summarizing the classes involved in the Calcite integration.

9
Introduction to Apache Beam

Apache Beam is a new programming model and library for portable massive-scale data processing—both batch and streaming. Using Beam, you can author data processing pipelines and execute them on various data processing engines, including Apache Apex.

In this chapter, we will cover the following topics:

- Introducing the technical vision of Apache Beam
- Explaining the most important concepts in the Beam programming model
- Discussing simple classic example—counting the occurrences of words in the works of Shakespeare
- Launching this pipeline on Apache Apex

Introduction to Apache Beam

Beam is a programming model—what does that mean, exactly? It means that Beam defines essential primitives, from which you can construct big data processing pipelines. By design, your processing logic is unified across batch and stream processing, infinite and finite, and bounded and unbounded. One important practical benefit is that Beam allows you to reuse your code for processing an incoming stream, reprocessing historical data (for example, after fixing a bug, or receiving a data dump), or running experiments or tests on samples of data:

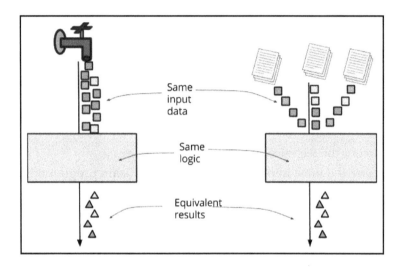

The essential structure of your computation is independent of what data processing engine executes it. Today there are **runners**—libraries for executing Beam pipelines on various data processing systems—for example, Apache Apex, Apache Flink, Apache Spark, Google Cloud Dataflow, and Apache Gearpump (incubating), with others underway for JStorm, Apache Tez, and nonTez Apache Hadoop MapReduce.

A Beam pipeline is also independent of what language it is written in. The library with which you describe your data processing pipeline is called an **SDK**. In addition to the basic wiring together of a pipeline, an SDK is how you specify implementations of user-defined functions, or **UDFs**, such as a custom Java function, to map over all elements of a data stream. Beam has SDKs for Java, Python, and Go, with varying levels of maturity. The Java SDK is well-supported on all runners, because most existing runners are also JVM-based and can easily execute Java UDFs directly. A major effort is underway to adapt all runners to use Beam's portability framework, which will make the Python and Go SDKs available to all runners, and all runners available to Python and Go aficionados.

The promise of portability of *any SDK on any data processing engine* is summarized in the following diagram, in which either a Java or Python *sum per key* program is translated to a portable format, and then can be executed on any of the pictured runners:

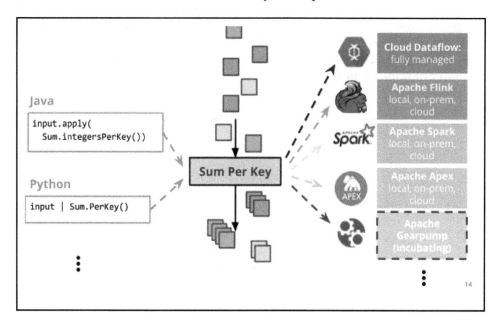

Beam's portability framework goes beyond *any language on any data processing engine* to *multiple languages in the same pipeline on any data processing engine*. This unlocks reuse of big data processing components across languages. For example, in Beam Java, there are many mature connectors to external systems, including HBase, Kinesis, Hadoop InputFormat, Tika, MongoDb, Cassandra, Elasticsearch, Apache Solr, MQTT, Kafka, Redis, and Google Cloud Platform (BigQuery, Pub/Sub, Bigtable, Datastore, Spaner). There is also a Beam SQL library based on Apache Calcite. Python and Go users can immediately have access to this growing library of transforms. Conversely, Python provides `tf.Transform`, a connector to the preprocessing library of TensorFlow:

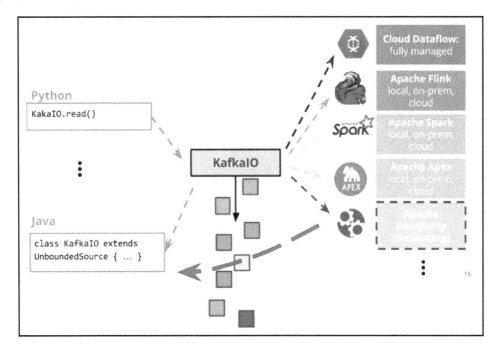

Having introduced the main technical vision of Beam, we will first walk-through the big-picture concepts before looking at the classic example pipeline: wordcount.

Beam concepts

The premise for using Beam (and Apex) is that you are processing some massive datasets and/or data streams, so massive that they cannot be processed by conventional means on a single machine. You will need a fleet of computers and a programming model that somewhat automatically scales out to saturate all of your computers.

Pipelines, PTransforms, and PCollections

In Beam, you organize your processing into a directed graph called a **pipeline**. You may illustrate it something like this:

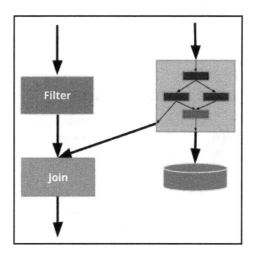

The boxes are parallel computations that are called **PTransforms**. Note how one of the boxes contains a small subgraph—almost all PTransforms are actually encapsulated subgraphs, including both Join and Filter. The arrows represent your data flowing from one PTransform to another as a **PCollection**. A PCollection can be **bounded** as with a classic static dataset like a massive collection of logs or a database snapshot. In this case, it is finite and you know it. However, a PCollection can just as easily be **unbounded**, which means that it may never end, and even if no data arrives, you don't know if some might arrive at any moment.

A PTransform is a parallel transformation on your data. In order to make it easy to assemble pipelines that scale effectively, Beam has only five core PTransforms, of which three (**Read**, **ParDo**, and **GroupByKey**) embody dominant parallel patterns of computation, one (Window) embodies our approach to out-of-order data processing:

- **Read**: This is the start of a pipeline, reading from an external source in parallel
- **ParDo**: This is for element-wise processing
- **GroupByKey / Combine per key**: This is for aggregating multiple input elements
- **Window**: This is for organizing your elements in event time
- **Flatten**: This is an administrative transform that just unites two PCollections

This chapter will go over ParDo and GroupByKey/CombinePerKey as parallel patterns of computation, and really dive into the details of windowing and triggering for effective stream processing. Flatten is uninteresting and you will not commonly use Read—instead, you would use a pre-existing connector to your data. In fact, you may often build your pipeline almost entirely from higher level transforms. However, to understand the Beam programming model, you first need to understand these patterns of massively parallel computation.

ParDo – elementwise computation

The most elementary form of massively parallel computation is *doing the same thing to every element* in a stream or massive dataset. In Beam, this computational pattern is called **ParDo**, short for **Parallel Do**. You might think of it as **Map** from **MapReduce** or similar to Apex's Transform operator (`http://apex.apache.org/docs/malhar/operators/transform/`):

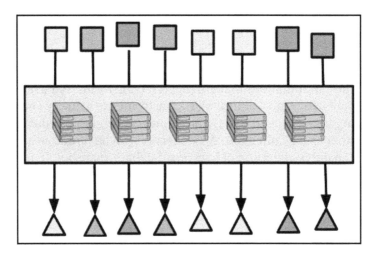

ParDo is *embarrassingly* parallel: there are no dependencies between the processing of each element. Every input element can be processed potentially in parallel on separate machines. This computational pattern applies to both the bounded datasets, such as a huge collection of files, or unbounded datasets, such as a stream from a Kafka subscription.

The Beam primitive ParDo is the basis for all per-element processing logic. It has many features and variations. Many common element-wise transformations are already provided with Beam, such as `MapElements`, `FlatMapElements`, and `Filter`, which you may know from functional programming, or more down-to-earth utilities such as string manipulation via `Regex`.

GroupByKey/CombinePerKey – aggregation across elements

The primary computational pattern for aggregation in Beam is to group all elements with a common key (and Window—but we'll get to windowing later), and then, to combine each group of elements using an associative and commutative operation. Like the **Reduce** from **MapReduce**, this originates in functional programming from the early 90s. In Beam, aggregation has been enhanced to work with unbounded input streams as well as bounded datasets.

When elements are grouped and emitted as-is, the aggregation is known as **GroupByKey** (the associative/commutative operation is just *bag union*). In this case, the output is no smaller than the input, so *Reduce* might be a misnomer.

However, often, you will apply an operation such as summation, where the output is significantly smaller than the input. In this case, the aggregation is called **CombinePerKey**. There are significant performance advantages to the latter, which is discussed in detail after we cover the basics.

In the following illustration, input elements are squares and outputs are triangles. Elements with the same color represent those with a common key and window. So all of the red squares are routed to the same place where they are aggregated, producing the red triangle as the output:

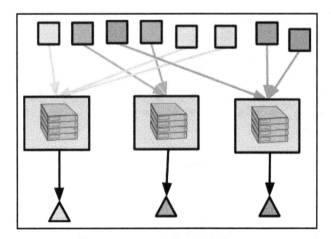

This pattern is embarrassingly parallel when you have plentiful keys. For example, if you are doing usage analytics, you might group by user ID.

This pattern also applies to unbounded input, but is more subtle. How do you know when all the elements for a key have arrived so that your aggregation is complete? Do you really want to wait for all your data to arrive before producing some output? These questions motivated two of the most innovative and powerful aspects of the Beam model: windowing and triggering. We will cover these in their own section.

Windowing, watermarks, and triggering in Beam

In global-scale stream processing including mobile devices and IoT with imperfect connectivity, the data you are processing will regularly arrive for processing in a different order than the order of the events that the data describes. Windowing, watermarks, and triggering together allow you to perform coherent aggregation over out of order data, and they tune your pipeline according to your latency requirements, your tolerance for incomplete data, and your willingness to pay for redundant computation.

Windowing in Beam

In the following diagram, there is a red element, a yellow element, and a green element that all describe events that occurred between 8:00 and 9:00 (let's say, UTC), as far as their users were concerned—these are the *even time* timestamps on the data. The time that they arrive for processing is on the horizontal axis:

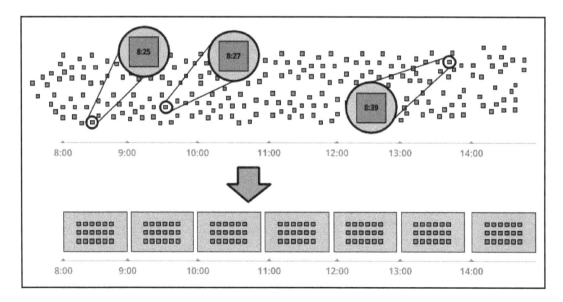

If we want to compute accurately about the events that occurred between 8:00 am and 9:00 am, we need all of these events gathered in one place. However, we won't actually receive all of the relevant data until well after 13:00. We might be willing to wait until 10:00, but probably not until 14:00. Also, even then, we can never be sure that another event might arrive even later.

A window in Beam is a grouping, such as an hourly grouping, that has a time as an upper bound. You know that you are waiting for events with timestamps under that upper bound, so it is possible to use appropriate statistical and heuristic techniques to estimate when all the data within that window has arrived.

In Beam, every element has a timestamp in event time associated with it, and every element resides within a window. In this way, event time and windowing pervades every aspect of Beam and always allow resources to be managed as windows expire. Of course, sometimes you are doing classical batch processing with no need for windowing—in this case, your data can have any timestamp you please and reside in the global window, which does not expire until your data is fully exhausted.

Watermarks in Beam

Simply putting it: a watermark is an estimate of the oldest data you expect to see. As real time passes during your pipeline's execution, a Beam runner (for you, Apex) maintains this estimate for each PCollection in your pipeline. In streaming applications, a watermark will generally track a bit behind wall-clock time and advance irregularly as incoming queued data is processed.

In the following illustration, **processing time**—the time that passes as your computation proceeds—is on the vertical axis. **Event time**—the time as recorded in your data stream—is on the horizontal axis. The red curve is the progress of the watermark. You can trace this by considering processing time proceeding upwards, while the estimate of Beam runner of your data's completeness evolves and progresses to the right. Elements that arrive for processing are the purple boxes; if they arrive after the watermark estimates there will be no more data, they are considered late:

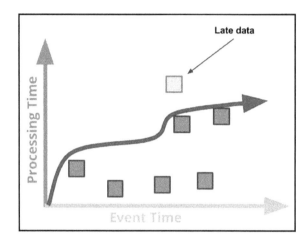

More abstractly, a watermark is a measure of the *completeness* of your data. When the watermark reaches a particular point in event time—for example, the end of an hour—then, aggregations over prior time ranges are considered complete. It is thus estimated that a proper answer may be emitted for those aggregations.

Triggering in Beam

Triggering in Beam governs when output is emitted by aggregations in Beam. It is not necessary to wait for your data to be complete, nor is it required to emit output when data is complete. Completeness is merely one input to the decision about whether an aggregation should emit a result.

More specifically, triggering aims at letting you control the trade-off, for your pipeline, between completeness of your results, latency of output, and cost due to excessive recomputation. Let's consider these dimensions for three common use cases: a monthly billing pipeline, a running total of a monthly bill prior to sending it, and an abuse detection pipeline. In the following figure, the blue column indicates the importance of complete data, the red column the importance of timely results, and the green column the importance of keeping costs low:

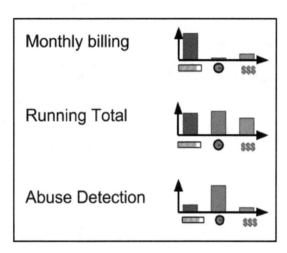

For monthly billing, completeness is an essential requirement, so the leftmost, blue, column is all the way up. Latency and cost are not really negotiable, so these columns are very small, indicating very little importance.

For a running total of a prospective bill, however, completeness is not terribly important. You want up-to-date data, but it isn't critical. Lower latency is fundamental for this use case, so the column for timeliness is much larger. Also, it would make little sense to spend much on a secondary noncritical feature; so the rightmost column is large, indicating that you need to keep costs in check.

In a complete different domain, consider building a model and using it for abuse detection, for example, a cloud service. Now, low latency is paramount—if you don't catch the abuse quickly, you are going to lose a lot of money. Since money is gained from timely results, you don't mind investing money, so cost is a lesser consideration. Completeness is possibly even meaningless—your model will converge in its effectiveness and constantly update. Anyhow, it is a statistical model, so it carries a good amount of built-in error; it doesn't make sense to wait long before issuing an updated model of abusive use.

While the whole catalog of triggers is too much for an overview chapter, let's look at two core triggers. We will use Java code even though we are still in a fairly conceptual discussion, because it is easier to have a concrete way of writing these down:

- `AfterWatermark.pastEndOfWindow()`: This is the fundamental trigger that emits aggregations when the watermark estimates that your data is complete. If you don't modify triggering in any way, this is Beam's default behavior. This is essentially the *windowing without triggering* choice.
- `AfterProcessingTime.pastFirstElementInPane(duration)`: The name is a mouthful, but this trigger is vitally useful. When data arrives for inclusion in an aggregation, the result will be emitted after a specified duration has passed. This trigger allows low-latency results with a cost determined by the duration you choose.

You can build more complex triggers in Beam by combining the primitives. The recommended way to do this is to specify triggering for speculative output and late output as augmentations of the default triggering. For example, to trigger speculative output every minute, but every second for late data, you would write this:

```
AfterWatermark.pastEndOfWindow()
    .withEarlyFirings(
        AfterProcessingTime.pastFirstElementInPane(
            Duration.standardMinutes(1)))
    .withLateFirings(
        AfterProcessingTime.pastFirstElementInPane(
            Duration.standardSeconds(1)))
```

To read more about windowing and triggering, visit the Beam documentation (windowing: `https://beam.apache.org/documentation/programming-guide/#windowing` and triggers: `https://beam.apache.org/documentation/programming-guide/#triggers`).

Advanced topic – stateful ParDo

Both ParDo and per key aggregation are standard patterns for parallelism that go back decades. When implementing these in a massive-scale distributed data processing engine, we can highlight a few characteristics that are particularly important.

Characteristics of ParDo:

- You write single-threaded code to process one element
- Elements are processed in an arbitrary order with no dependencies or interaction between processing of elements

Characteristics for per key aggregation:

- Elements for a common key and window are gathered together
- A user-defined operator is applied to these elements

Stateful ParDo is a computational pattern that combines aspects of each of these:

- Elements for a common key and window are gathered together
- Elements are processed in arbitrary order
- You write single-threaded code to process one element or timer, possibly accessing state or setting timers

In the following illustration, the red squares are gathered and fed one by one to the stateful, timely, DoFn. As each element is processed, DoFn has access to state (the color-partitioned cylinder on the right) and can set timers to receive callbacks (the colorful clocks on the left):

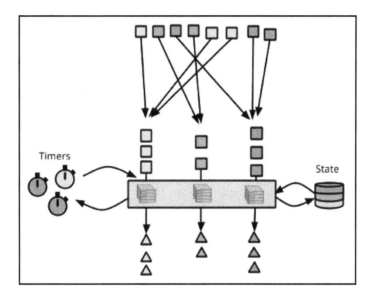

This is a lower-level primitive without the guarantees of associativity, commutativity, or unlimited parallelism. Few or no automatic optimizations can be applied to a stateful ParDo. However, by giving up higher level structure and automated optimization, you gain tight low level control over the computation. Examples of transformations that require this low level control include the following:

- Assigning an arbitrary sequence number to each element
- Output only when the result has change a statistically significant amount

- Output based on other characteristics of the input data stream—Beam's triggers are data-agnostic
- Sharded stream join algorithms, supporting customized garbage collection of candidate tuples
- Batching RPCs to external systems

If you have written a custom operator in Apex, this pattern of computation may be more familiar than the rest of Beam. In effect, this is how you can drop *down to the metal* and write a custom operator in Beam.

Now, one of the raisons d'être for Beam is correct processing of out-of-order event data via event time windowing. A user of your stateful operator may specify windowing into fixed window of one hour, or overlapping 30 minute windows that slide by 10 minutes:

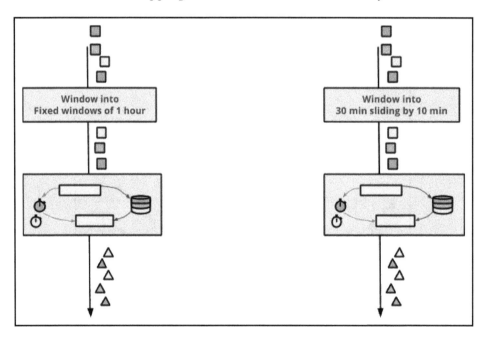

This works in Beam automatically, because state and timers are partitioned per key and window. Within each key and window, the stateful, timely processing is essentially independent. As an added benefit, the passing of event time (also known as advancement of the watermark) allows automatic release of unreachable state when a window expires, so you often don't have to worry about evicting old state.

WordCount in Apache Beam

Now that we have introduced the big picture and concepts of Beam, we'll walk through the basic example of Beam WordCount in Java, run it first in a testing runner, and later on Apex. Since you have already seen this on Apex elsewhere in the book, we will jump right into the Beam code.

Here is the entirety of the example we call *minimal word count*:

```
PipelineOptions options = ...
Pipeline pipeline = Pipeline.create(options);
pipeline
    .begin()
    // Read some data (parallel connector that ships with Beam)
    .apply(TextIO.read().from("gs://apache-beam-
samples/shakespeare/*"))\
    // Split into "words" (elementwise transform)
    .apply(FlatMapElements
        .into(TypeDescriptors.strings())
        .via((String word) -> Arrays.asList(word.split("[^\\p{L}]+"))))
    // Drop empty strings (elementwise transform)
    .apply(Filter.by((String word) -> !word.isEmpty()))
    // Count per words (per key aggregation)
    .apply(Count.<String>perElement())
    // Format output into a string (elementwise transformation)
    .apply(MapElements
        .into(TypeDescriptors.strings())
        .via((KV<String, Long> wordCount) ->
            wordCount.getKey() + ": " + wordCount.getValue()))
    // Write to text files (complex composite shipped with Beam
.apply(TextIO.write().to("gs://YOUR_OUTPUT_BUCKET/AND_OUTPUT_PREFIX"));
    p.run().waitUntilFinish();
```

This is a very sparse example just to give you a taste of Beam and to allow us try to explain the technical nitty-gritty of running a Beam pipeline. It shows the most basic concepts:

- Beginning a pipeline
- Reading data
- Element-wise computation
- Aggregation
- Writing data

Most importantly, it does not illustrate windowing and triggering. At `https://beam.apache.org/get-started/wordcount-example/`, you can find variants using windowing and more full driver programs for the pipeline.

However, let's now walk through the code and connect it with the core Beam concepts.

Setting up your pipeline

The first thing you will do when writing a Beam pipeline is to get your hands on a `Pipeline` object. You do this by instantiating it with `PipelineOptions`, so that you can create programmatically or parse from the command line:

```
Pipeline pipeline = Pipeline.create(options);
```

Reading the works of Shakespeare in parallel

The first transform applied to the beginning of the pipeline reads the works of Shakespeare from a public bucket on Google Cloud Storage:

```
TextIO.read().from("gs://apache-beam-samples/shakespeare/*")
```

This outputs a PCollection containing one string element for each *line* of all the works of shakespeare. `TextIO` is a built-in connector for reading collections of lines stored in many text files. The reading will be split across files and also within a file, so this supports both numerous files and extremely large files.

Splitting each line on spaces

In order to count the words, we have to get the words. For simplicity, we will just hand-craft a regular expression for splitting, and not even take into account any text file formatting:

```
FlatMapElements
        .into(TypeDescriptors.strings())
        .via((String word) -> Arrays.asList(word.split("[^\\p{L}]+")))
```

Here, `FlatMapElements` accepts a function that takes one input and results in possibly many outputs. It is identical to `flatMap` you may be familiar with from functional programming.

Eliminating empty strings

Our naive way of splitting can easily result in empty strings, so we filter them out with another element-wise transform:

```
Filter.by((String word) -> !word.isEmpty())
```

Counting the occurrences of each word

The one and only user-visible aggregation in the WordCount pipeline is for counting words (of course):

```
Count.<String>perElement()
```

This is a composite transform that is a very thin wrapper on a basic per-key aggregation. The input collection of words is transformed into a collection of key-value pairs, where the key is the word and the value is the integer 1. Then, a per-key sum is performed.

Format your results

Formatting demonstrates another simple library transform that ships with Beam—mapping a one-input-to-one-output function over all input elements:

```
MapElements
        .into(TypeDescriptors.strings())
        .via((KV<String, Long> wordCount) -> wordCount.getKey() + ": " +
wordCount.getValue())
```

Writing to a sharded text file in parallel

Finally, we invoke the TextIO.write() library transform to write our results to a sharded file. The output will not be a single file, but many—they will be idempotently written in parallel to a temporary location (some writes may fail and be restarted), and then, idempotently moved to their final location. You should replace the output destination with some location that you establish for writing the output of word count:

```
TextIO.write().to("gs://YOUR_OUTPUT_BUCKET/AND_OUTPUT_PREFIX")
```

Testing the pipeline at small scale with DirectRunner

As you work, you want quick feedback about how your pipeline is working. You can run the whole pipeline in a local process using `DirectRunner`. This is an in-process Java runner that runs extra checks to help ensure that your pipeline will be robust when it is really deployed.

For demonstrating the invocation, we will switch to the more full `WordCount` example that supports command-line configuration. You can get a project set up to run this by following `https://beam.apache.org/get-started/quickstart-java/`. For our purposes, run this command:

```
mvn archetype:generate \
    -DarchetypeGroupId=org.apache.beam \
    -DarchetypeArtifactId=beam-sdks-java-maven-archetypes-examples \
    -DarchetypeVersion=2.2.0 \
    -DgroupId=org.example \
    -DartifactId=word-count-beam \
    -Dversion="0.1" \
    -Dpackage=org.apache.beam.examples \
    -DinteractiveMode=false
```

Then, to run the pipeline on `DirectRunner` via Maven, you issue this command:

```
mvn compile exec:java \
    -P direct-runner \
    -D exec.mainClass=org.apache.beam.examples.WordCount \
    -Dexec.args="--inputFile=gs://apache-beam-samples/shakespeare/* --
output=/tmp/output-direct/ --runner=DirectRunner"
```

The command-line arguments to the main program are within the `-Dexec.args` argument to `mvn`. They are fairly self-explanatory:

- `--runner`: This selects `DirectRunner`
- `--inputFile=gs://apache-beam-samples/shakespeare/*`: This selects the works of Shakespeare
- `--output=/tmp/output-direct`: This indicates where to write the output

You should now find files in `/tmp/output-direct`, containing the counts of all the words in the works of Shakespeare!

Running Apache Beam WordCount on Apache Apex

As the next step toward running on Apex, you can also run your pipeline on a local Apex cluster, for a testing scenario that is slightly more similar to production:

```
mvn compile exec:java \
    -P apex-runner \
    -D exec.mainClass=org.apache.beam.examples.WordCount \
    -Dexec.args="--inputFile=gs://apache-beam-samples/shakespeare/* --
output=/tmp/output-apex/ --runner=ApexRunner --embeddedExecution=true"
```

Again, you should find output files in /tmp/output-apex. The number of files may differ, but their overall contents will be the same. Unless you request particular sharding, it is up to the Beam runner to decide the parallelism of the write step.

Now, we should run this on a real YARN cluster; if you are not already in an environment with a cluster available, it is easy to set one up with Google Cloud Dataproc or AWS EMR. To do so, there is no special treatment needed.

Now, let's spin up a Dataproc cluster and run this via those instructions:

```
mvn compile exec:java \
    -P apex-runner \
    -D exec.mainClass=org.apache.beam.examples.WordCount \
    -Dexec.args="--inputFile=/tmp/input/pom.xml --output=/tmp/output/ --
runner=ApexRunner --embeddedExecution=false --configFile=beam-runners-
apex.properties"
```

Check out https://beam.apache.org/documentation/runners/apex/ for more details on how to use the Apex runner for Beam.

Summary

This chapter has been a whirlwind tour regarding the core concepts of Apache Beam and how to run a basic WordCount pipeline using Apache Apex as a backend. Specifically, we looked at the following topics:

- The technical vision of Beam—any language on any data processing engine
- The main parallel processing patterns of Beam—ParDo and GroupByKey
- The features of the Beam model that support unbounded data—windowing, watermarks, and triggers
- A basic Beam pipeline to count occurrences of words
- Launching a Beam pipeline using Apache Apex on a YARN cluster

For more details on both Beam and the Apex runner for Beam, visit the Beam website at `https://beam.apache.org`. Also, follow `@ApacheBeam` on Twitter and join our user mailing list at `user@beam.apache.org` by following the instructions at `https://beam.apache.org/get-started/support/`.

10
The Future of Stream Processing

This closing chapter will take a look at the road ahead for stream processing in general. The space has seen a lot of innovation over the past few years. Apache Apex, natively built for streaming, has contributed unique features such as distributed checkpointing, dynamic scaling with on-demand resource allocation, and runtime modifications to pipelines. At the same time, the stream processing technology is rapidly evolving, and organizations are still just getting started with applying the technology to use cases. There is significant opportunity to make adoption and infrastructure integration easier.

The order of topics here will go from being more developer focused to operational. We will cover the following topics:

- How a wider audience can access stream processing
- The role of SQL and programming language APIs
- Machine learning integration
- State management capabilities
- Management and operability support

Lower barrier for building streaming pipelines

Stream processing platforms overall need to become more accessible. Considering how databases today can be accessed from virtually every programming language and with a wide variety of tools, similar support will be needed in the streaming space.

Traditionally, most projects provide their native primary API with the language that they were also written in, which predominantly, in the big data space, is Java or Scala. The resulting level of abstraction may be appropriate for data engineers with a solid background in distributed systems. However, this skillset is not widespread and hard to acquire, resulting in an excessively high entry barrier. There are various trends and efforts to address this, including visual tools, higher level DSLs (domain-specific languages), and more general programming language bindings.

Visual development tools

The bottom of the stack use cases, such as simple data movement or basic ETL, can be addressed with visual development environments that come with the promise of building data processing pipelines without writing code. There have been products in this area for a long time; notable recent efforts include vendors such as StreamSets and Talend.

Often, it turns out that while initial, basic requirements can be met by such a tool, development soon bumps into the ceiling of functional limitation and lack of expressiveness. Development teams that originally did not want to write code ultimately find themselves maintaining a growing list of custom plugins or other custom code repositories.

An alternative that may offer a more attractive trade-off between simplicity and expressiveness are higher level languages. Several of the projects in this space offer higher level, declarative APIs. Nevertheless, those are still reserved for programmers, and even programmers would prefer alternatives for certain tasks. Perhaps this can be roughly compared to the choice between SQL and stored procedure in the world of databases. It is unlikely that one would write a stored procedures unless the problem at hand justifies the effort.

Streaming SQL

Recently there has been renewed interest in SQL, and stream processing communities are working on bringing SQL to data in motion.

Apache Calcite is central to most of these efforts. It proposes extensions to express streaming semantics (especially windowing) with SQL and has already been adopted by multiple projects (Apex, Beam, Flink, and Storm to name a few). An example using the Apex integration of Calcite was discussed in `Chapter 8`, *Example Project – ETL Using SQL*.

Here are some useful links:

- `https://calcite.apache.org/`
- `https://calcite.apache.org/docs/stream.html`
- `https://calcite.apache.org/docs/powered_by.html`

Apache Kafka (which stores data in topics) was recently given its own flavor of SQL, namely, KSQL (currently in developer preview). It is positioned as an SQL engine that enables stream processing on top of Kafka. KSQL will become an interesting option for a category of less complex processing needs. It also looks attractive for ad hoc exploration of data in Kafka topics, something that pretty much every developer that works with Kafka will at some point need to do. Such exploration was typically done by writing a custom consumer or using the primitive console consumer, neither of which is as convenient for searching as KSQL is.

The early efforts to bring SQL to streaming are promising. They will eventually enable a host of existing tools and products that speak (some dialect of) SQL to interoperate with streaming systems, similar to how Hive or Impala have brought BI tools to data at rest. In the future, it may not even be necessary to wait for data to be at rest, when SQL can be used to ask questions while data is in motion. Before streaming SQL is ready for that, systems need to become smarter though. In the typical data warehouse project, SQL developers and administrators spend significant time with query optimization, indexing, and similar activities. Streaming platforms today have an even larger array of options that require manual tuning for good performance. SQL for everyone will require that much of this gets automated.

Better programming API

While DSLs can certainly cover a significant spectrum of stream processing use cases, more complex logic will be built using programming languages. All of the streaming engines have their own flavor of native API, which can be broadly categorized into declarative and compositional (or higher level and lower level, respectively). An overview of Apache streaming technologies can be found here: `https://databaseline.bitbucket.io/an-overview-of-apache-streaming-technologies/`.

In addition to that, some platforms and frameworks offer multi-language APIs (Apex has declarative and compositional API in Java; refer to `Chapter 1`, *Introduction to Apex*; development of a Python API is in progress).

Given the proliferation of API styles and languages, where does that leave users? Adopting one of the frameworks requires learning the respective API and library since there is no common standard for such APIs. For example, while the API of Apache Flink and Apache Spark Streaming may look similar, they are semantically quite different.

This is where Apache Beam (introduced in `Chapter 9`, *Introduction to Apache Beam*) comes into the picture. As described at `https://beam.apache.org/`, it is *An advanced unified programming model* to *Implement batch and streaming data processing jobs that run on any execution engine:*

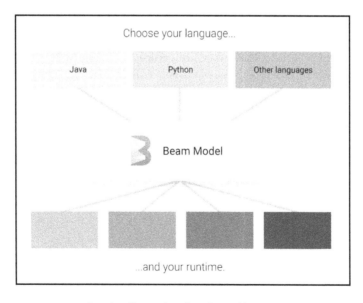

Source: https://beam.apache.org/images/beam_architecture.png

The vision of Beam is to support different programming languages (and higher level DSLs) based on a unified model (for **B**atch and St**ream**) that abstracts the underlying runners. For current details about supported runners and capabilities refer to: `https://beam.apache.org/documentation/runners/capability-matrix/`.

The Beam approach would allow users to learn one unified API (hopefully in their language of choice), and use one of several different execution engines to implement that API based on the runtime characteristics of the engines. Besides the unified API, Beam has actually contributed quite a bit in terms of concepts and terminology to the underlying runner API. For example, the windowing concepts of Beam have been adopted in the native APIs of Apache Apex and Apache Flink. The portability promise of Apache Beam has potential to simplify things for pipeline developers.

Beam provides not only the API and future DSLs (Calcite-based SQL support has recently been added), it also has an expanding library of connectors. Developing these integrations is not trivial and they take time to mature. Once this occurs, Beam with a large development community would offer an important benefit over individual platforms that have to replicate such efforts individually.

At the same time, Beam needs to expand its model and API to cover important capabilities that some of the frameworks natively have and that are currently missing in Beam, such as support for iterative processing (the loop in the processing graph). This is also indicative of a tradeoff-portability and flexibility against the optional custom differentiating capabilities of the runners that may not be accessible via the unified API.

Bridging the gap between data science and engineering

Data scientists work with data for exploration, often in an ad hoc manner. Data engineering builds data pipelines that run continuously, so operability and production readiness are important concerns. While the two camps look very different and work with different tools and different methods, large organizations often have both work for a common objective. It is also not uncommon that successful data science experiments eventually result in data engineering projects.

An important reason for the popularity of Apache Spark is that its entry barrier is perceived as low and the platform as not limited to Java/Scala developers and distributed system experts. Spark was first to offer support for interactive notebooks, Python-based programming, and machine learning that are easy to get started with. Databricks was first to offer these features, even integrating them better into the cloud. This has attracted many users and a huge community with broad vendor backing to Spark, despite the frequently cited challenges on the operability front and nonoptimal streaming architecture.

Most of the other stream processing projects are focused on production pipelines. The question is whether a more inclusive approach could lead to broader acceptance. Many production pipelines eventually started with early experiments. What if, for example, the logic that was already developed in Python (and depends on NumPy or other libraries) can be reused instead of requiring a rewrite in Java by another team? The Apache Beam language portability effort may be a step forward in this direction. Projects like Apache Apex certainly need to step up efforts in this area.

Machine learning integration

Machine learning (**ML**) has become a popular topic, so let's consider how stream processing and machine learning can work together. The Apex approach in this area has been to let the data scientist community work with the tooling of their choice (which often is Python or R), and focus on the data engineering aspects of reliable and efficient production pipelines. Instead of reinventing ML libraries as part of the stack, the approach therefore is ML integration.

Apache SAMOA (`https://samoa.incubator.apache.org/`) explores distributed online machine learning (the training of a model with continuously arriving data). SAMOA aims to allow for ML development without having to focus on the intricacies of the underlying stream processing system, and Apex is one of the supported engines. However, this "inline ML" approach has its limitations. To work with a stream processor, the ML algorithm would need to be written in a language that the engine supports, which, as discussed earlier in this chapter, often isn't what data scientists work with. The algorithm also needs to allow for incremental, distributed execution.

Additionally, it may be necessary to preselect/filter the streaming data in a special way before it can be applied to learning. On the stream processor side, ML usually requires the ability to define a loop in the processing graph (which means it isn't strictly a DAG any more). The Apex engine supports this construct with iterative processing through a special delay operator, which involves special treatment for streaming windows.

More information on this type of ML integration and the SAMOA / Apex combination can be found here:
`https://www.slideshare.net/DataTorrent/machine-learning-support-in-apache-apex-next-gen-hadoop-with-apache-samoa`.

Another form of ML integration is online scoring through the use of an existing model that was built offline by a specialized platform. Online scoring is, for example, used in fraud prevention systems. It still requires the ability to evolve the model (albeit not real time), combined with low-latency scoring and production-grade reliable processing that can be provided by a stream processor such as Apex. The streaming pipeline has to allow for updates to the model, for which Apex with some of its dynamic update capabilities provides basic building blocks. It would be possible, for example, to update a scoring model in HDFS (whether that is a script or JVM bytecode), and switch it to live with dynamic property change of the scoring operator.

Today Apex has support for R (generic operator + example application in the Apex library), and it can be integrated with an ML framework that generates Java code (like H2O). Support for native Python is in-progress, as shown here:

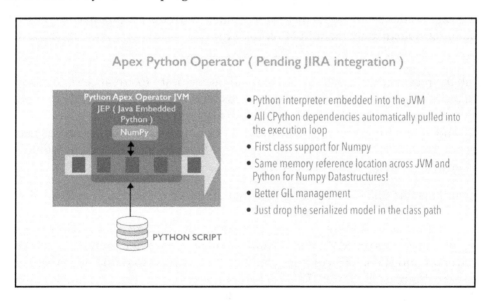

The proposed Python operator illustrates how Apex would focus on the streaming and delegate the ML aspect to a Python model, which is the result of the offline data scientist work. This model will be used for scoring as opposed to transcoding. In other words, time to market can be a core differentiator in Apex following such an approach, as most of the data scientist community today is mostly using Python or R. For more information about this integration approach refer

to `https://www.slideshare.net/ApacheApex/low-latency-polyglot-model-scoring-using-apache-apex`.

State management

Managing the state of the streaming pipeline in a way that scales (also dynamically) and guarantees accurate results (even in the event of failures), is one of the key challenges in building a streaming platform. We discussed in `Chapter 5`, *Fault Tolerance and Reliability* how Apex manages the state, and in `Chapter 4`, *Scalability, Low Latency, and Performance* how it also supports elasticity (or dynamic scaling). Apex has been a pioneer in this area. Apache Flink is actually quite similar in its checkpointing approach, and recently has built interesting capabilities to utilize its distributed state snapshots for pipeline upgrades (for a good primer on state management in Flink refer to

`http://www.vldb.org/pvldb/vol10/p1718-carbone.pdf`).

Despite all the recent advances, there is plenty of opportunity to advance state management in stream processing. State management backends have room for improvement. Both, Apex and Flink today assume that data is stored in a distributed file system to guarantee durability and access from every worker node. Apex only reads/writes blocks as needed and does not need to do a wholesale state copy on a failover. Still, file access would be much faster when state is "local" to the worker.

Storage solutions like EBS offer performance that is similar to local disk and can also provide
fault tolerance for worker failure; the building blocks for doing so are available today. If the streaming platform runs on AWS, and resource management understands the relationship between worker and state, EBS volumes could be (re)assigned to workers/containers and state access be dramatically faster. This isn't any different from how one might manage Kafka brokers and topic log volumes in an EC2 deployment.

Another area is elasticity. Dynamic scaling for a streaming pipeline needs some form of dynamic state sharding. Ideally, the user should be able to scale a system dynamically without having to lock in a fixed set of partitions for parallelism, upfront. Besides, allocating the resources on-demand, stream processors need to be able to reshard the state to do that. Currently, this is not supported in most projects (also not for Kafka topics). It would be nice if platforms understood state semantics well enough to automatically redistribute state when parallelism changes either through user intervention or algorithmically, similar to how Google's Dataflow can dynamically scale workers along with their state.

Exploring if (in the spirit of Beam) state management for stream processors can be abstracted to be reusable and pluggable would also be interesting. If there are several projects that use flavors of distributed snapshots, could they share a state management component that provides a set of state primitives, such as defined in Beam (ValueState, CombiningState, MapState, and so on), with an API to be notified of events such as "checkpoint occurred" or "checkpoint committed"? Perhaps there could also be portable state/checkpoint formats that allow for interoperability. Also, maybe this can be taken to cross-data centre support. Support for cross-cluster checkpointing might enable future architectures with better operability characteristics that cater for resumption of processing across data centres or A/B upgrade or testing scenarios, for example.

State query and data consistency

In Chapter 6, *Example Project – Real-Time Aggregation and Visualization*, we looked at an example for visualization of streaming computation in Apex. It was based on the idea that since the streaming platform manages the state, it can be accessed directly instead of having to load it to a separate external system first (which also has its own performance constraints).

The idea today is represented under different names such as *Queryable State, Interactive Queries*, or *Stream Processor as Database* in a number of ecosystem projects, each with its own implementation flavor and semantics. It will be interesting to see how users will potentially adopt this concept and understand it as true database alternative. There is no doubt about the scalability benefit, large volumes of state can be accumulated by distributed workers in-memory and accessed very fast. Stream processors have become much better with consistency guarantees for their state (via distributed checkpointing/snapshots or transactions).

Future advances could provide consistency guarantees to the query (similar to isolation levels in databases). Just like with triggers in windowing, it may be interesting to query partial results or only final results, and the user may want control over them. It would also be interesting to explore if (streaming) SQL could be an interface to queryable state (and how that would be different from statically expressing a pipeline with SQL).

Containerized infrastructure

Apex works very well on YARN, but at the moment that's also still the only supported option for cluster orchestration and resource management. The complexity of setting up and maintaining YARN clusters is a hurdle for adoption, especially when it becomes a prerequisite for starter stream processing projects and isn't a strategic part of the larger enterprise infrastructure.

The trend toward containerized services and cloud infrastructure management solutions is clear, and big data streaming will be part of it. Apex needs to have a good story for Docker-based deployment, and then, support other cluster managers such as Kubernetes, DC/OS, or Docker Swarm/Enterprise. With Apex internal architecture that cleanly abstracts away the cluster manager interface, it won't be hard to support other cluster managers and adapt to changes in a fast evolving space.

Management tools

Running streaming pipelines in production requires good management tools and infrastructure. Existing offerings focus predominantly on functional aspects (APIs and libraries) and performance. A large portion of infrastructure for a successful project has to cover build, source control, continuous integration, testing, deployment automation, upgrade, monitoring, and so on. Today, this involves expert skill sets, expensive custom architecture, and development. From a user perspective, this needs to become much simpler, and it presents an area with potential for vendor differentiation (especially in the cloud).

Some examples where integrations in Apex could benefit operations are as follows:

- **Better integration for metrics**: Apex provides system and custom operator metrics as well as the Apex master REST API, but the only metric sink that is currently supported is the Apex specific web socket reporter. Users typically need integration with their monitoring infrastructure with alerts and metric repositories. Metric sinks for frequently used protocols and systems (DataDog, Graphite/InfluxDB, and JMX) will be useful.
- **Log file analysis**: Problem root cause analysis in distributed systems can be challenging, it often involves going through log files on individual machines. Specialized logger sinks and/or integration for distributed tracing (Zipkin/OpenTracing/HTrace) would help here.
- **Disaster Recovery (DR) Strategy**: Most production deployments require a **Disaster Recovery** (DR) strategy. It is not trivial to replicate a stateful streaming pipeline (efficiently) across data centres at the user level. If the Apex state management / checkpointing can be aware of clusters, then DR and possibly other use cases, such as blue/green deployments, could be more effectively managed.

Efforts for operationalized streaming in general are still early, and we can expect to see much innovation in this space going ahead.

Summary

The rise of stream processing is one of the big technology shifts in recent years, which is driven by the need to react to ever more complex events in a timely manner by analyzing large-volume, infinite, and continuous data streams as they occur, with growing sophistication. Technology in the stream processing space has evolved rapidly. Apache Apex has been one of the projects on the forefront of the trend.

In this final chapter, we took a look at some of the possibilities ahead and presented ideas and opportunities to extend the reach of stream processing and projects such as Apache Apex.

Index

reference link 92
JDBC Poller Input Operator
  reference link 92
join 108
JSON 31

K

Kafka input operator
  about 80, 82
  reference link 220
Kappa Architecture
  about 13
  reference link 13
Kinesis operators
  references 84
Kinesis streams 84

L

Lambda Architecture 12
load balancing 112
log4j configuration 72
  reference link 72
low-latency
  versus throughput 131

M

machine learning (ML) 262
machine learning integration
  management tools 266
Managed State 103, 109
map transform
  about 96
  references 96
MapReduce 243
Maven project
  creating 44
MergeAccumulation 105
minGap 100
modus operandi 112

N

native S3 API
  reference link 90
NoSQL 77

O

operator state 116
operator
  reference link 87, 90
operators
  about 25
  aspects 136
output operator
  references 92

P

parallel instances 112
parser
  about 95
  references 95
partition keys 115
partition mask 115
partitioning 112, 220, 221
partitioning toolkit
  about 117
  configuring 117
  StreamCodec 119
  triggering 117
  unifier 123
partitions 112
PCollection 241
performance optimizations
  about 128
  affinity 129
  anti-affinity 129
pipeline
  about 241
  empty strings, eliminating 253
  occurrences of word, counting 253
  results, formatting 253
  setting up 252
  sharded text file, writing in parallel 253
  splitting, on spaces 252
  testing, at small scale with DirectRunner 254
  works of Shakespeare, reading in parallel 252
Powered by Apache Apex page
  reference link 15
prebuilt accumulations
  reference link 106

www.ingramcontent.com/pod-product-compliance
Lightning Source LLC
Chambersburg PA
CBHW080630060326
40690CB00021B/4876